BUY THIS BOOK . . .
OR WE'LL SUE YOU!

BUY THIS BOOK . . . OR WE'LL SUE YOU!

OUTRAGEOUS LAWSUITS, OUTLANDISH VERDICTS

LAURA B. BENKO
AND ATTILA BENKO

CITADEL PRESS
Kensington Publishing Corp.
www.kensingtonbooks.com

CITADEL PRESS BOOKS are published by

Kensington Publishing Corp.
850 Third Avenue
New York, NY 10022

All Kensington titles, imprints, and distributed lines are available at special quantity discounts for bulk purchases for sales promotions, premiums, fund-raising, educational, or institutional use. Special book excerpts or customized printings can also be created to fit specific needs. For details, write or phone the office of the Kensington special sales manager: Kensington Publishing Corp., 850 Third Avenue, New York, NY 10022, attn: Special Sales Department, phone 1-800-221-2647.

Citadel Press and the Citadel Logo are trademarks of Kensington Publishing Corp.

Design by Leonard Telesca

First printing: September 2001

10 9 8 7 6 5 4 3 2 1

Printed in the United States of America

Library of Congress Control Number: 2001093051

ISBN 0-8065-2233-X

To Pam,
For the idea and inspiration

To our mother, Ida,
Who always said, "Why don't you just write a book?"
(Well, here it is!)

To our father, Stephen,
For his enduring support

To our brother, Istvan,
An honest attorney

CONTENTS

ACKNOWLEDGMENTS

This book has been a richly rewarding collaborative effort, with several people making important contributions to our work. We would like to personally thank Bob Shuman, our editor, whose dedication and incisive suggestions improved the quality of our book considerably, and to Shannon Seta for lending a much-needed hand with the research. Joel Fishman, our former agent, also deserves much gratitude. He was the first to put faith in our project and was largely responsible for its getting beyond the early planning stages.

In addition to these acknowledgments, which we share equally, each of us would like to mention individually those who have been closest to us during our work.

I owe a tremendous debt to my beautiful wife, Pam, who has contributed invaluably to everything I have done here. Her critical listening to ideas as they took shape, her thoughtful comments on them, and her patience with the often preoccupying nature of the task made my work on the book possible.
—A.B.

I would like to give heartfelt thanks to my heffa and dearest friend, Angela Gomez, for her unwavering support and for always helping me through the rough patches. (Believe me, there were plenty of them!) Also deserving a special mention are the members of my writers' group, Paul Almond, Tammy Delatorre, Rex King, and Pamela Ranger. Their wisdom and creativity astound me. Finally, I would like to express my deepest gratitude for the inspiration and encouragement of my friends and fellow writers Brian Gibson, Brian O'Connor, and Matthew Robinson. They have contributed more than they know.
—L.B.

INTRODUCTION: FIT TO BE TRIED

Whether the bone of contention is a crippling injury, a constitutional right, or a surprise missing from a box of Cracker Jacks, Americans are streaming to civil court in record numbers. In 1999, a whopping 15.4 million lawsuits—one for every seventeen Americans—hit state and federal court dockets at a cost of almost $200 billion in settlements, jury awards, court expenses, and attorney fees. And this surge in litigation shows no signs of abating. Health maintenance organizations are now being hauled to court under federal antiracketeering laws originally designed to bring down mob figures like John Gotti. Tobacco companies are up to their cigarette butts in lawsuits, ducking for cover under multibillion-dollar settlements, while gun vendors face a barrage of claims for, well, selling guns. Even McDonald's, Starbucks, and several other seemingly benign food chains have hunkered down against litigious customers who would rather douse themselves with Colombian Supremo, it appears, than drink it.

Let's face it, lawsuits have become a way of life. Anyone, from grade-schooler to convicted killer, can file them; no one—

not even a former president—is immune to them. Employees are suing their bosses. Students are suing teachers, teachers are suing students. Friends are suing friends, men are suing their mothers, mothers are suing their daughters, daughters are suing their lawyers, and lawyers are suing on behalf of their dogs. In short, we're all fit to be tried.

Which is where we step in.

Never passing up the chance to take a well-deserved poke at human folly, we've decided to share with you some of the most outrageous lawsuits to have crossed our desks as a reporter and insurance claims administrator. Most of these suits have been published in newspapers around the country, having caught the interest of the media simply by their chutzpah. Many of them have also eventually faded away into the sunset—rightly so—without ever being heard from again. Others are still winding their way through a legal labyrinth of discovery, motions, hearings, and settlement negotiations. But for those that have had their day in court, we've made sure to note the verdicts—many of which are as outrageous as the claims themselves, such as the cat burglar who was awarded $260,000 for falling through a skylight while trying to break into a school.

Knowing what a prickly bunch the plaintiffs can be, we've elected to withhold the names of the parties involved. (We found that their names didn't add to the absurdity of their actions, anyway.) We've also opted to refrain from referring to these interesting and unusual lawsuits as "frivolous." In an effort to appear magnanimous—and in the hope of avoiding any interesting and unusual lawsuits being leveled at us—we've decided to let you judge which lawsuits are simply laughable and which qualify as downright frivolous.

To help the discerning reader along, here's how California's Code of Civil Procedure defines *frivolous:* "(A) totally and completely without merit, or (B) for the sole purpose of harassing an opposing party." So why all the absurd suits? Some are drawn up simply to ease a bruised ego or make a petty point, such as the one filed in 1993 by the parents of a nine-year-old Indiana girl who found no prize in her Cracker Jack box. The vast majority of outlandish lawsuits, however, have a far more opportunistic motive: money. Most injuries these days can only be soothed with a liberal salve of legal tender. A profound apology, a box of chocolates, or a bouquet of flowers with a Hallmark card tucked between the leaves won't work; when it comes to compensation, most won't settle for less than a generous dollop of cash, and what better way to ladle it up than with the help of a lawyer?

Enterprising attorneys have found a lucrative business in filing frivolous claims. Armed with an arsenal of hyperbolisms, such as *wanton disregard for* and *intentional infliction of,* lawyers can transform even the most mundane grievance into a matter for the Supreme Court. Sure, this legal buffoonery creates more laughs than we could shoehorn into a Bible-sized tome, let alone this book. But it also carries with it a number of serious consequences, not the least of which are more taxes, higher prices, and fewer services. Then, of course, there's the deeper cultural aftereffect: Personal responsibility is being eroded in this country. It's easier—and often more profitable—to simply blame someone else.

Having said all this, a well-placed disclaimer may now be in order. It's not our intention to ridicule a particular plaintiff or attorney—though sometimes it's tempting. Rather, we believe the lawsuits themselves serve as adequate ridicule for anybody associated with them. So if you recognize yourself as a plaintiff in any of the following cases, well, what did you expect? On the other hand, if you identify yourself as a defendant, you have our sincerest condolences. And to those of you who are too busy making a living to be filing wacky lawsuits and are merely reading this out of curiosity, thank you.

1

WATCH YOUR STEP: PERSONAL-INJURY LAWSUITS

This trial is a travesty; it's a travesty of a mockery of a sham of a mockery of a travesty of two mockeries of a sham. I move for a mistrial.
—Woody Allen in *Bananas*

It's amazing how so many well-intentioned ideas end up becoming a parody of their original designs. Take airlines' coach-class seating. Originally intended as a way to provide an economical way to travel, the idea has been taken to such extremes that passengers now get little more than a no-frills cattle-car ride. The same can be said for the American tort system, which was created as an equitable way to resolve disputes. It has since evolved into a virtual circus of legal tricks and sideshow polemics.

Tort, as defined in *Black's Law Dictionary,* is: "A private or civil wrong or injury . . . for which the court will provide a remedy in the form of an action for damages." Read, *financial compensation.* More specifically, a *personal tort* is "one involving or consisting of an injury to the person or to the reputation or feelings, as distinguished from damage to real or personal property. . . ." Hence, personal-injury lawsuits.

Somewhere along the line, society had the great idea that if somebody causes a "civil wrong or injury," that person should be held accountable to compensate the injured party. Fair enough. But unfortunately, the ever-present opportunists soon discovered that this well-meaning remedy could be manipulated into a source of easy money. This is accomplished by grossly exaggerating damages and distorting the idea of negligence beyond any semblance of its definition. In the process, accountability is stretched to grotesquely contorted proportions.

So what was once intended as compensation for actual harm is now mostly a market for subjective "whiplash" or, in millennial parlance, "soft-tissue" injuries—ones that are unprovable and, better yet for the plaintiffs, impossible to disprove. Roughly two-thirds of medical claims resulting from auto accidents, for example, are believed to be, if not outright bogus, at least grossly exaggerated. Minor fender benders are inflated into pseudo-scientific dog-and-pony shows for a jury's consumption. Dramatic testimony by medical professionals, accident reconstructionists, and a plethora of other "experts" is often used to rivet the jury. And the jurors, caught up in the pomp and circumstance of the court proceedings, are routinely swayed into believing that they are benevolent benefactors endowed with the duty of showering the victims with pain-relieving cash. The result? To offset these costs, the average driver pays an additional $250 in annual insurance premiums.

It shouldn't be surprising, then, that enterprising personal-injury attorneys can take virtually any situation and make a case out of it. They know that a court victory hinges not so much on clearly defined law or logic as on compassion, emotions, beliefs, and the myriad obscure human interests that are part of the jurors' makeup. Probably the most famous case of jury fuzziness is the O. J. Simpson criminal trial. In that case, it seems clear that the jury was swayed not simply by hard, cold facts, but by personal sentiment.

Yet in civil cases, the main objective is to sway a jury for financial gain. The result is more than sixty thousand personal-injury lawyers in the United States alone. All are making a living off their clients' "injuries"—injuries sustained in auto accidents, premises-liability mishaps, and slip-and-falls. Many of these injuries carry over into other areas of litigation such as product liability and class actions; and with the advent of "emotional distress" as a compensable "injury," personal injury has become an appendage to just about every lawsuit there is. The word is out—and has been for a long time—that given the right spin, any accident, be it serious or trivial, can mean money in the pocket.

Finally, since the almighty dollar has become the primary objective of lawsuits, it's essential for the purported victim to know if the targeted party has plenty of money to go around. One favorite ploy is to go after only those who have the best means to pay, typically defendants with high-limit insurance policies, corporations, and government entities. These "deep pockets" usually end up being pulled into lawsuits regardless of how remotely they may be connected.

DEEP POCKETS

McDefendant

We can all recall the lawsuit filed in 1994 by the little lady from Albuquerque, New Mexico, who decided to balance a cup of steaming coffee between her legs while riding shotgun in her grandson's sports car. The seventy-nine-year-old granny spilled the coffee and burned her tush, and the rest is history—history being a jury award of $2.7 million in damages (which a sagacious judge later slashed to $480,000). We're reminded of her public service every time we buy a cup of coffee at McDonald's and see the warning on the cup that declares: "Caution: Contents Are Hot." (Personally, we've noticed the coffee seems a bit more on the lukewarm side these days, but better safe than sorry.)

As it turns out, you don't even have to be the person who spills the drink to reap the rewards of the mishap. In another McDonald's case in 1995, a spill-happy customer purchased a chocolate milk shake, hamburger, and fries at a drive-through window and drove off with the shake between his legs. As he leaned over to reach into the bag of food, his legs tightened, popping the lid off the shake and sloshing it onto his lap. Startled, he looked down and slammed into the car in front of him. The driver of the other car, evidently displeased with the shake spiller's lack of auto insurance, decided to fish around for another defendant that could more adequately compensate him.

Bingo! He sued McDonald's. Why? For not having a warning on the milk-shake cup instructing customers not to "drink and drive." The plaintiff contended that if McDonald's had printed the disclaimer on the cup, the milk-shake-drinking customer would not have been slurping and driving, would not have spilled his shake, and, therefore, would not have rear-ended the plaintiff. To which we could add, using the same logic: had the defendant never been born, he would never have been driving behind the plaintiff and in turn would never have rear-ended him. So why not sue the shake sipper's obstetrician?

Outcome A New Jersey Supreme Court judge didn't quite buy the guy's argument, either. He dismissed the lawsuit, but also denied McDonald's request that the plaintiff reimburse the company for the $10,000 it had spent on attorney's fees. In the judge's words, the plaintiff was "creative and imaginative and shouldn't be penalized for that."

Look Out Below

Is a Coco Loco too hard to hold? One woman in Ann Arbor, Michigan, thought so. The forty-nine-year-old university professor filed a federal lawsuit against Royal Caribbean Cruises in 1998 after being hit on the head by a Coco Loco tropical cocktail during an "Island Night" party on a cruise en route to San Juan, Puerto Rico.

Apparently, the unlucky plaintiff was floored by the twelve-ounce mixture of coconut milk, pineapple juice, and rum served in a coconut husk after the concoction slipped from the hands of a passenger standing on an upper deck. In her deposition, the woman said she and her husband were standing on the lower deck of the *Zenith* cruise ship in March 1997 when he left to get a plate of ribs. Suddenly, she felt something strike the crown of her head, fell to the floor, felt blood and "saw stars." On his return from the buffet table, her husband found his dazed wife lying beside a coconut shell and suspicious pile of slush.

Suffering from a concussion that affected her memory and balance, the plaintiff sued the cruise line for more than $2 million in damages. She claimed the company should have foreseen that a person holding the cumbersome Coco Loco by the ship's railing might drop the drink, hitting someone below. Her lawsuit went so far as to quote an "expert" from New York's International Bartenders School, who called the tropical drink "a recipe for disaster, an accident waiting to happen."

For its part, Royal Caribbean argued that Coco Locos had been served on its ships for years without any other coconut-related injuries. As such, the accident was not foreseeable, the cruise line's lawyers argued, and hence the company could not be held liable for the carelessness of a single passenger.

Outcome No news yet on the outcome of this "nutty" lawsuit. But don't be surprised if your next Caribbean cocktail comes served in a Dixie Cup.

Crash Course

In November 1971, a couple of lovebirds were enjoying a magical day at Disney World in Florida. They decided to try the Grand Prix ride, in which patrons steer miniature race cars around a railed track at breakneck speeds approaching six miles an hour. The woman drove off first, with her then-fiancé following closely behind in his own car. As they rounded the course, the fiancé, who apparently hadn't mastered the fancy footwork involved in applying the brakes, managed to rear-end his girlfriend's car. The woman sued Disney World for whiplash.

Outcome A jury assessed the woman's injuries at $75,000, but decided that the theme park was liable for only 1 percent of the damages. It determined that the plaintiff was 14 percent at fault for stopping her car abruptly, while her fiancé was 85 percent at fault for ramming into her. Sounds fair, but there's a twist: The fiancé claimed he was unable to pay his portion of the damages—so the court ordered Disney World to pay it for him. In other words, the theme park was forced to cover 86 percent of the woman's award, even though it was only 1 percent at fault! Stranger still is the fact that the bumper-car couple then got married—so the new husband actually ended up enjoying the $63,750 that Disney had covered him for!

Taking a Bite Out of Justice

In 1996, a New Hampshire woman dropped by her friend's apartment for a visit. While the two were chatting, the tenant's pit bull jumped on the woman, biting her numerous times on the arms and legs. The victim faced roughly $40,000 in medical bills after the attack. But did she sue her friend, the owner of the vicious dog? Why, no. She sued the owner of the apartment building—for allowing pets!

Outcome Even more outrageous is the fact that a jury actually awarded the mauled woman $2.1 million.

Reaching

A New York family may have reached even farther in 1995 when it filed a $35-million lawsuit in the state's supreme court following a car accident. Of course, the other vehicle didn't carry $35 million worth of insurance. But that wasn't a problem for the ingenious plaintiffs, who simply named a defendant that did: Motorola Incorporated. Why? Because the driver of the car that hit them was reaching for her Motorola cellular phone when she lost control of her car!

Outcome No news on the outcome of this crank suit, but it sure gives new meaning to the old phone phrase "Reach out and touch someone." (It's worth mentioning that in June 2001, New York became the first state to ban the use of handheld cell phones by drivers. Similar laws are now under consideration in at least forty other states.)

Santa Suit

A New Jersey reporter sued a shopping mall in October 1992, two years after she was injured by a throng of excited children waiting for Santa to appear. The woman accused Rockport Mall of failing to adequately control the crowd of youngsters who had gathered outside the mall in December 1990 to see St. Nick fly in from the North Pole with two penguins in a helicopter. She demanded that the mall pay her $2,500 for the dislocated kneecap she suffered when she was bumped by "one of the young patrons." Her husband also claimed that he had been "deprived of her care and services" because of the injury.

Outcome No news of the outcome of this lawsuit, but we're pretty sure the plaintiff is going to get a lump of coal for Christmas.

Taking the Fall

Counting down his final days of second grade, an eight-year-old Massachusetts boy climbed a schoolyard tree with some friends, hanging from branches and horsing around. But the fun ended abruptly when a classmate pulled the boy's leg, causing him to fall ten feet. He broke his wrist and spent a miserable summer in a cast. That was in 1997.

Fast-forward three years. The little tyke was doing fine—swimming, playing basketball, and even climbing the occasional tree. Meanwhile, his parents were suing the city of Boston, the Boston School Committee, and their son's teacher at Emily Fifield Elementary School, arguing that the accident was caused because the class had not been properly supervised. Their lawsuit, filed in July 2000, demanded monetary compensation for medical care and the time their son lost that summer when his arm was in a sling.

Outcome No verdict yet. In simpler times, however, most parents would have viewed the accident as a "boys will be boys" mishap and moved on. But that was then. Nowadays, when a boy tumbles from a tree, it's usually some deep pocket that takes the fall.

The Flying Nun

There's nothing like a leisurely softball game to bring friends together for a good time. Usually it's fun and rather uneventful. That wasn't the case in one particular ball game, however, which escalated into a full-blown lawsuit involving the entire league and the city of Syracuse, New York.

The trouble started in July 1994 when one of the players ran for home plate and collided with the catcher. Unfortunately, it ended with the catcher breaking her right leg, then voicing a few well-phrased expletives before being transported out of shouting range by an ambulance. Being the good sport that she was, the foulmouthed catcher went on to sue the player who had bowled her over. She also sued the city, which owned the softball field, as well as the corporate sponsor of the other team.

Ironically, the main defendant, who had hit the home run, happened to be a Roman Catholic nun. Should she be the one to pay $500,000 in damages for "negligently, carelessly, and recklessly" bowling over the catcher? No doubt the sister believed these prayers were misplaced at best. And the team's sponsor, which had contributed more than $12,000 annually to various teams, dropped out of the sponsorship business altogether from that point on.

Outcome No news on the outcome of this "Hail Mary" lawsuit. We suspect, however, that a jury will find the defendant to be a credible witness on her own behalf.

POOR SPORTS

Can you figure out what role the sponsor of the softball team, or the city of Syracuse for that matter, played in this legal fiasco? Clearly, the only reason they were hauled so unceremoniously into court was because of an ability to pay more money. Undoubtedly, trying to squeeze $500,000 out a nun would have been an exercise in futility. But by naming some faceless company or government entity, the chances of swaying a jury into doling out cash were far better than mugging the sister.

Sporting lawsuits like these are actually quite common, though they do require some creativity by the plaintiffs to stretch the blame. The defense usually has a good liability argument, namely the "assumption of risk" by the participant. If someone goes skiing, for example, it means that the skier is aware of the risks involved and assumes those risks by proceeding downhill anyway. This logic, though, is rarely a deterrent for imaginative attorneys, as the following cases show.

First Down

A female athlete at Francis Scott Key High School in Union Bridge, Maryland, knew the ins and outs of football well enough to play on the guys' team. It seems, however, that she overlooked one basic premise of the contact sport: you can get hurt.

In 1989, the seventeen-year-old athlete became the first female running back in the school's history. Although the school's board members shuddered at the thought of the young lady buried under a heap of thick-necked tacklers, they knew that forbidding her to play would violate a federal law banning discrimination based on gender. So they crossed their fingers and waved her onto the field.

Unfortunately, the running back didn't make it past the first scrimmage. Tackled moments after kickoff, she suffered a swift knee to the stomach, an injury that eventually resulted in the loss of her spleen and half her pancreas. Three years later, in October 1992, the sidelined sportswoman sued the Carroll County Board of Education for $1.5 million. Her claim: No one had explained to her "the potential of serious and disabling injury inherent in the sport." Based on what she had seen on television, she had believed she was unlikely to suffer much more than "a twisted ankle or something." Seems this sports enthusiast had never watched *Monday Night Football*.

Outcome The waylaid running back failed to score any points with the judge, who ruled against her.

All Washed Up

In 1991, a water-skier who fell and was hit by his own ski sued the skipper of the boat that was pulling him. He claimed that the boat's movement made the water choppy, causing him to lose his balance.

Outcome A judge thought the sportsman's argument was all wet. He dismissed the case, stating that the plaintiff, by choosing to take part in a competitive sport such as waterskiing, had assumed any foreseeable risks—like falling. In 1997, a Texas court of appeals refused to reinstate the suit despite the water-skier's insistence that he wouldn't have fallen had the helmsman not been pulling him. For that matter, he wouldn't have been waterskiing, either.

Pint-Sized Tonya Harding

In 1999, a twelve-year-old girl was skating at a public ice rink in Berkley, Michigan, when she bumped into another skater, knocking her over. Embittered by her resulting knee injury, the fallen skater sued her preteen assailant for "reckless endangerment."

Outcome A trial court dismissed the case, ruling that skaters assume certain risks by stepping onto the ice—a surface reputed for being hard and slippery. Sadly, our plaintiff managed to persuade a state court of appeals to reverse that decision and allow the case to proceed to trial. After much ado, the state supreme court ultimately stepped in and reversed the appellate court's ruling. The justices stated, "When one combines the nature of ice with the relative proximity of skaters of various abilities, a degree of risk is readily apparent."

Knockdown, Drag-Out Suit

A Florida woman filed a lawsuit against a Boca Raton nightclub for coercing her into joining a tag-team boxing match in which she was then knocked out. The twenty-year-old had never boxed and had no intention of starting in September 1997, when she walked into Club Boca on a Monday, known to patrons as "fight night." The club had contracted with a Fort Lauderdale promotions company to hold shortened but otherwise full-fledged boxing matches to draw Monday-night crowds. All volunteer boxers were required to sign waivers and wear headgear and oversized boxing gloves to prevent injuries. But apparently those precautions weren't enough.

An emcee in search of a fourth woman for a two-on-two match picked our plaintiff out of the crowd. She claimed that she was "physically pulled into the ring," cheered on, and placed under "extreme pressure" by a rowdy crowd. According to her lawsuit, the plaintiff landed a couple of punches herself, then ran out of steam. When she turned her back, she got hit from behind and fell unconscious into the ropes.

Outcome At trial in 1999, the club's owners denied wrong-doing, arguing that the plaintiff had assumed the risk of injury by signing a consent form and stepping into the ring. But after a knockdown, drag-out court battle, the jury awarded the plaintiff $16,750 for her injuries.

Wesson or Crisco?

An accountant in Oakland Park, Florida, sued the Pure Platinum strip club in 1991, claiming that he was beaten and kicked senseless while oil-wrestling two bikini-clad women at his bachelor party. Apart from needing stitches to his lip, the plaintiff claimed he suffered "mental anguish and the loss of capacity for the enjoyment of life."

Outcome No news on this slippery case. As a side note, though, one of the female wrestlers once knocked out Geraldo Rivera on his syndicated television show and is known professionally as The Banshee. Sounds like the plaintiff got what he paid for.

Net Proceeds

New York's Richmond Hill High School got tangled up in a lawsuit after one of its student athletes tripped while trying to bound over a volleyball net.

Practice was just getting under way one afternoon in April 1988. The school's volleyball coach instructed his players to hoist the net while he stepped out of the gym for a moment. Naturally, the teens took his brief absence as an opportunity to horse around, and began jumping over the net while teammates held it at increasing heights. One particularly enthusiastic teen took a running start from some thirty feet away. Tragically, he caught his foot on the top of the net, hit the parquet floor headfirst, and fractured a vertebra in his neck. He then sued the school for leaving him unsupervised.

Outcome The jury, clearly sympathetic toward the wheelchair-bound youth, awarded him $18.8 million in damages. In March 1997, however, a New York appellate court spiked the entire award, causing the teen to lament in the press, "I accept part of the blame, but what about the responsibility of the teacher and the school?"

DIFFERENT STROKES FOR DIFFERENT FOLKS

Fore in golfing parlance is a polite way to alert fellow duffers of incoming balls. Since most golfers need not worry about being hit by their own balls, the customary warning is usually intended for the benefit of others. Yet there are a rare few who may need to start yelling "heads up" to themselves before flailing at the ball, as shown by the following golfer lawsuit.

Teed Off

A woman in Maine actually sued the Fort Kent Golf Club in 1995 after managing to hit herself on the nose with her own ball. She happened to be playing on a fairway that had old railroad tracks running across it. Not exactly Pebble Beach, but as far as hazards go, no worse than the standard trees, ponds, and sand traps that are part and parcel of most golf courses. Yet somehow, when she hit her ball, it ricocheted off the tracks, hitting her in the schnozz.

Her attorney argued that the golf course had a "free lift"

rule, which allowed golfers to lob balls that landed near the railroad tracks to the other side. By virtue of that rule, he reasoned, the golf course had acknowledged that the railroad tracks were indeed a hazard. Of course, this didn't explain why the plaintiff had opted not to toss her ball over the tracks and had chosen instead to take a swipe at it, tweaking her honker in the process.

Outcome The golfer scored a hole in one in the courts, where she received a $40,000 jury award. She probably could have received another $100,000 from *America's Funniest Home Videos* had she only videotaped her ricochet shot.

Eagle Eye

We're not sure if the previous golfer was yelling "fore," "aft," "duck," or "yikes" when she popped herself in the face. But we do know of a woman in Madison, Wisconsin, who filed a lawsuit arguing that "fore" be used at all times.

Here's what happened: In 1999, the plaintiff was sunbathing asleep on the deck of her condominium, about 140 yards from a neighboring golf course. A golfer hit his ball, which crashed through a row of pine trees shielding the condo from the golf course and smacked the sunbather in the eye. She sued the condo owner, the condo association, and the golf course for having trimmed the trees too low to stop errant balls. She also sued the golfer for failing to warn her by yelling "fore."

The case against the condo owner was thrown out, while the condo association and the golf course both settled out of court for undisclosed sums. That left just the golfer. In court, his attorney questioned why a golfer would yell "fore" if he saw no one in the area. He also pointed out that the golf ball had taken less than 2.9 seconds to travel from the tee to the plaintiff's reclining head—too short a time for the sunbather to have reacted, even if she had been awake.

Outcome The jury took only fifteen minutes to decide in the golfer's favor. His attorney summed it up by saying, "The truth is it was a fluke shot. The ball had to find its way through those trees, through the deck with a fence around it, and to the woman who was reclined with her feet facing toward the fairway, presenting an incredibly small target."

Toasted Caddie

A wild and crazy golfer sued the Men's Club in Houston, Texas, in 1994 after he ruptured an Achilles tendon in a spill from a golf cart. It turns out his "designated caddie" and driver was an exotic dancer who was so soused that she rolled the golf cart into a drainage canal. In case you're wondering why a stripper was caddying for the plaintiff, well, that was all part of the fun at the club-sponsored tournament.

Outcome Apparently unimpressed by the golf course's creative choice of caddies, a jury awarded the plaintiff $30,000 for his troubles.

Par for the Course

Here's another golfer who should probably take up a tamer sport. In 1996, this Wisconsin athlete tripped on his own golf-shoe spikes and took a nosedive onto the brick path of the Indianhead Golf Course in Wausau. It was no small tumble, either, given that he ended up requiring nine root canals and twenty-three dental crowns after his bout with the walkway.

The golfer sued the owner of the golf course, claiming that his spikes had gotten caught between the bricks in the path.

The golf course was negligent, he said, because it hadn't made the walkway out of smooth concrete. The golf course owner, on the other hand, argued that the plaintiff was slightly inebriated. As it turned out, the plaintiff had actually consumed thirteen drinks and had a blood-alcohol level of about 0.29—three times the legal limit for driving—at the time he kissed the pavement.

Outcome Of course that didn't matter, since golfers seem to be a sympathetic bunch with the courts, which in this case awarded the plaintiff $41,540 to put a smile back on his face.

What's Your Handicap?

Considering all the injuries involved in golf, maybe the club-wielding sportspeople should be required to wear full face helmets. Here's a seventy-four-year-old southern California golfer who could have benefited from one: He filed a lawsuit in 1994 after a 750-pound pine branch fell on him. He ended up with a broken nose and contusions; but far worse, the golfer claimed, the accident had aggravated his erectile dysfunction.

He sued the Oaks North Golf Course in Rancho Bernardo, claiming it failed to properly "safety trim" a large pine tree that bordered the ninth fairway. Had the tree just been clipped properly, he argued, the branch wouldn't have hit him—and in turn he would not have required the painful injections and suppositories he now needed to reach coitus with his wife of fifty-three years.

The defendants claimed the accident was an "act of God" and that his impotence had existed long before the accident. In fact, the plaintiff had a medical history dating back ten years in which he had voiced complaints of his little problem.

Outcome Be that as it may, a jury decided to placate not only the golfer but also his frustrated wife. He received $55,000 for his troubles; she pocketed $5,000 for loss of consortium. She's probably thrilled with the results of his golfing.

SEX APPEALS

If you thought *that* guy's sex life took a questionable turn after a knock on the noggin, consider the next few plaintiffs. Their personal-injury claims are pretty suspect, too.

Cable Car Named Desire

Although undoubtedly a sign of the times, outrageous lawsuits aren't purely a recent phenomenon. In fact, Americans can take pride in a long history of legal looniness. Take one high-profile case of 1970, which the media promptly dubbed "The Cable Car Named Desire." An aspiring dancer was riding a San Francisco cable car when it rear-ended an auto. The young woman, who was standing on the running board, lost her balance in the jolt, tumbled onto the pavement, and hit her head. She sued the city, claiming that the fall, of all things, had turned her into a nymphomaniac!

Outcome Sound nutty? The jury didn't think so. The sex-crazed commuter strolled away with $85,000.

A Surprise Outing

Sometimes all it takes is a little nudge to come out of the closet. Take the man in Michigan who filed a lawsuit in 1994 claiming that he turned into a homosexual after being "rear-ended" (talk about a double entendre!) by a pickup truck. The twenty-seven-year-old plaintiff sued the truck's driver for $200,000, alleging that the accident left him unable to have sex with his wife. The fateful fender bender, he added, also forced him to start frequenting gay bars and perusing homo-erotic magazines.

Outcome The jury bought the plaintiff's collision/conversion theory. Not only did it award him the $200,000, but it granted his wife $25,000 as well.

Satisfaction Guaranteed

It was Thursday night at St. Florian's Catholic Church in Milwaukee, Wisconsin, and the bingo game was in full swing. The announcer plucked white Ping-Pong balls from the machine and called out the numbers, oblivious to what was about to transpire . . .

A seventy-three-year-old parishoner seated at the front of the hall scanned her cards for the winning combination, pen poised, heart pounding in anticipation; she needed only one more number to win. Just then, the three-hundred-pound electronic bingo board gave way and toppled on her head.

Fortunately, the stricken senior escaped with no more than a bruised arm and a small bump on the gourd. Yet in her lawsuit, filed against the church in 1990, she claimed she had sustained $90,000 in more permanent "injuries"—namely, uncontrollable "spontaneous orgasms." Starting shortly after the accident, they apparently wracked her body in tingly "clusters" numerous times each day. To confound matters, the churchgoing granny also claimed the knock to her noggin made her sexually attracted to women for the first time in her life.

Outcome The circuit court judge who heard the case wasn't, well, satisfied. "It is unexplained in modern medicine how a bump on the head can alter sexual orientation or cause recurring orgasms," he declared. The judge, therefore, ordered the woman to undergo a psychological exam, but she refused and filed an appeal. The case remained tied up in court for six years before it was finally dismissed in April 1996. Since then, rumor has it, no less than a dozen seniors have hurled their heads against bingo scoreboards in hopes of suffering similar "injuries."

Knockout Knockers

A physical therapist went for all or bust when he sued a top-less nightclub for whiplash. The thirty-eight-year-old plaintiff claimed he suffered back and neck injuries at a 1996 bachelor party after being "slammed" in the face by a dancer's prodigious sixty-HH breasts. "It was like two cement blocks hit me," he testified. The man sought $15,000 for the reimbursement of medical expenses and what he alleged was nearly two years of "pain and suffering."

Outcome Alas, the plaintiff got another slap in the face when a judge ruled against him. As it turned out, the judge had sequestered the stripper in a room with a female bailiff, who put the defendant's beasts on a scale. She found each one to be about two pounds and of average firmness—hardly enough to inflict grievous injury to the plaintiff.

Workaday Grind

A Florida phone-sex operator sued her employer for a hefty workers' compensation package in 1999, alleging that she was injured from pleasuring herself too often at work. The forty-year-old telephone titillater claimed she had developed carpal tunnel syndrome, a repetitive motion injury, in both hands from giving herself an orgasm as many as ten times a day while speaking with callers! Her lawyer said she deserved weekly benefits of $267 plus $30,000 in medical expenses. "She was told to do whatever it takes to keep the person on the phone," he argued.

Outcome The plaintiff probably wasn't yelling "yes, yes, yes!" when she settled out of court for undisclosed "minimal damages."

ROYAL PAINS

Hot Buns

In 1997, a deliveryman for a machine shop in Los Angeles was stopped at a red light while on a routine trip across town. Noting the warmth from the engine beneath his buttocks, the driver soon realized he was sitting on top of a potential gold mine. He immediately slapped his employer with a workers' compensation lawsuit, claiming he had developed hemorrhoids because the seat of his truck was too warm.

Outcome No news on the verdict, but our guess is the judge will find the case to be a big pain in the rear.

Cool Stool

Believe it or not, that isn't the only lawsuit involving the illegal infliction of hemorrhoids. An inmate at the Centralia Correctional Center in Illinois claimed in 1995 that the state had violated his civil rights by replacing an old porcelain toilet seat with a stainless-steel one. Apparently, the new seat was so cold that it gave the prisoner a bad case of piles.

Outcome The crazy case was thrown out faster than you could say *Preparation-H*.

A Pain in the Foot

A Santa Rosa, California, woman managed to bamboozle a dozen jurors into awarding her a princely sum for a mysterious pain in her foot. The injured plaintiff's tale of woe began in 1995 at Berry's Market, where she went to buy some beer. When she opened the cooler, a wayward six-pack of long-necked bottles dropped from the shelf onto her left foot. She pulled off her sandal and sock to inspect her toes. There were no cuts, bruises, or other readily apparent signs of injury, so she bought another six-pack of beer and left the store.

Two months later, the woman called the store complaining of ongoing pain in her foot. Shortly thereafter, she filed a lawsuit against the store, demanding $2.5 million for future medical costs, lost lifetime wages, and damages.

According to her filing, she suffered from "reflexive sympathetic dystrophy," a nerve disorder that caused her constant pain. This rare "disease," her attorney argued, "left her with not much of a life." Interestingly, in her effort to get to the bottom of her mystery pain, the plaintiff consulted eleven different specialists, including podiatrists, neurologists, orthopedic surgeons, and even a psychiatrist—none of whom could find anything wrong with her—until she found the diagnosis that suited her best.

Outcome The charitable twelve-pack of jurors apparently suffered from a malady of their own—possibly a reflexive generous compensation disorder. After brainstorming for a good two days, they awarded the plaintiff $475,000 in damages. They decided the store employees hadn't acted negligently in causing the accident, since another customer had probably moved the six-pack into its precarious prefall position without their knowledge. But the jurors determined the store manager and the clerk had erred when they failed to preserve an in-house videotape recording the incident. Further, they concluded, the store failed to have a written policy on how to handle such mishaps and therefore, somehow, aggravated the injury. Hence, the jury's verdict: "Madam, we feel your pain."

Needless to say, the owner of Berry's Market was rather dismayed at being on the hook for half a million dollars. "I've tried to make sense of it but this, to me, is a case of lawsuit abuse and the need for tort reform," he told the local media.

Sir, we feel *your* pain.

Foot Foul II

Our second limping litigant wasn't so lucky after going toe to toe with a neighbor in court. This pain-in-the-foot plaintiff from California dropped some iron security bars on her toot-sie, then blamed her next-door neighbor, who had been help-ing her carry them. The neighbor's insurance company offered to settle the dispute by paying her medical bills, but she wanted more. She filed a lawsuit in 1997, demanding unspeci-fied damages for her "pain and suffering."

Outcome This time, the jury took just seventeen minutes to unanimously decide that the woman had only herself to blame for her flattened foot. The neighbor, however, ended up paying $4,700 in defense costs. The two are rumored to no longer be friends.

Death Grip

A Utah elementary school teacher sued the parent of a student for shaking her hand so hard during a parent-teacher conference that she had to undergo surgery, wear a hand brace, and drop out of advanced teaching classes. Filed in March 2001, the lawsuit charged the enthusiastic parent, a forty-eight-year-old homemaker and mother of two, with "vigorously pumping [the plaintiff's] arm up and down," causing "pain and suffering" to the tune of $250,000 in damages!

Apparently, the manhandling had forced the thirty-nine-year-old teacher not only to miss work and incur $3,000 in medical bills, but also to drop a university class, making her ineligible for a pay raise of $2,000 a year. "When she squeezed my hand and jerked it, she rubbed the bones and cartilage together," the plaintiff told the *Salt Lake Tribune*. "There was muscle and nerve damage."

Outcome No verdict yet. But if these two women go *mano a mano* in court, we're betting on the defendant.

Six Digits for One Digit

In 1999, a dental hygienist was kicking up her heels at a Georgia nightclub when her dance partner decided to try an impromptu "shag-style spin move." They twirled, their hands got twisted, and the woman broke her finger. She then sued her partner for having caused the accident.

Outcome Astonishingly, an Atlanta jury awarded the plaintiff a record $220,000 for her damaged digit. Up to that point, the state's largest verdict for a broken finger had been $20,000, won by a tennis instructor who was hurt in a 1990 car accident.

Man Versus Material

Can a direct hit by a T-shirt really cause a quarter million dollars' worth of injuries? A man from Cincinnati, Ohio, wanted a jury to think so. He sued the NBC network, the *Tonight Show,* and its host Jay Leno, claiming he was "battered" and "forcefully struck" in the eye on September 11, 1998, when a warm-up comedian before the show launched a souvenir T-shirt into the audience with an air gun.

The plaintiff, who chose to represent himself, claimed the flying garment was traveling at a near-supersonic eight hundred feet per second when it made "harmful and offensive contact with him." He sought $250,000 in compensation plus unspecified punitive damages for his pain and suffering, disability, lost wages, emotional distress, humiliation, and embarrassment.

Outcome The plaintiff's lawsuit hit a wall when experts pointed out that eight hundred feet per second amounted to 545 miles per hour, or the speed of a jetliner. An object traveling at that rate would have done a lot more than injure his eye—it would have torn off his head. The case was dismissed.

Talk About Hidden Charges

Let's face it, banks simply don't provide the same personal service they used to. Most are buying up their competitors, then replacing them with automated teller machines and on-line banking. Some seem like they couldn't care less about their customers. In fact, one bank gave a woman in Tampa, Florida, a heart attack.

Yes, this unfortunate bank customer had her life savings, approximately $20,000, stashed away in her account. When she received her monthly statement in May 1995, she eagerly tore open the envelope to see how much interest she had accrued. What she found instead was a zero balance. Hence the heart attack.

It's okay, though, because she bounced back and sued the

bank, despite its assurances that the big goose egg was simply a printing error.

Outcome No word on the outcome yet, but we're pretty sure the plaintiff is in store for some free checking.

PLEASE PASS THE BLAME

Attorneys suffer no shortage of buffoons to represent. Virtually anyone's crazy conduct, it seems, can be not only justified but also manipulated to shift responsibility onto others. And far too often, these blame games turn out to be highly profitable, too.

Swan Dive

In 1993, a man in Toronto, Canada, was getting a thrill from jumping off the roof of his friends' house into their swimming pool. Despite the homeowners' repeated protests, the thirty-six-year-old man repeatedly climbed through a window, ascended to the roof, and leaped into the water. On his fourth jump, however, he hit the side of the pool and broke his neck. After recovering, he sued his friends for negligence.

Outcome Despite the fact that his own lawyer called his high-diving antics "idiotic," the plaintiff was awarded $2 million for his injuries.

Asleep Under the Wheel

A Washington man got drunk one night in 1994, then tried to stumble his way home. The walk must have been quite tiring because, rather than waiting to reach his bed, the man curled up in the middle of an arterial road and dozed off. As you can guess, it wasn't long before an unsuspecting motorist, in a squeal of brakes, ran over the street sleeper and nearly killed him. The man, by then fully awake, sued not only the driver but also the city.

Outcome A jury awarded the plaintiff $120,000. Maybe now he can pay for a cab ride home.

Hey, Who Put That Road Block There?

If the previous case didn't prove that liquor and litigious bozos don't mix, this one might. In 1985, a Texas man, who had a few too many drinks at a party, decided to show himself home for the night. He managed to find his car and start it, but that's where his cleverness ended. While speeding home at a mere seventy-five miles an hour, the blitzed driver missed three signs directing drivers to a detour and a fourth pertaining to a forty-five-mile-per-hour speed limit. He careened into a barricade where road construction was under way, suffering a concussion and broken bones.

Eight hours after the accident, the driver still had a blood-alcohol level of 0.09 percent, enough to be deemed legally drunk in many states. Yet rather than slinking off to the nearest AA meeting, thankful to be alive, what did he do? You got it: he found someone to sue. Although everyone else on the road that night had managed to avoid bashing into the barricade, the plaintiff somehow came to believe that there were others to blame for his injuries—namely the state highway department, the engineering firm that designed the detour, the utility company that owned the adjoining property, the road contractor, and four subcontractors.

Outcome Five years later, after spending exorbitant amounts on legal fees, the defendants finally settled the case by paying the man $35,000. So while the engineering firm, a small company with fifteen employees and $2 million in annual revenue, was stuck with $200,000 in legal bills, our plastered plaintiff walked away with enough for a new car and several kegs of beer.

Fiddling on the Roof

A cat burglar in Redding, California, sued the local school district in 1984 after taking a plunge through a school's skylight. According to the foiled prowler, the school had failed to warn him that the skylight was unsafe to walk on. (Maybe it should have provided a rope ladder with instructions, too.) Okay, the poor dope did get severely hurt, but then again, whose idea was it climb onto the school's roof and do a tap dance on the skylight anyway?

Outcome The court rejected the plaintiff's $3-million demand, but came up with a nice compromise instead. It awarded the clumsy cat burglar $260,000 plus $1,200 a month for life.

Freeway Fun

A twenty-eight-year-old dentist was cruising down a California interstate in 1994 when she lost control of her car. She veered from lane to lane, spun around to the point where she was cruising backward, then completed her joy ride by piling into another car. What did this freeway menace do next? She sued the motorist that she had plowed into, claiming that he should have been paying more attention to avoid the accident!

Outcome Fortunately, a more sensible judge dismissed the death-defying dentist's case.

Caught in the Headlights

A man who hit a deer while driving along a semirural stretch of road in Brazoria County, Texas, sued the local subdivision association in 1989, demanding that it compensate him for his back injury and whiplash. The man's lawyer alleged that some of the subdivision's homeowners had taken to feeding the deer and, therefore, could be held responsible for the animals' presence in the area.

Outcome When the local residents kicked up a fuss, the plaintiff backed off, announcing that he would not pursue the suit against them "at this time."

See No Evil

Few things could be less civil than the civil suit filed by a Florida minister and his wife against a Seeing Eye dog charity in 1995. Southeastern Guide Dogs was the only company of its kind in the region to raise, train, and provide Seeing Eye dogs for free to the visually impaired. One day, Freddy, a guide dog, was leading his new master, a blind man, on a training exercise to determine if the two would work well together. An instructor for the fourteen-year-old school supervised the team as they practiced at a shopping mall outside Tampa. A woman, who apparently had nothing better to do, stopped to watch. According to several witnesses, the nosy shopper made no effort to step aside as the blind man approached, because she was curious "to see if the dog would walk around her." The dog did, but the blind man failed to react fast enough and accidentally stepped on the woman's toe.

Apologies were exchanged, and life went on—that is, until a year later when Southeastern Guide Dogs learned it was being sued by the woman. She claimed her toe had been broken by the blind man and demanded $80,000 for medical bills, pain and suffering, humiliation, and disability. And as if that weren't enough, the woman's husband, who happened to be a minister, sought another $80,000 for loss of his wife's care, comfort, and companionship.

Outcome Fortunately, the case never made it to court. After being ridiculed in newspapers and on television, the plaintiffs eventually dropped their uncharitable suit.

Up in Smoke

Robbing banks was probably a much simpler vocation in the days of Bonnie and Clyde. These days, with all the high-tech security systems and booby traps to contend with, what's a career bank robber to do? For starters, he or she can do some lawful plundering when the old ways prove less than fruitful.

Take the Oakland, California, bandito who was on parole for a previous bank robbery when, in 1993, he decided it was time to hit the local savings and loan. He held up the teller, took the money roll given to him, shoved it in his pants, and made his getaway. He didn't get too far, though, because the money roll contained a Security Pac, which released tear gas and red dye, ultimately throwing a crimp into his departure plans.

The stickup artist then began robbing the legal way. He sued the bank, the Security Pac manufacturer, the city of Oakland, the local police, and the hospital—because, according to his complaint, he received third-degree burns around his genitals when the smoke bomb exploded in his pants.

Outcome The plaintiff moved for a summary judgment—that is, an immediate ruling in his favor. But when the court rejected his request, he eventually dropped the suit. Interestingly enough, had the desperado simply stuck with tradition and provided the teller with the customary bag to fill up, the smoke bomb would have blown up in the sack, the neck of which would have been firmly clutched in his hands, thereby sparing his privates. Of course, considering the plaintiff, that wouldn't have necessarily prevented a lawsuit.

Smoking in the Boys' Room

Gone are the days when troublesome pupils were slapped with rulers; now they're simply slapped with lawsuits. Believe it or not, a math teacher at Liverpool High School in New York sued an eleventh-grade student in March 1999 for smoking in the rest room!

The teacher alleged that the cloud of smoke he encountered in the school's lavatory left him with a sore throat, watery eyes, and head congestion. He sought $57 for a doctor's visit and allergy medication he claimed he needed after inhaling the smoke-filled air, in addition to an unspecified amount in punitive damages. "I was fed up with getting sick," the teacher said, adding that his real motivation in the case was to teach the rebellious teen a lesson. Well, thanks for making a federal case out of it!

Outcome The school board suspended the litigious instructor for ten days then relegated him to the math resource room, charging him with conduct unbecoming a teacher. The lawsuit against the student was dropped, but in March 2001, the teacher turned around and sued the school for not allowing him back into the classroom. No news on the outcome of that suit, but we suspect the plaintiff has gained quite a reputation as the teacher you don't want to mess with.

Temper Tempered

Who says smoking isn't bad for your health? Just ask the southern California smoker who tried to purchase a pack of cigarettes from a local Thrifty Oil convenience store in 1996.

When the customer was denied his smokes, he didn't take kindly to the unexpected crimp in his habit. The frustrated customer displayed his dissatisfaction by putting a fist through the glass door on his way out. In so doing, he managed to not only break the glass, but cut his right triceps as well.

The cashier called the local police, who showed up to deal with the situation. After speaking to both parties, the officers came up with a generous compromise. The ornery smoker promised to pay for the broken glass door and, in return, Thrifty Oil wouldn't prosecute him for vandalism.

But after the convenience store sent a repair bill to the jab-happy customer, he promptly filed a lawsuit alleging that Thrifty Oil had not complied with the Uniform Building Code, because it had used polished wire glass in an "ingress/egress door." Had the door not contained polished wire, he reasoned, he would not have cut his arm. Therefore, he demanded $147,000 to compensate him for his self-inflicted injuries. Needless to say, Thrifty Oil declined this generous offer and decided to duke it out in court.

Outcome After a four-day trial and two days of deliberations, the jurors awarded the surly plaintiff $17,000, but conceded that he was 60 percent responsible for his injuries. Therefore, he was entitled to only 40 percent, or $6,800, of the full award! Apparently, the plaintiff was to blame for punching the glass, and Thrifty Oil was at fault for having glass that cuts.

The Ninny-Bomber

Every family has at least one member who, through his or her antics, stands out from the rest of the clan. We all know the types—the Beaver Cleavers, Bart Simpsons, and Patty Hearsts of the family.

So when this Pontiac, Michigan, man went to his parents' home for a July Fourth celebration in 1986, it's easy to picture him as an adult Dennis the Menace. He was having a jolly old time playing with fireworks, which he had purchased from a coworker and brought to the party. Fun guy that he was, this thirty-two-year-old family jester was also imbibing on the side and was soon drunk. He then lit one of the fireworks. When it appeared to fizzle out, he bent down to inspect it—and it exploded in his face.

Aside from destroying one of his eyes, the firecracker also seems to have blown away any common sense he may have had prior to the incident. Deciding compensation was in order for his miscue, the man sued his parents in 1988. After all, they shouldn't have allowed him to use fireworks when he was "visibly intoxicated." He also sued his coworker for selling him the fireworks. And if that didn't cover all angles, he also filed a lawsuit against his employer for *allowing* the coworker to sell explosives on business property!

Outcome No news on the outcome of this case, but we're expecting fireworks in the courtroom if it ever goes to trial.

What a Blast

In another "explosive" case, a cleaning woman from Grand Haven, Michigan, sued for more than $25,000 in 1998 after being singed by a firecracker she stole from a condominium that she had cleaned. The plaintiff had apparently mistaken the stick of TNT for a decorative candle and, later that night, lit it at a restaurant while dining with friends!

Burned in the surprise explosion that followed, the cleaning woman sued the owners of the condo for leaving the firecracker behind without a warning on it. For their part, the condo owners said they had placed the device, which looked like a "huge firecracker," in a cupboard to keep it away from the children after someone had left it at their home during a party.

Outcome An Ottawa County Circuit Court judge dismissed the suit in June 2000, ruling that the pilfering plaintiff had it coming.

Flaming Cucaracha

In yet another legal flare-up, two wise guys entered a Texas bar in 1993 and ordered "La Cucaracha," a rum and tequila drink that in Mexico is typically served flaming. But because the club had a rule against serving liquid fire hazards, the patrons received their drinks unlit. Rather than having their fun spoiled, though, the men whipped out their cigarette lighters and, despite repeated warnings from the bartender, proceeded to light up. On his third round, one of the aspiring pyromaniacs put a flame to his La Cucaracha and—boom!—it exploded. The man, who was burned in the incident, sued the bar for serving him the combustible concoction.

Outcome The plaintiff was burned again in 1996 when the jury decided he was to blame for his own injuries.

Did the Earth Move for You?

There's no question that the life of a transient is tough. Little pleasures are often hard won for these peripheral members of society. Perhaps it's heartwarming, then, that in December 1992 two homeless people fell in love and decided to consummate their union by taking a romp in the hay. Unfortunately, the two New York lovebirds did so by dragging an old mattress onto the tracks of the local subway.

Well, with life being what it is, it's not hard to guess what happened next. Yes, an intrusive subway train barged in on the couple's intimate interlude and—spladap! Fortunately, it was a slow-moving train preparing to stop, so instead of running them over, it merely gave the preoccupied pair a good bump.

Here's the strange part: The couple sued the state transit authority for "carelessness, recklessness, and negligence," because it did not prevent access to the railroad tracks. Their attorney added, "Homeless people are allowed to have sex, too." Sure, but on public subway tracks?

Outcome After pleading their case, neither the couple nor their attorney was heard from again. We guess they suspected that they were in for a bumpy ride.

POTTY PLAINTIFFS

Some people seem to have the hardest time doing the simplest things—such as remaining perched atop a toilet seat long enough to take care of business. It's a problem the following four plaintiffs had in common. Okay, so they tumbled off their respective toilets, but is it necessary to sue? You be the judge.

Shattered

The first potty acrobat was a woman in South Carolina who, in December 1994, was using the ladies' room at Children's

Hospital in Charleston. She claimed that the toilet shattered beneath her, causing her to fall and hurt her back. Unfortunately, we don't have a physical description of the plaintiff, but judging by her version of the incident, either she must have weighed as much as a sport utility vehicle or she was doing something she didn't want anybody to know about. Was she attempting a full gainer? We'll never know, but we do know she sued.

Outcome Nothing on the outcome of this lawsuit, but we advise the hospital to invest in reinforced-steel toilet bowls.

Rest Room Rodeo

Our second toilet tort involves a New York woman who sued McDonald's in December 1994. Much like the previous plaintiff, she seems to be one of those folks who can turn life's simple matters into profound mysteries. She claimed that the fast-food restaurant's toilet was unsteady, causing her to be "thrown" against a wall when she sat down. The incident allegedly caused injuries to her arm, shoulder, and chest. Not about to take her lavatory launch sitting down, the plaintiff expected McDonald's to compensate her for the "pain and suffering, humiliation, and emotional distress" she endured.

Outcome No verdict at this time, but we suspect the judge may question whether the toilet was really the bucking bronco that the plaintiff claimed it was.

Exploding Commode

Our third bathroom blunder involves a bank president in St. Paul, Minnesota. It was June 1989, and he had just completed his executive business in the men's room when he bent over and flushed. Unexpectedly, the toilet blew a geyser of "200 to

300 gallons" of raw sewage right into his torso "with such force it stood him right up."

The peeved president sued a local construction company, claiming that it had caused the explosion by turning the sewer line off and allowing pressure to build up in the pipes. He demanded $50,000 for the "humiliation and embarrassment" he had to endure once word of his bathroom fiasco leaked out. The construction company offered to pay for the replacement of his soiled clothes, but argued that the bank was largely at fault for the eruption. Apparently, the bank building had a sewage holding tank and a pump that forces the tank's contents into the city sewer lines, but it was missing a crucial mechanism that stops the pump when the line is shut.

Outcome A judge thought the plaintiff's case was all wet. Dismissed!

Pinched Appendage

Our fourth and final bathroom bungler is a Canadian tourist who sued a Starbucks for $1.5 million, alleging that a highly private part of his anatomy was crushed when it got caught between the toilet seat and bowl at the New York coffee shop. The thirty-seven-year-old plaintiff was reportedly seated on the commode in March 2000 when he turned to grab some toilet paper. As he leaned forward again, the toilet seat apparently clamped his, well, manhood. The guy demanded that Starbucks pay him $1 million for what he described as "dire and permanent" injuries to the pinched appendage. His wife demanded an additional $500,000 for deprivation of his spousal services.

Outcome No verdict yet. Just be glad, though, that the plaintiff wasn't sitting on a Lawn-Boy power mower.

DOUBLE-DIPPING

One profitable ploy for attorneys is to represent people hurt on the job. The goal here is to do a little double-dipping. First, the employee is usually paid for his or her injury through the employer's workers' compensation insurance, regardless of who was at fault for the accident. Technically, this compensation is designed to cover only the employee's medical bills and loss of earnings, but is often manipulated to compensate for disability, as well. The trick is to then also sue a third party that may or may not be responsible for the injuries, and try to collect again from that defendant.

A Raw Deal

A convenience store in Charleston, West Virginia, got just such a raw deal when it was forced to pay a former employee a mind-boggling $2.5 million after she sprained her back opening a jar of pickles.

In 1991, the then–assistant manager claimed that the strain of prying off the jar's lid had revived an old back injury. She continued to work at the store for several months, but eventually stopped and began receiving workers' compensation benefits for "temporary total disability." A year later, the woman told her employer, Sheetz Incorporated, that she could return to work if she didn't have to do any heavy lifting. The manager told her that the job functions listed by Sheetz required employees to be able to lift up to fifty pounds and stand for eight hours a day. In addition, the company's liability policy prohibited injured employees from returning to work before they were completely recovered.

The woman finally returned to work in April 1995. On her first day back, she was asked to restock a cooler, a task that required lifting no more than a six-pack or two-liter bottle of soda. Within twenty minutes, though, she was incapacitated by "back spasms."

The next morning, the woman was once again out on workers' compensation leave. And sure enough, she also filed a lawsuit against Sheetz, claiming the store had failed to accommodate her disability and that the company's request that she stock a cooler violated the state's Human Rights Act.

Outcome Apparently, the jurors saw it that way, too. After a three-day trial, they awarded the woman $130,066 in compensatory damages, $170,000 for "emotional distress, upset, embarrassment, and humiliation," and $2.7 million in punitive damages! That's quite a pretty penny considering that the only proof of the woman's emotional distress was her own testimony that she felt "real bad." Although the state supreme court called this evidence "meager," it later slapped down an appeal by Sheetz and upheld $2.5 million of the verdict.

One supreme court justice was soured by the outrageous sum, however. In his dissenting opinion, he stated, "I know an excessive punitive damages award when I see one, and I see one here. I would call this one hard-core."

The Invited Police Officer

There's a luckless restaurateur in Lakeview, Texas, who called the police for help—then got sued by the responding officer.

In August 1994, an unruly customer kicked up a fuss for not being served after midnight and refused to leave. The restaurant employees then called the local police to give the guy the heave-ho. Enter the plaintiff, an eleven-year veteran and sergeant of the Lakeview Police Department. She carried out the job she had been dispatched to do by escorting the combative customer away from the restaurant. Unfortunately, in the process, she tripped and fell in the parking lot, breaking her wrist.

The city of Lakeview paid for her medical bills, lost time from work, and disability under its workers' compensation policy. Considering her fall was not in the course of any action-packed pursuit, it appears to us that she was adequately compensated for her misstep. But she didn't seem to think so.

The sergeant sued the now-defunct Croc's restaurant more than two years later for failing to maintain the premises "in a reasonable, safe condition for invitees who entered upon the premises." This uniformed "invitee" also sued the company that managed the restaurant, as well as two other companies belonging to the restaurant owner. She wanted $500,000 for her medical expenses (which the city had already paid for), as well as for the "physical and mental anguish," "physical impairment," and "disfigurement" she suffered. Upon being served the lawsuit, the owner of Croc's lamented, "It's concerning to call a policeman and in turn be sued for his injuries. Do firemen and policemen, if you call them for assistance, have the right to file on you when you're supposed to be paying them to protect you?"

Outcome No news on the outcome of this "Croc" of a lawsuit, but it seems the restaurant would have fared better with a robbery than having "invited" the local constabulary onto its premises.

Who Invited You?

Take consolation that the previous officer was at least "invited" onto the premises—unlike the next policeman who, in

1986, took it upon himself to enter an unsuspecting home-owner's property, then sued the homeowner.

This fleet-footed patrolman from Anaheim, California, was in hot pursuit of a burglary suspect when he tried bounding over the homeowner's fence and tripped on an old rotted post. Like the Texas sergeant above, he was compensated by the city's workers' compensation insurance, but then decided he was entitled to far more riches. He filed a $1-million lawsuit against the homeowner—who, incidentally, wasn't obligated to have any fence at all, let alone maintain one in hurdle-proof readiness for uninvited police officers.

Outcome In 1997—a full eleven years later—a jury finally cleared the homeowner of blame and refused to award the officer any of the $1 million he had requested. Maybe he'll fare better in the future if he waits to be invited onto someone's property.

Jackpot Cop

Another policeman in West Covina, California, fared far better with his double-dipping lawsuit than did the uninvited officer above. In 1996, this cop responded to an alarm that had gone off on the defendants' property. Since the homeowners were away, he checked around the house, then proceeded up to a wooden deck on the second floor to look through a sliding glass door leading to the master bedroom. While he was heading back to the stairs, one of the wooden boards gave way, causing his leg to become lodged in the opening.

The police officer radioed for help and had a lieutenant, a corporal, and a sergeant extricate him from his mess. Trained investigators that they were, they promptly took photos of the scene and removed the broken board as evidence. Yes, evidence. Apparently, they were no longer interested in intruders, but rather in making a case for their fallen comrade.

A subsequent investigation revealed that two years prior to the incident, the homeowners had a termite company inspect their property. The exterminator allegedly recommended that several boards of the balcony be replaced. But the homeowners claimed the company had also offered an alternative: to scrape and treat the fungus and dry rot. This was what they had chosen to do.

The policeman, however, sued the homeowners—and the exterminator—anyway. Like the two preceding officers, he also received workers' compensation benefits. In fact, two years after the incident, the thirty-six-year-old officer was deemed incapable of handling his duties as a patrolman due to his injuries. He was then put on disability retirement, under which he was entitled to receive half of his pay, about $2,000 a month, tax-free, for the rest of his life. The workers' compensation carrier also paid his medical bills and $34,000 for the disabled officer's lost time from work.

But in a grand show of double-dipping, the officer wanted more from both the homeowners and the termite company. His suit claimed that he had undergone surgery on his right and left shoulders for nerve impingement, yet admitted he had fully recovered in the left shoulder and almost fully in the right. The defendants, via their independent medical examiner, argued that neither shoulder operation was necessary. A biomechanical engineer also testified that the officer could not have been injured in the way he had described.

Eventually, all this information was introduced at trial, except for the part about the lifetime payments the officer was already set to receive. This, for some legal reason, was kept from the jurors, lest it influence their decision. And, lest we forget what this lawsuit is really all about, we should reiterate that this trained and armed guardian of the peace was doing his job—in a profession that makes no guarantees of safety—on the property of citizens who didn't even know he was there.

Outcome A jury decided that the homeowners should pay the thirty-six-year-old plaintiff—who was almost fully recovered yet retired on disability—the hefty sum of $268,872. That's on top of the $50,000 the termite company paid to avoid going to trial, and on top of his lifetime stipend. All this to someone who can now go out and get another full-time job.

Encore

One final police story: In 1990, a patrolman in Wheeling, Virginia, was called to the home of a seventy-six-year-old widow who thought she had heard a prowler late at night. When the officer arrived on the premises, he promptly slipped and fell on her front steps. After collecting his workers' compensation, the patrolman then sued the elderly woman, claiming he had hurt his back, head, "body chemistry," and "psyche." He demanded $1.4 million for his heroic response to the defendant's 911 call.

Outcome The lawsuit was eventually settled for an undisclosed sum. To which we add, if the officer received more than a nickel, he was overpaid.

Going Postal

Neither rain nor sleet nor snow. . . . Well, it seems the average postal worker isn't quite as rugged these days. A case in point is the Los Angeles mail carrier who, in 1996, was foiled on his appointed rounds, not by harsh weather—but by some leaves. Yes, this thirty-eight-year-old postman was delivering letters to a duplex where some leaves had accumulated in the driveway. He slipped on them and hurt himself, collected workers' compensation—then sued the owner of the duplex.

We all know what the building owner did wrong: nothing, except perhaps failing to run outside with a butterfly net every time a leaf dropped toward the driveway. The postman, however, had a better theory. By letting the leaves pile up, he argued, the duplex owner had "created a hazardous condition."

Outcome Letting nature take its course, a jury ruled unanimously for the defendant in just one hour. The two-day trial, however, cost California taxpayers roughly $12,500.

I'VE FALLEN AND I CAN'T GET UP

All this goes to show that the old slip-and-falls, trip-and-falls, and even the oops-I've-conked-my-head claims are still highly popular forms of personal-injury lawsuits.

Next Stop, Mount Everest

It's doubtful there are any drivers who don't consider speed bumps a royal pain. But the little asphalt bumps serve their noble purpose—namely, ensuring that pedestrians are kept safe from speeding cars. So it might be considered a bit ironic that a shopping center in southern California was sued by a pedestrian who tripped over one such speed bump.

After her fateful stumble, the fifty-eight-year-old woman claimed she suffered from constant pain and was unable to stand or walk for more than an hour. She also said she could not sit in one position or kneel for extended periods. She blamed the Laguna Hills Plaza Shopping Center for having failed to "maintain" the speed bump in its parking lot. The defendant, on the other hand, argued that she had simply failed to lift her foot to step over it.

Outcome The jury rejected the woman's plea after a five-day trial, which included expert testimonies from a civil engineer and a "certified industrial/commercial safety professional" who contended that there was nothing particularly dangerous about the speed bump. These experts were no doubt paid handsomely for their professional opinions on the intricacies and social ramifications of speed bumps.

In God We Trust

A Michigan woman sued the Abundant Life Fellowship Church in 1990 after tripping on a concrete tire stop in the church's parking lot. The plaintiff, who broke her arm in the fall, sued for thousands of dollars in damages. She claimed that the church's tire stops, used to mark parking spots, were "haphazardly placed." Church officials said they gave the woman money for her medical bills, but refused an insurance settlement because they thought she was seeking more than she deserved.

Outcome The state supreme court apparently thought so too, dismissing the case a full ten years after it was filed. The court ruled that churches—unlike stores, banks, and other businesses that lure customers for a commercial purpose—hold less of a responsibility to make sure their property is safe. "We conclude that church visitors who are attending church for religious worship are more like social guests than business visitors," one of the justices wrote in his majority opinion.

Sticky Situation

We're forced to question the motor skills of our next plaintiff. The woman from El Paso, Texas, sued Furr's Supermarket for premises liability in 1995 after tripping over a piece of dried chewing gum on the sidewalk outside the store.

Outcome Before dismissing the case, the trial judge pondered aloud, "How does one trip over gum? How many times has everyone in this room stepped on gum without tripping?"

Fancy Footwork

A seventeen-year-old student and his father sued the town of Shrewsbury, Massachusetts, in February 1999 after the teen tripped on his own pant leg during gym class. Their lawsuit claimed the town was liable for the young plaintiff's "severe and debilitating" injuries because town teachers had required him to engage in physical activities without proper gym clothes. As a direct result, Twinkle Toes allegedly tripped over his trousers and suffered "great personal and permanent injury and loss of function of his foot."

Outcome No news on the outcome of this case. But given the plaintiff's troublesome trousers, we're surprised he made it all the way to gym class before tripping.

Technical Foul

A Michigan man sued a homeowner in 1998 after tripping over some decorative rocks while playing a game of pickup basketball in the driveway of the defendant's house. At trial, some of the other players testified that the injured b-baller had not only noticed the rocks but also pointed them out to his teammates. For his part, the hapless plaintiff denied seeing the rocks, but admitted that if he had glanced up while dribbling he would have undoubtedly seen them.

Outcome A judge ruled that the property owner was free of fault since the rocks were in plain sight. The plaintiff took another shot in appellate court but was rejected again.

Do Not Be Afraid, Monsieur

Here's a construction site that was left in not-so-capable hands after dark. The security guard on duty was diligently walking his post, checking for vandals, thieves, and other trespassers, when he stumbled across a real stinker of a situation: He spotted a skunk. So what did this trained night watchman do? He ran and leaped into a hole. In so doing, he managed to evade any pungent onslaughts from the invading varmint but, sadly, injured himself.

In 1995, the security guard then sued the engineering firm that designed the construction site, which in turn filed a cross-complaint against the construction company, which also filed a cross-complaint, and on and on it went. By then, everybody was pointing fingers at everybody else, except at the skunk and the dauntless guard.

Outcome No telling what the outcome of this putrid lawsuit will be, but we can certainly recommend a far better security system for the construction site: hire Mr. Le Pew.

Blue Light Special

Attention Kmart shoppers. It's raining blenders in aisle nine! Thanks to a fifty-four-year-old cafeteria worker, that is. The woman was browsing in a Northridge, California, Kmart store in 1997 when she spotted a blender she wanted. Unfortunately, the blenders were stacked four high on an upper shelf and out of her reach—well, almost. The woman jumped up and grabbed the bottom box in the stack. As she pulled, the three blenders above came crashing down onto her head.

The woman sued the retailer for failing to warn customers not to take stock from the upper shelves and for stacking the boxes too high. She also claimed the incident had caused her to suffer "neck, shoulder and back pain, and bilateral carpal tunnel syndrome." Strange, considering that carpal tunnel is a condition that develops in the wrists, usually after years of repetitive movements such as typing. In fact, there are more than twenty-seven causes of carpal tunnel syndrome, none of which is a falling blender.

Outcome Regardless, the plaintiff never managed to convince a jury. Her admission that she knew the boxes would fall, along with the fact that she didn't ask for help, did not set well with the jurors. They sided with Kmart after less than thirty minutes of deliberation.

Using the Old Noggin, Part II

Heads up! Here's another southern California shopper who used her noggin while shopping in a discount store. But this one, rather than butting a shower of blenders, decided to use her cranium to straighten a shelf.

The shopper had bent over to look through a box of merchandise on a lower shelf. When she tried to straighten up, she rapped her bean on the shelf above. She sued the store in 1996, claiming that it was negligent by not having merchandise occupying all available shelving space. In other words, by having half-filled shelves, the store presented a hazard to customers.

Outcome A jury decided the plaintiff's case had some serious gaps in it, too. It sided with the retailer. Nonetheless, the three-day trial cost California taxpayers roughly $18,500.

IF ONLY I HAD BEEN WARNED

Another popular avenue for attorneys to stretch the bounds of negligence is to argue that their clients weren't properly "warned" by the defendants.

Hey, Watch Where I'm Going!

A California woman who attended a barbecue at a friend's house filed a personal-injury lawsuit in 1996 after learning the hard way that there's often more than meets the eye.

When she arrived at the host's home, our plaintiff was shown through a sliding glass door into the backyard, where the guests had gathered. She walked back and forth through the open door several times over the next few hours, sometimes to fill her plate or chat to a friend, other times to use the bathroom. Yet later, the pacing partygoer headed inside once again—and marched face-first into the glass door, which someone had slid shut during the course of the evening.

Now, most people in her situation would have simply rubbed their noses and perhaps given themselves a swift kick for being so clumsy. Then they would have slid open the door and proceed with their day, hoping their face plant had gone unnoticed.

Not so here. The woman claimed her nose had been injured in the incident. How badly we don't know, given that she waited almost three months before seeing a doctor. It didn't take nearly as long, though, for her to sue her friend—for failing to warn her of the glass door! (We can only wonder whether the same warning would have been required for the surrounding walls and trees.)

Outcome It took the jury just one hour to see through the case and rule in favor of the homeowner. The four-day trial, however, cost California taxpayers about $24,500. Not exactly the cheapest way to tell someone to watch where they're going next time!

Attack of the Sleeping Dog

It's not unusual to find dog owners being sued for the antics of their beloved pets. Usually, the incidents entail the fun-loving pooch knocking a neighbor down or chewing on a postal worker's leg. Rarely, though, can we expect to find a dog owner being sued because the dog was lying around minding its own business in its own home.

Yet that's precisely what happened to one Raymondville, Texas, man in July 1996. It seems the unfortunate homeowner made the mistake of letting a visitor amble into the kitchen, where his dog was enjoying a nap. The unobservant visitor promptly tripped over the sleeping dog and injured himself.

The visitor then sued the homeowner for $25,000 because, according to his lawsuit, he should have been warned that he was "walking on the floor at his own risk." He also argued that the owner should have cautioned him about "the dog's propensity of lying in certain areas."

Outcome No word on the outcome of this boneheaded lawsuit, but we hope the dog filed a cross-complaint for the trauma of being kicked awake by the bungling visitor.

Look Mom, No Warnings!

A three-year-old boy and his sister were playing in the living room of their second-floor apartment in San Bernardino, California, while their mother chatted on the phone in the kitchen. Since it happened to be a warm March day, the windows were left wide open. It's not hard to guess the rest, save to say that the boy broke his leg after his free fall to the pavement below.

The indignant mom sued the owner of the apartment building for $90,000, claiming the window should have had a label warning residents that they could fall out. She also claimed the window should have had bars—not to keep intruders from breaking in, but to prevent residents from flying out. Finally, she argued that the window sill was too low to the floor, making it a dangerous condition.

Outcome The jury threw out the case in 1997, deciding the careless mother was lucky to still have her son in one piece.

Contest Casualty

A sixty-seven-year-old man in Norwood, Ohio, sued a local bar for more than $1 million after an "all-you-can-drink" contest left him falling-down drunk. The plaintiff won a Super Bowl 2000 drawing at Lieb's Cafe, which entitled him to free, unlimited alcohol for one day. His victory, however, quickly turned into one heck of a hangover, when he became so rip-roaring drunk that he fell over, hit his head, and was knocked unconscious. Hospital tests showed he had a 0.31 percent blood-alcohol level, three times the state's legal limit.

In January 2001, the plaintiff sued the owner of the bar for $1 million in punitive damages, accusing the bartenders of being "reckless" by continuing to serve him alcohol after he was drunk. He also demanded an additional undetermined sum exceeding $25,000 for past and future medical bills and pain and suffering.

Outcome No news yet on the outcome on this doozy of a lawsuit. It seems, though, that the defendant was in a no-win situation. Had the bar denied the plaintiff his promised drinks, it probably would have ended up in court for breaching its contest's terms.

Foul Ball

A woman in Connecticut dragged an eight-year-old little league pitcher to court for hitting her in the face with a baseball. The boy was warming up on the sidelines; he went for the windup, released too early, and sent the ball flying off course— on a direct trajectory with the woman's nose. In her subsequent lawsuit, filed in 1999, she claimed the boy was careless, failed to warn her, and threw the ball at a "dangerous speed." (Just how fast could an eight-year-old actually throw?)

Outcome The case was eventually thrown out on a technicality. The plaintiff had named the boy as the sole defendant. Since eight-year-olds can't be sole plaintiffs under the law, the boy's attorney argued that the same should hold true for defendants. The judge agreed.

SAY, THAT COFFEE'S HOT!

As we mentioned earlier, one of the country's best-known "lack of warning" lawsuits resulted in the colorful "Caution: Contents Are Hot" disclaimer found on McDonald's coffee cups these days. That historic coffee-spilling caper of 1994 has also inspired a slew of copycat sloshings around the nation. Shrewd imitators that they are, however, these self-scalders often try to avoid the obvious by targeting other hot-drink servers.

To celebrate this innovation in litigation, we have chosen to close this chapter on personal-injury lawsuits with an award commemorating spill-and-sue lawsuits. Admittedly, we were at a loss for what to call this award. Several ideas were bandied about, including the "Oops, I've Burned Myself!" award. Another was "Buddy, Can You Spare $2.7 Mil for a Cup of Coffee?" We even considered the not-so-subtle "Just Call Me Butterfingers." But we finally settled on "Say, That Coffee's Hot!"

So, here are the six finalists for the prestigious "Say, That Coffee's Hot!" award.

Fireman Bob

Our first nominee is a sixty-five-year-old retired firefighter from southern California. Given his profession, it seems he would be an expert at dealing with heat, fire, burning buildings, and such. But no, he too fell victim to a "too hot" cup of coffee.

This nominee bought his cup of joe in April 1994 from a Starbucks shop in Malibu, California. He returned to his van, placed the cup on his dashboard, and drove off. When he stopped suddenly, the coffee fell from its perch and splattered on his right foot.

Nominee No. 1 sustained a second-degree burn to his tootsie, which, with an infection, escalated to a third-degree burn. We suspect that the injury wasn't quite as bad as he wanted the jury to believe, though, because his medical bills amounted to only $500. Nonetheless, the former fireman sued Starbucks, claiming the coffee was "unreasonably hot" and "therefore dangerous." (How comforting, a firefighter who considers hot coffee dangerous.)

Desired compensation $60,000.

Outcome The jury decided the plaintiff's injury was the result of his own carelessness and ruled in favor of Starbucks.

The Cocoa Kid

Our second nominee is a thirteen-year-old boy from Sherman Oaks, California. He bought a hot chocolate (okay, so it's not coffee) and some candy from a 7-Eleven convenience store in January 1995 before catching a ride with his carpool. While in the backseat, he clutched the cocoa between his legs so that he could free his hands to munch on the candy. The car stopped short, the hot drink spilled, and junior grilled himself. The injuries amounted to second- and third-degree burns to his left foot.

Nominee No. 2 then sued the 7-Eleven store because the drink was served "unreasonably hot." Sound familiar? He went on to allege that there was a breach of implied warranty and a design defect in the cup. Finally, the youngster's lawyer claimed there was "a failure to warn" him of the possible consequences of perching hot cocoa between his pubescent legs.

Desired compensation $235,000.

Outcome The jurors tossed out the case, apparently realizing that it doesn't take a fireman to know that hot drinks can burn.

Cocoa Case II

Our third nominee is a man from Fayetteville, Oklahoma, who sued Braum's restaurant in October 1998 after receiving second-degree burns on his thigh when he spilled a hot-chocolate drink that he had bought at the restaurant's drive-through window. His lawsuit is unique in that it claimed the burn left him unable to apply his van's brakes, therefore causing him to slam his vehicle into park to avoid hitting other cars. His transmission was damaged as a result.

Desired compensation $1 million.

Outcome A federal judge threw out the case in March 2000, noting that the plaintiff was a regular cocoa drinker and should have known his drink was hot enough to burn. He went on to add, "The court observes that, while it hesitates to characterize a case as frivolous, the degree of that hesitation in this case is quite minimal."

And the Kitchen Sink

Our fourth nominee filed a lawsuit against the Oasis Truck Stop, a popular highway rest stop in Hartland, Michigan, in 1998 after dousing herself with a cup of coffee she had purchased from the store's vending machine. What vaults this plaintiff into the top echelon of spill-and-suers, however, was her decision to also file negligence suits against the makers of both the coffee machine and the coffee cup.

The customer's lawyer argued that the truck stop and coffee-machine manufacturer were at fault for making coffee that was too hot, although an investigation found the temperature of the brew to be exactly what it should have been based on accepted industry standards. Meanwhile, the cup manufacturer was accused of a design defect (one that apparently allowed liquids to flow out of the cup when dropped).

Desired compensation $62,500.

Outcome Again, the jurors didn't go for it. They threw out the case, figuring the plaintiff could have prevented the mishap by simply holding on to her cup a little tighter.

Big Bucks from Starbucks

Our fifth nominee is a twenty-eight-year-old woman from New York. She purchased her fated cup of java in 1998 from a Starbucks in Manhattan's Upper East Side. Nominee No. 4

has an edge on the other spillers in that she didn't even make it out of the front door of the coffee shop before scalding herself. The woman simply removed the cup's lid to add milk and sugar. In the process of doing so, a drop of the hot coffee dribbled onto her finger, causing her to drop the cup and splatter the contents over her ankle. She, too, alleged second-degree burns.

Like those of the others, Nominee No. 4's lawsuit claimed that the temperature of the coffee was "dangerous" and "unsafe." She receives bonus points, however, for originality: she added a new twist by also alleging that "too much" coffee had been poured into her cup.

Desired compensation $1 million.

Outcome No word on the outcome. We suspect, however, that the plaintiff's case, unlike her coffee cup, won't hold "too much" water in court.

Mother Made Me Do It

Our sixth and final nominee is a woman from southern Illinois who apparently didn't take heed to the now-famous "Caution: Contents Are Hot" warning on her McDonald's coffee cup. The woman, who was a passenger in her mother's car, ordered a cup of coffee from a McDonald's drive-though window in 1998. As she placed the drink in the car's cup holder, it spilled and burned her ankle. Claiming the coffee was served at a temperature "hot enough to scald the human body," the woman filed a lawsuit in January 2001 against not only McDonald's but also Wal-Mart, which made the cup holder, as well as her own mother! She accused her mom of negligence, claiming that she was responsible for the safety of others riding in her vehicle.

Desired compensation $450,000.

Outcome The case has yet to go to trial, so there's no telling who'll get burned.

And the winner of the "Say, That Coffee's Hot" award is . . . well, there are no winners. Except, of course, the trusty defense attorneys, who are paid regardless of the outcome of the lawsuit. The plaintiffs and their attorneys, gamblers that they are, roll the dice and sometimes win, sometimes lose. So simply because the diva of the spilling craze received a resounding award doesn't mean all her impersonators will fare as well. The defendants, on the other hand, are always losers. And Joe Consumer? *Loser!*

2

CRIME PAYS:
INMATE LAWSUITS I

One of the biggest lies in the world is that crime doesn't pay. Of course, crime pays.

—G. Gordon Liddy

Believe it or not, there may be one institution that breeds more aspiring attorneys than the American bar—the slammer. No sooner do criminals land behind bars, it seems, than they gain a newfound appreciation for the finer points of the law.

Take the guy convicted of murdering five teenage girls with ice picks, sledgehammers, and coat-hanger garrotes. This jailhouse "lawyer" filed a federal lawsuit from his prison cell on death row. His complaint? That jailers had subjected him to "cruel and unusual punishment" by serving him soggy sandwiches!

Then there's the former Florida firefighter who was sentenced to seventeen years in prison for stabbing his roommate and dumping her body in a shallow grave. After his conviction in 1995, this frequent filer sued the Palm Beach County Sheriff's Department, the sheriff, and three detectives who investigated him. He served the victim's mother with a letter accusing her of fraud and demanding that she pay him $15,000. And he slapped a libel and slander suit on the lawyer who won a civil wrongful-death judgment against him. The ironic part is that he could be released for good behavior after serving just six years.

Sadly, these two convicted killers aren't the only ones trying to get away with murder. In 1999, prisoners filed a whopping 56,603 lawsuits in U.S. district courts, 33 percent more than in 1990 and 143 percent more than in 1980. Each case costs taxpayers anywhere from $1,000 to $6,000—even though more than half are thrown out as "frivolous" and 96 percent of those that remain are eventually found in favor of the defendant.

Sure, some lawsuits are valid, like the one filed in January 2000 by four female inmates in New York who spoke out about being raped by prison guards. The vast majority, though, are baseless gripes filed by contentious felons who have nothing better to do than harass prison officials, their victims' families, and anyone else unlucky enough to cross their minds. Take the rambunctious rapist who decided to sue the *wife* of one of the jurors who convicted him.

Repeat Offender

This Missouri convict claimed that a juror's spouse, whom he had never met, was part of a broad "extrajudicial conspiracy" against him. That's no surprise, really, given that virtually everyone he came in contact with after being arrested in 1997 had somehow lied, committed fraud, or conspired to deprive him of his rights.

From his cell in a high-security penitentiary, the inmate churned out half a dozen lengthy, handwritten lawsuits, naming nearly thirty people as defendants. The filings asked for millions of dollars in damages for wrongs done to him after he was accused of rape—for a second time—by what he called a "rejected vengeful paramour."

Police caught the wise guy in his "paramour's" Kansas City apartment after a neighbor heard a struggle. He claimed that they were friends, but addressed her by the wrong name.

Seventeen years before, the convict had been charged with rape in South Carolina. He claimed consensual sex in that case, too, and sued the state Department of Corrections seven times from 1989 and 1995. Within months of his release from prison in South Carolina, the inmate was then re-arrested in Kansas City—and launched a second filing frenzy.

He sued the prosecutor, as well as the judge who sentenced him to eighty-eight years in prison. He sued the Johnson County sheriff and nineteen members of his department. He claimed deputies at the jail refused to sharpen his pencils. They gouged him for legal pads and wouldn't provide postage for his mail. And they didn't give him a desk to write on. The prisoner even taped an inch-and-a-half-long pencil stub to a filing to demonstrate what he was given to write with. When prison officials provided a pen, he put it to heavy use. One suit listed 119 reasons why he thought his lawyer didn't properly represent him.

As the district attorney who prosecuted him so aptly put it, this repeat offender "seems to be one of those individuals who devotes his life to making things miserable for other people. It's one of those few times I feel sorry for the inmates who have to be around him."

INDIGNANT INMATES

What is it about the state pen that turns lawbreakers into relentless litigants? Perhaps filing laughable lawsuits helps them whittle away the time. Or maybe it's simply an effective way to be a pain in the legal briefs. Whatever the reason, prison has an uncanny way of transforming even the most hardened criminals into defenseless victims, often with the frailest sensibilities. Here are just some of the myriad "injustices" suffered.

Left Out

An Arizona inmate filed a lawsuit claiming he suffered emotional distress when he was not invited to a pizza party that prison employees held for a guard who was retiring.

Rise and Shine

A convicted killer in Massachusetts sued two prison guards for $100,000 after being woken up too early on the morning of his parole hearing. The cranky criminal claimed his 5:00 A.M. wake-up call made him too tired to present his usual sunny self to the parole board, which ultimately rejected his bid for freedom.

All Choked Up

An ungrateful car thief in Colorado filed a lawsuit after a female guard tried to administer the Heimlich maneuver as he choked on a piece of meat. The guard was too small to wrap her arms completely around the malfeasant's midsection, so an inmate sitting nearby stepped in and saved his life. The choked-up thief's suit accused the guard of having given another inmate authority over him.

Don't Sue the Messenger

A San Quentin death row inmate sued the state of California, claiming his rights were violated when his packages were sent via United Parcel Service instead of the U.S. mail.

You Mean That's Illegal?

A woman serving a fifty-four-year sentence for kidnapping and armed robbery sued an Arizona prison for "losing contraband" sent to her by family members. Didn't anyone tell this jailhouse genius that illegal activities are frowned upon in prison?

Concerned Viewer

A perspicacious prisoner convicted of killing five people sued a Florida prison after lightning knocked out the facility's satellite dish. He argued that, because he no longer had access to public television, he was forced to watch network TV that contained violence and profanity.

Just the Facts

An Oregon inmate filed a $3-million lawsuit against a Portland TV station for the "mental frustration" he suffered when the station misidentified a fourteen-wheel tractor as an "eighteen-wheeler."

Fumbled!

An Arkansas prisoner accused the state of cruel and unusual punishment when he was forced to miss the National Football League playoffs.

We Beg Your Pardon

Eleven hospitalized criminals in Ontario demanded legal compensation for having been "inconvenienced" after a prison guard union staged a walkout. Incredibly, the union agreed to pay $45,000 to soothe the disgruntled cons. The leader of the eleven, a psychotic murderer, got $2,250.

Prize Patrol

A Michigan prisoner filed a lawsuit claiming that a sweepstakes mailing wasn't provided to him in time. If it had been, the incarcerated optimist argued, he would have won the multimillion-dollar jackpot.

Life Is Hard

An inmate sued after his Nebraska prison limited the number of complaints he could file monthly. The convict had been inundating prison officials with complaints such as "when it rains, puddles form that I have to walk around."

The Price of Incarceration

A New York convict filed a lawsuit claiming that, because he was serving as an inmate-paralegal in the prison law library, he should be paid the same wage that lawyers make.

Ditty for a Dodo

A Texas prisoner sued *Penthouse* magazine in December 2000 on the grounds that its layout of Paula Jones wasn't sufficiently revealing. The felon, who was serving fourteen years for robbery and assault and identified himself as the Minister of Law for the Mandingo Warriors prison gang, sought $500,000 in damages, alleging he had been "very mentally hurt and angered" when the magazine's pictorial didn't live up to his expectations.

A judge tossed out the case, using a little creative license in the process. U.S. District Judge Sam Sparks wrote:

> *Twas the night before Christmas and all through the prison, inmates were planning their new porno mission.*
>
> *The minute his Penthouse issue arrived, the Minister ripped it open to see what was inside.*
>
> *But what to his wondering eyes should appear—not Paula Jones' promised privates, but only her rear.*
>
> *Life has its disappointments, some come out of the blue. But that doesn't mean a prisoner should sue.*

3

THIS BLOWTORCH IS NOT A TOY: PRODUCT-LIABILITY LAWSUITS

WARNING: To avoid danger of suffocation, keep away from babies and children. Do not use in cribs, beds, carriages or playpens. THIS BAG IS NOT A TOY.

> —Warning label on the plastic wrapping around a Black & Decker coffeemaker

Have you ever wondered why the directions on your toaster, hair dryer, and blender warn against use in water? Could it be that manufacturers actually think consumers are clods? Quite possibly. Yet while they may sincerely want to ensure we don't injure ourselves, the real reason all those product warnings seem to be written with Homer Simpson in mind is because of the big P: product-liability lawsuits.

We live in a highly litigious society in which people, when injured, would sooner point fingers and run to the courts for compensation than admit that they were simply unlucky or forgot to use their heads. It's gotten so out of hand that makers of everything from chain saws to Q-tips are trying to anticipate any possible misuse of their products purely to avoid being sued. Nowadays, you can't even dry your hands without running smack-dab into a disclaimer. For instance, a warning on a cloth towel dispenser in one restaurant bathroom reads: "Use only to dry hands and face. Do not hang from towel. Intentional misuse can be harmful or fatal." The warning was written in both English and Spanish.

And that's just the tip of the liability iceberg. Fast Track Torpedo snow sleds now carry labels that warn, "Avoid trees, steep inclines and cliffs"—as though these words of advice were the only things keeping sledders from careening off the nearest precipice. Conair's Pro Style 1600 hair dryer reads, "WARNING: Do not use in shower. Never use while sleeping." Stickers on public toilets declare, "Recycled flush water unsafe for drinking." And printed on the box of a Batman Halloween costume is the choice phrase "PARENT: Please exercise caution. Mask and chest plate are not protective; cape does not enable wearer to fly."

Then there's the cryptic caveat accompanying a chain-link basketball net made by Lifetime Products: "All players must wear a mouth guard while performing slam-dunk maneuvers to avoid getting teeth caught in net." Wacky, right? It gets worse. The warning was the result of an actual lawsuit. Here's the story.

High Jinks

A fourteen-year-old Shaquille O'Neal in the making learned to keep his mouth shut on the basketball court—the hard way. The Nashua, New Hampshire, teenager was practicing his slam-dunk moves in the family's backyard in 1994. Impressively, he soared to the hoop and stuffed the ball. On his way down, however, his two front teeth got entangled in the net . . . and out they came.

The little jammer ended up needing $1,100 in dental work. So his parents sued Lifetime Products, the maker of the basketball net for, well, making the net.

Outcome Obviously, the boy's parents had some slick moves of their own. In November 1995, they netted a $50,000 settlement for their son's slam-dunk slipup.

SAVE ME FROM MYSELF

Whatever happened to good old accidents? Years ago, injuries happened either because of your own fault or someone else's. If it was someone else's error, you sought to recover your medical expenses, not to retire. But nowadays, you can't even have a freak mishap—like getting a piece of sporting equipment lodged in your mouth—without calling in lawyers to secure a whopping settlement and then some. Since 1993, the median jury award in product-liability cases—not including punitive damages—has more than tripled, from $500,300 to over $1.8 million in 1999, according to LRP Publications, a nonpartisan group that tracks cases. Here's just a smattering of unfortunate product-related slips, falls, cuts, and sprains (and a few of untimely deaths thrown in for good measure) that people have thought to cash in on.

Overreaching

A do-it-yourselfer in San Diego, California, was using an aluminum stepladder in his garage in 1998 when he fell and fractured his elbow. Despite admitting that he used the ladder without incident for at least eighteen months prior to the accident, he sued both the ladder manufacturer and Home Depot, which had sold him the wayward product.

Aside from his physical injuries, the fallen homeowner claimed to have suffered "loss of consortium" from his wife, who supposedly divorced him due to problems resulting from his tumble. Further, he alleged his stepdaughter suffered emotional distress because of the divorce, so she, too, needed compensation. According to the plaintiff, none of this would have happened if the manufacturer hadn't built the stepladder with its four feet "unsquare," or what we presume to mean lopsided. Allegedly, it was this negligent design that caused the ladder to pitch forward and drop the plaintiff like a bad habit. And as for Home Depot, it should have known better than to sell the product.

The defendants, however, claimed the plaintiff fell simply because he was "overreaching and overleaning."

Outcome A neurologist, an orthopedic surgeon, an engineer, a biomechanical engineer specializing in sports injuries, and a consulting engineer of ladders all testified during the seven-day trial. The jurors, after scratching their heads for a couple of minutes, told the plaintiff he was once again overreaching. They dismissed the case.

Balancing Act

Another daredevil do-it-yourselfer in Iowa took a lucrative fall after dragging a ladder to the top of a scaffold to paint the side of his house. In the midst of his high-wire home-improvement act, the assemblage gave way. The man fell to the ground holding on to the ladder, which broke on impact.

Outcome In 1997, the man won one lawsuit against the ladder manufacturer and another against the retailer—for failing to point out the disadvantages of putting a ladder on a scaffold.

Dangerous Dung

Apparently, some folks' understanding of ladders and their limitations leaves much to be desired. No, chances are they won't remain standing if placed on unstable or slippery surfaces, and that goes double for horse dung. Yes, it's true: in November 1981, a Pennsylvania farmer placed a ladder on top of a pile of frozen manure while working in his barn on a chilly day. When the sun came out, the droppings thawed, causing the ladder to slip out from under him. So whom did the fallen farmer sue? The weatherman? The horse? No, the ladder maker. His lawyers claimed the manufacturer had failed to "anticipate" the circumstances of his accident and to warn him that it might occur.

Outcome And no, the jurors didn't pooh-pooh the claim. They awarded the farmer $200,000 in damages.

The Test of Time

A couple in Oakland County, Michigan, sued a swing-set manufacturer for a "design fault" after their six-year-old son took a tumble in a public park. The parents claimed the boy fell from the swing in 1998 because its seat was wobbly and loose. Never mind that the swing set was twenty years old and that the washers used to keep the seat stable had been stolen!

Outcome A judge dismissed the case, ruling that the swing-set maker couldn't be held responsible for the condition of play equipment that was two decades old. If anything, he added, the park was negligent for not having maintained the swing in better condition.

Test of Time II

An Illinois construction worker was using a thirty-three-year-old pipe-bending machine in 1992 when a hose on the machine burst, spraying him with hydraulic fluid. The man slipped on the oily liquid and injured himself, then sued Teledyne Pines, the manufacturer of the machine. He claimed that the rupture had been caused by the old age of the hose.

Outcome The judge agreed, but ruled that the machine maker was not required to use hoses that were impervious to the wear and tear of old age. If any breach of duty had occurred, he added, it was that of the plaintiff's employer, who had failed to keep the three-decade-old machine in good working condition by replacing worn hoses. The case was dismissed.

Slippery When Wet

A man slipped on a wet floor while entering a San Antonio, Texas, cafeteria in 1996. After changing into a dry pair of pants, he sued the Justin Boot Company, claiming that his rubber-soled boots were defective because they should have kept him from falling.

Outcome A jury threw out the case, deciding that it was the water, not the boots, that had foiled the plaintiff. Think he'll sue the water company?

Attack of the Killer Sneakers

A New York orthopedic surgeon sprinted to the courts to sue Nike for $30 million after tripping on what she called a "defectively designed" cross-training shoe. The woman, who considered herself a serious competitive runner, was jogging in a pair of Nike Certitude sneakers when the right shoelace apparently hooked around the back tab of the left shoe, causing her to fall and hurt her wrist. Her lawsuit, filed in April 2000, accused Nike of product liability, negligence, and breach of warranty because the leather tab, used to pull the shoe onto the foot, was allegedly "larger and more rigid" than it should have been. The suit went on to claim that the sporting-goods giant had carelessly "designed, manufactured, assembled, inspected, tested, and distributed" the shoes the plaintiff was wearing and had "failed to warn" her that they were hazardous.

Outcome No verdict yet. We fear, though, that this footwear fracas will result in rather unsightly "Wear at Your Own Risk" labels plastered onto everything from stilettos to flip-flops.

Slap on the Wrist

If you bash your thumb with a hammer, who's to blame? Why, the guy who made the hammer, of course. At least that's what our next plaintiff would most surely surmise, given that she filed a lawsuit in December 1996 that makes just about as much sense.

The former executive secretary for the Port Authority of New York and New Jersey claimed she had developed a chronic form of carpal tunnel syndrome, a repetitive stress injury, from typing too much on her computer keyboard. Repetitive stress injuries have become common workers' compensation claims at virtually every company where employees perform repetitive tasks. Assembly-line workers who have to attach the same widget to the same doodad for hours on end can suffer from the condition, as can butchers, carpenters, and, of course, typists.

But no dummy she, our sore-wristed secretary didn't bother

to sue the Port Authority. She went after an easier target—the keyboard maker, Digital Equipment Corporation. And rather than merely asserting that the keyboard was defective and therefore led to her injury, the plaintiff's lawyers contended Digital Equipment was to blame because it "neglected to warn users about the dangers of typing."

Outcome Agreeing, the jury gave Digital Equipment more than a slap on the wrist. It awarded the plaintiff a whopping $5.3 million in compensation!

Now let's get something straight. Repetitive stress injury can be caused by many things. Improper workstation layout, poor posture, lack of exercise, and even chairs that are too high or too low often can contribute to the stresses that cause the condition. To claim that the keyboard maker "caused" the woman's carpal tunnel is like blaming a hammer manufacturer for a hand injury. And if tool makers got sued every time someone bashed himself on the thumb, we'd all be using rocks to pound in nails.

Give Her a Hand!

An eighty-year-old woman took to the courts when her Clapper gave her no reason to applaud. The stricken senior filed a product-liability lawsuit in December 1993 against Joseph Enterprises, which makes the sound-activated electrical switch. She claimed that she had to clap so hard to turn her appliances on and off that she injured her hands. "I couldn't peel potatoes when my hands hurt," she said in court. "I never ate so many baked potatoes in my life. I was in pain."

Outcome A New York appeals court rejected the suit, ruling that the clap-happy claimant had simply failed to adjust the device's sensitivity controls. One might also wonder why she repeatedly chose to clap her palms raw instead of simply flipping the appliances' "on/off" switches by hand.

Muscle Man

In the early 1980s, a California bodybuilder decided to show off his strength by running in a footrace with a refrigerator strapped to his back. Unfortunately, he slipped in the process and was injured when the four-hundred-pound kitchen appliance crashed down on him. He sued not only the television company that produced the event, but also the maker of the strap. He claimed that the accident would never have happened if the strap had held the refrigerator more securely to his back.

Outcome The strap maker was ultimately cleared of blame. The production company, however, settled out of court for a cool $1 million.

Toddler Travesty I

A California man was tossing his two-year-old son up and down in the family's living room. The more the tot shrieked with pleasure, the higher the father tossed. But the playful parent went a tad too far when he propelled the boy's head straight into the overhead ceiling fan . . . which was on at the time.

Rather than accept responsibility for his child's injuries, pop passed the blame. He sued the manufacturer of the ceiling fan in 1984, claiming the company had failed to warn him that the fan's whirling blades could harm his son.

Outcome No news on the outcome of this one, but we suggest that the plaintiff invest in a parenting class.

Toddler Travesty II

In 1991, a fourteen-month-old girl was left unattended in the bathroom of her family's Illinois home. The curious tot crawled into the sink, turned on the hot-water faucet, and unfortunately scalded herself on the legs. Shortly thereafter, the girl's parents sued Westinghouse, the maker of the sink's water heater. They claimed that the heater made the water excessively hot and that the company should have warned consumers of the danger of being burned.

Outcome An Illinois judge threw out the case, ruling that the danger of being scalded by hot water was "open and obvious." He added that it was reasonable to assume people would mix hot and cold water to wash their hands, and that the likelihood of being burned was minimal when the sink was used properly.

A Red, White, and Blue Mess

A Texas man was driving down the street in August 1987 when he noticed a flag being lowered in the parking lot of a local building. Alarmed that part of the massive flag might touch the ground, the man pulled over and offered to help the employees lower it. But while doing so, a powerful gust of wind billowed the banner and yanked it into the air. The Good Samaritan was tossed seventy feet and injured.

Two years later, the man sued the Dixie Flag Manufacturing Company, claiming that the flag was an "unreasonably dangerous product" and should have carried warning and instruction labels.

Outcome The head of the company was relieved when it turned out that his firm hadn't made the flag in question. In fact, the company had no connection whatsoever to the bizarre accident except that, coincidentally, it happened to make flags. But Dixie's insurance company eventually settled anyway, for $6,000. Why? Because the plaintiff had sued under the "joint and several liability" doctrine, in which all defendants in a lawsuit can be assessed damages, regardless of their relative blame.

Ironically, the company that actually sold the flag was not even included in the lawsuit. It was a one-man business operating out of the back of a pickup truck and had no insurance and little money. But two other flag makers, in addition to Dixie, were sued—neither of which sold the flag—and settled for $14,000 and $1,500, respectively. That means the plaintiff extracted at least $21,500 from three small businesses, none of which were involved in any way in the incident, without ever having to prove his claim in court.

Depth Perception

A thirty-one-year-old man in Illinois dived into a swimming pool, struck his head on the bottom, and, tragically, was paralyzed. He sued the pool manufacturer in 1996 for failing to warn him of the dangers of diving into the pool.

In his deposition, the plaintiff admitted that he knew diving was potentially dangerous and was aware of the location of the shallow end of the pool. His lawyers, however, argued that markers should have been placed at appropriate intervals in the pool to indicate every foot change in depth. They also claimed that additional markers should have prohibited diving and warned that paralysis could occur.

Outcome A judge dismissed the case. He ruled that because the risk of injury from diving into water of uncertain depth was "open and obvious," the manufacturer had no duty to make explicit warnings. The judge also pointed out that the plaintiff had been swimming in the pool for more than ninety minutes prior to the accident and should have been able to determine its depth by then.

Grapes of Wrath

In the early 1980s, an Illinois man was arrested for raping his neighbor after drinking a bottle of low-alcohol wine. The rapist's wife then sued the wine maker for $10 million in punitive damages, claiming that the wine had caused the crime by intoxicating her husband.

Outcome A Madison County court dismissed the case, ruling that there were no grounds for the complaint. Perhaps the wife had indulged in that intoxicating wine herself before filing suit.

EAT AT YOUR OWN RISK

One type of product that seems to be more liability-prone than most is food. Whether we're chewing it, drinking it, or simply holding it, even the most benign of edibles, such as a milk shake—or just plain milk, for that matter—can become the basis of a red-hot court battle.

Milk-Shake Madness

A woman from Medina, Ohio, sued McDonald's for $8,500 in August 1991, after a "foreign body" allegedly became lodged in her throat while she was slurping a chocolate milk shake.

The woman had taken a few sips of the shake when "all of a sudden, I took another sip and something sharp stuck in the back of my throat," she told the *Cleveland Plain Dealer*. "I thought it was a piece of ice, so I swallowed. But it wouldn't move." Then, "I thought to myself, 'A chocolate milkshake, who the hell ever chokes on a milkshake?'" (Funny, we were wondering the same thing.)

The plot thickens: "I don't know what it was," the plaintiff went on to say. "All I know is that this thing lay in my throat for two and a half hours. Nothing would push that thing down." The woman drove herself to Medina General Hospital, where she was examined by a doctor, had a series of X rays taken, and underwent an endoscopy, in which a fiberoptic tube is inserted into the throat. Yet no one could find anything wrong. "The doctor said he couldn't prove anything," she said. "I could have swallowed it by the time he did the endoscopy. The doctor said it probably let go when the muscles in my throat relaxed."

When McDonald's refused to pay her $1,900 for her medical bills, the woman sued the fast-food chain for $8,500.

Outcome No news on the outcome of this case. However, it seems that the plaintiff's legal wranglings weren't limited to her mishap with the milk shake. On the same day in August 1991, the woman also filed a lawsuit stemming from a September 1989 car accident, which she claimed left both her and her husband with permanent neck and back injuries that would require "continual medical treatment." The plaintiff was reluctant to talk about that lawsuit, but told the *Plain Dealer* that she had simply run into a streak of bad luck. "When it rains, it pours. It's one thing after another."

Bone of Contention

An unemployed truck driver sued McDonald's and two other companies in 1989 after allegedly biting into a bone while eating a boneless McChicken sandwich. According to his lawsuit, the forty-two-year-old plaintiff from Stanton, California, had taken three bites out of the sandwich when he suddenly felt an "explosion" inside his head. He claimed a one-inch bone had become vertically lodged between his teeth. The following day, his jaw became swollen and made "clicking and popping" sounds. Soon after, his ailment was diagnosed as "temporomandibular joint dysfunction," a malfunctioning of the hinge mechanism in the jaw.

It was all downhill from there. The out-of-work trucker claimed he could eat only soft foods, such as oatmeal and peanut butter on bread, for the next five years. This restricted diet caused him to lose twenty pounds. Worse yet, he developed slurred speech, which was all the more unfortunate given that he used to be a backup singer in a rock-and-roll band and could no longer carry a tune.

All these problems left the ex-singer with no choice but to file lawsuits against McDonald's, the chicken-patty manufacturer, and the trucking company that delivered the patty. According to his attorneys, all were guilty of violating the "expressed warranty" of the boneless sandwich. They sought $40,000 in medical expenses, along with unspecified compensation for the pain and suffering the plaintiff had endured.

The defendants' lawyers, however, argued that the plaintiff had suffered from a jaw ailment long before he bit into the breaded chicken-patty. They pointed out that he had visited a dentist only twice over the prior twenty-five years. Hence, any problems with his jaw were strictly the result of years of dental neglect.

Outcome In 1994, a twelve-member jury in Orange, California, cleared McDonald's and the trucking company of any liability for the "chewing accident." It did, however, force the chicken-patty maker to pay the plaintiff a whopping $175,000. Hopefully he'll use some of the loot on a visit to the dentist.

Burnin' Gherkin

In another inventive attack on the Golden Arches, a woman and her husband filed a $125,000 lawsuit in October 2000 over a "defective" pickle on a McDonald's hamburger. The Knoxville, Tennessee, couple claimed an "extremely hot" pickle slice slid out of the Quarter Pounder the woman was chomping, landed on her chin, and left a permanent scar. In their lawsuit, they alleged that the pickle had breached an "implied warranty" of safety by being "in a defective condition or unreasonably dangerous to the general consumer."

The woman demanded that the restaurant pay her $110,000 for lost wages, medical bills, physical pain, and mental anguish. Her husband, whose life had apparently been turned upside down by the pickle fiasco too, sought $15,000 for being "deprived of the services and consortium of his wife."

Outcome McDonald's settled the lawsuit out of court in April 2001. The company said it admitted no wrongdoing in the pickle debacle, but kept all other details of settlement confidential.

Udder Nonsense

Jaws dropped in America's dairyland upon news of a lawsuit that branded cows as little more than accomplices to Joe Camel. A Seattle resident filed a product-liability lawsuit against Safeway food stores and the Dairy Farmers of Washington, claiming that a lifetime of drinking whole milk gave him clogged arteries and caused a minor stroke he suffered in 1994. The self-proclaimed "milkaholic" complained that milk was "addictive" and asked a federal court to require that cartons carry "hazardous to your health" labels like those found on the sides of cigarette packages. "If tobacco products can be required to have warning labels, why not dairy products?" the plaintiff told the *Milwaukee Journal Sentinel* after filing his suit in June 1997. "I think milk is just as dangerous as tobacco."

The sixty-one-year-old milk guzzler asked for reimbursement of his medical expenses and cash for his troubles. He demanded that Safeway, where he habitually obtained his lactic fix, put labels on all its dairy products, warning consumers about the dangers of fat and cholesterol. And he insisted that the dairy industry be forced to pull its deceptive "Milk does a body good" ads off the air and compensate public health-care agencies obligated to care for milkaholics. Much of the country's health problems might have been avoided, he claimed, had the "Got milk?" guys simply come clean. "They push their dairy products without warning you of the hazards. It's underhanded," argued the plaintiff, who admitted downing milk "like some people drink water."

Outcome In 1998, the milk man's case turned sour. The judge took one look at his grocery list of grievances and promptly asked, "Got sense?" She dismissed the case, pointing out that the artery-sparing information the plaintiff was seeking is already on the carton: A recommended daily diet includes up to sixty-five grams of fat. One eight-ounce glass of whole milk contains eight grams of total fat. The same amount of 1 percent milk contains 2.5 grams. It says so in black and white.

Sometimes You Feel Like a Nut

An Oberlin, Ohio, man demanded $500,000 in damages for injuries he sustained while biting into a plain M&M. The nutless candy had apparently found its way into the bag of peanut-filled M&Ms that the sweet tooth was munching on. Having adjusted his biting force in anticipation of a hard nut, the man was apparently rendered helpless when his teeth unexpectedly connected with the softer, pure-chocolate morsel. The surplus force caused him to bite straight through the candy and into his lip, causing enough damage to require stitches.

In November 1996, the man sued both the maker of M&Ms and the Family Dollar Store in Cleveland where he bought the wayward bag of goodies. He blamed the store for failing to "inspect" the candy and selling "defective and mislabeled merchandise."

Outcome This nutty case was dismissed.

THAT'S WHAT DIRECTIONS ARE FOR

Most Americans are probably aware that the steadily rising number of lawsuits adds hundreds of dollars to the cost of a car, about 10 percent to the cost of a ski lift ticket, and so on. Offsetting these costs, however, is the widespread feeling—aided by the lawyers who earn their money from these suits—that there are some compensating benefits to our wacky liability system. Many believe, for instance, that our lives are made safer by the system because it makes companies more careful.

Interestingly, there is no known evidence of this. The idea was examined in meticulous detail by the Brookings Institution, where twenty experts assessed the impact of liability law on product safety and innovation. The findings: There was no demonstrable improvement in safety for Americans compared with nations that have less stringent liability laws. In fact, our legal system may make things worse by slowing the introduction of some safety improvements. Swiss Industrial Company, for instance, planned to stop selling handguns in the United States due to litigation-driven increases in the cost of product-liability insurance. Ironically, SIG would have been the first to market "personalized" handguns, which include an electric locking system designed to allow only authorized users to fire. Such locking mechanisms are among the innovations being demanded by plaintiffs suing gun makers.

Here are some product-liability lawsuits that are hardly blazing a trail for improved safety and innovation.

Looks Can Be Deceiving

An Adel, Georgia, man sued the maker of Liquid Fire drain cleaner for $100,000 after the contents oozed out of his home-made container and seriously burned the skin on his legs. The drain cleaner comes in a spill-proof container. The plaintiff, however, was rattled by the warning labels, which he said "were alarming and violent, with skulls and crossbones, and exclamations of severe burns and violent eruptions of acid." So, to protect himself, he decided to transfer the chemical solution into his own "safer" container—from which it eventually spilled. His lawsuit, filed in June 2000, claimed that Liquid Fire's original package created "the impression of flimsiness" and, therefore, forced him to use his own container.

Outcome No news on the outcome of this one. But we suggest that, next time, the plaintiff simply call a plumber.

Hold on Tight

An Illinois firefighter sued a fire-truck manufacturer in 1994 for injuries he suffered when he fell out of the truck's open seating compartment while en route to a fire. At trial, the plaintiff admitted that he had forgotten to wear his seat belt, but claimed that this detail was only a "contributory" factor in his accident. He argued that the fire truck should have been made in such a way as to prevent people from falling out, whether they are strapped in or not.

Outcome A judge doused the plaintiff's argument, ruling that the firefighter would have most likely have stayed in his seat had he simply buckled his seat belt as required. The case was dismissed.

Timber!

A Washington State lumberjack was killed when a four-hundred-thousand-pound redwood tree fell on his head. This tragedy was made all the more macabre when the victim's family devised an ingenious way to cash in on his untimely demise: They sued the manufacturer of the lumberjack's hard-hat in 1996, claiming that the product must have been defective because it did not provide adequate protection—against two-hundred-ton trees!

Outcome The outrageous argument must have felled the jury's common sense, because the plaintiffs collected $670,000!

Malaria Madness

Former U.S. congressman Ed Mezvinsky was indicted in March 2001 on fifty-six federal counts of fraud for bilking banks and investors out of more than $10 million. One day after his indictment, Mezvinsky filed a lawsuit against the Swiss pharmaceutical giant Roche Holding AG, a Philadelphia hospital, a pharmacy, and his own doctor. He claimed that the psychiatric side effects of the antimalaria drug Lariam, which he took while on business trips to Africa in the 1990s, caused him to run up huge debts and to subsequently swindle others to make up his losses. According to his lawsuit, "As a result of the psychiatric syndrome caused by his long-term use of Lariam, he invested rashly in bad investments . . . and depleted his own financial resources, his wife's financial resources, as well as his wife's inheritance." The former congressman, who represented Iowa from 1973 to 1977, sought $200,000 in damages and demanded that the four defendants pay off his creditors. "It's not a question of passing the buck. It's a case of making those responsible be held responsible," his lawyer said. "Clearly, the responsibility lies with the manufacturers." Clearly?

Outcome No verdict yet, Dr. Livingston.

Please Pass the Jelly

A woman in Philadelphia decided to take some precautionary measures to avoid an unwanted pregnancy. Unfortunately, in doing so, she showed that a cranium need serve no other purpose than as a swell spot to place a hat.

It seems that the woman, a former model and cheerleader for a professional basketball team, purchased a tube of contraceptive jelly from a local drugstore in 1997, and then used it before having sex. It didn't work, and given the circumstances it's not surprising. Apparently, she had interpreted *jelly* in the very American sense of the word—and spread it on toast and ate it!

She then sued the pharmacy that sold her the birth-control product, because it failed to keep her from becoming pregnant! Sure, she made a mistake, but according to her meandering mind, the drugstore was at fault for not telling her that eating the jelly wouldn't prevent pregnancy. After all, "The company should call it something else, and the pharmacy shouldn't sell it without telling each and every customer who buys it that eating it won't prevent you from getting pregnant," she told reporters. And as far as the instructions go, "Who has time to sit around reading directions these days, especially when you're sexually aroused?" Indeed! Rather than sitting around reading directions, it's far easier to lope into the kitchen, make some toast, spread a glob of "jelly" on it, wolf it down—and then make whoopee!

The woman's attorneys contended that she was swindled and lied to by implication, based on false advertising and truth-in-labeling laws. And for her hardships, they claimed, the plaintiff deserved $500,000, of which a not-so-small percentage was surely earmarked for the champions of her cause.

Outcome No news of the outcome of this crazy case. Sadly, some folks believe the plaintiff may actually prevail with her lawsuit because, as one legal expert put it, "With the courts bending over backwards to please consumer groups, the temper of the times is perfect for these crackpots to bring legal action against businesses—even a moronic legal action like this."

We Feel Your Pain

Once again, a customer who didn't have time to read the instructions before sexual intercourse tried to pass the consequences on to the manufacturer. Or rather, tried to reap some rewards instead.

In 1996, a twenty-two-year-old college student sued a contraceptive-sponge maker due to some penile pain he was experiencing. The poor guy claimed he suffered from a persistent ache in the crotch and could no longer perform—all after only a single episode of lovemaking, too. According to the student, the sponge maker did not warn him of possible irritation from exposure to spermicide. However, the manufacturer argued that neither the plaintiff nor his partner took the time to read the listed warnings. (They were probably making toast in the kitchen at the time.) The sponge manufacturer also claimed the plaintiff's disability was grossly exaggerated, given there was no scientific evidence that his alleged symptoms had anything to do with the spermicide.

Outcome It took the jurors just two hours to decide that the plaintiff's arguments didn't stand up; they ruled in favor of the defendant. The ten-day trial, however, cost California taxpayers $60,500!

Don't Point That Thing at Me

A woman sued her seventy-year-old common-law husband for dumping her after he became rejuvenated by the much-publicized love drug Viagra. According to her lawsuit, the defendant left her for a younger woman, proclaiming, "It's time for me to be a stud again."

The Garden City, New York, couple had been together for ten years when the retired millionaire first popped the blue wonder pill on May 1, 1998. The two had shared an opulent lifestyle, dividing their time among homes in Long Island and Hilton Head, South Carolina, an apartment in Manhattan, and a luxury yacht. Initially, the sixty-three-year-old plaintiff was delighted when her partner told her he had seen a doctor and received a prescription drug to cure his impotence. Two days later, they made love for the first time in four years. But things soon took a bitter turn.

On May 5, the reinvigorated tycoon packed up his bottle of Viagra, penned a "Dear Jane" ending their relationship, and left. The less-than-eloquent note read, "Hi Bobbi. Sorry but I am leaving. Be back in a few days. Use Nations Bank money to move your belongings and my Mercedes for a couple of days. Sorry but it just isn't working out. Love Sonny." He later moved in with his new girlfriend in New Jersey.

The jilted plaintiff sued her unfaithful partner in Nassau County State Supreme Court, demanding $2 million, plus emotional damages, the New York condo, their marital assets, life and medical insurance, and legal fees. She claimed the couple was considered married under the common law of South Carolina, where they met in 1988.

Yet oddly enough, the plaintiff didn't hold her partner solely accountable for his fickle heart. She also considered filing a lawsuit against Pfizer, the manufacturer of Viagra, for "failure to give notice that the drug could be dangerous for marriage." We've personally never heard of an inanimate object breaking up a perfectly good relationship. But as for the love drug, the plaintiff claimed, "It's like giving a loaded gun to someone who has not been trained to shoot."

Outcome The plaintiff dropped her case a year later—after the couple reconciled.

LETDOWN LITIGANTS

As shown by the previous case of penile empowerment, not all product-liability lawsuits involve physical injury. Some litigious types will sue manufacturers for letdowns, affronts, or the mere disappointment of discovering that products aren't exactly as they're expected to be. Take the following examples.

Pedal to the Metal

A doctor in Birmingham, Alabama, was driven to legal excess when he discovered that his brand-new 1990 BMW had been "touched up" before he bought it.

Initially, the man was delighted with his $40,000 Beemer.

He drove it everywhere, and he continually polished and fussed over it. It was only when he drove the beloved car to a detailing shop to make it look even snazzier that things took a nasty turn. Our autophile was apparently blindsided when the shop attendant pointed out a four-inch tape line on one of the fenders—evidence that a small portion of the BMW had been repainted before it was sold.

It's common practice among carmakers to have a refinishing facility cosmetically touch up vehicles that might have been scratched or dinged on their way to the dealership. The idea is to restore them to factory condition. In fact, BMW maintains a strict policy: if the cost of the repair exceeds 3 percent of the car's retail price, the vehicle is used only as a company car and then later sold as used. Our disgruntled driver, however, wouldn't hear of it. He decided to sue the German automaker for fraud and breach of contract.

That's when things really spun out of control. The plaintiff's lawyer deduced that even a perfectly refinished car was diminished in value by 10 percent; so that's $4,000 in compensatory damages. But the attorney also decided to factor into the equation the owners of the thousand or so other cars that BMW had touched up over the prior ten years. By these fancy calculations, he determined that his client deserved $4 million in punitive damages for the minor restoration done to his car!

Outcome Steered by this ridiculous argument, the jury granted our mistreated motorist the $4 million. The case was appealed before the Alabama Supreme Court. BMW argued that only fourteen of its cars had been refinished and sold in Alabama within the last ten years. So, the automaker claimed, its right of due process had been violated when it was held liable for the cars sold in twenty-one other states, where BMW's restoration policy met current standards. In essence, BMW was being punished for obeying the law. The highest court in Alabama agreed—in part, that is. It admitted that $4 million was too much for a four-inch mark on a bumper. Yet it decided that a $2-million award was "reasonable."

Fortunately, in 1995, the U.S. Supreme Court threw its act into gear and tossed out the $2-million award.

Buyer Beware

An Illinois man was shopping around for a used car in 1993 when he stumbled upon just the right one. Unfortunately, the vehicle of his dreams had a sign on its windshield that read SOLD AS IS. The man decided to take his chances and bought the car anyway. But when the vehicle broke down days later, the angry shopper sued the car dealership for breach of implied warranty.

Outcome A judge threw out the case, ruling that the plaintiff had agreed to buy the car in its present condition, flaws and all. In other words, the term *sold as is* is simply another way of saying "buy at your own risk."

Bearded Lady

A New York woman can testify that Rogaine really works— just not the way she intended. The balding publishing consultant sued the maker of the popular hair-growth cream for $1.5 million after she sprouted a beard instead of a healthy coif. In her filing against the Michigan-based drug company Pharmacia & Upjohn, the seventy-three-year-old plaintiff said she noticed a "heavy, dark, substantial beard-like growth" on her face in July 1996, roughly two months after she began using the product.

From there, it seems her transformation was as rapid and

complete as that of the famed werewolf of London. According to the suit, her beard started at "about eyebrow level" and extended down "to the chin area and on the upper cheeks under her eyes." The hair kept growing even after she stopped using the product, which contains minoxidil, a medically approved drug known to reverse baldness. The plaintiff charged that the beard caused her "discomfort, disfigurement, professional difficulty, embarrassment, and emotional distress." Adding insult to injury, what little hair did crop up on her scalp later fell out.

Rogaine carries a label warning users that unwanted hair can appear if applied frequently to areas other than the scalp. The plaintiff insisted the product was unsafe, however, because it failed to elaborate on the potential side effects—like a five o'clock shadow.

Outcome No news on the outcome of this "hairy" case. Either way, though, it seems the plaintiff is a winner. If she wins the $1.5 million, she'll be able to buy a lifetime's worth of razors. If she loses, she could still make a mint in the circus.

This Bud's Not for You

A Michigan man who apparently mistook Budweiser for a love potion sued Anheuser-Busch for false advertising. He claimed that he suffered physical and mental injury as well as emotional distress from the "implicit promises" of popularity made by the brewing company's TV commercials, in which male beer drinkers were surrounded by beautiful women. According to his 1998 court filing, when he drank the advertised beverage, not only did he fail to become a hit with the ladies, he also got sick.

Outcome The jury awarded him a cool $10,000 for his sob story! And although the verdict was later overturned by an appeals court, it just goes to show that those beer ads may be truthful after all: it seems drinking the right brand *can* make you rich and famous.

THE CHICKEN OR THE EGG

Sadly, not all product-liability lawsuits are so trivial or so laughable. Many center on violent crimes and pose serious threats to our freedom of speech and expression. In recent years, for example, a number of lawsuits have charged the producers of various forms of media—from books and films to music and Internet sites—with "inciting" ordinary consumers to commit criminal acts. With these lawsuits comes the implicit suggestion that people are just empty vessels whose behavior is determined by the right or wrong measure of media input— input that can override family values, social mores, or the existence of an individual soul. Granted, many movies, records, and books seem to revel in their explicit content and tone. But aren't those who blame these products for their crimes misplacing their criticism? It's the old chicken-and-egg question revisited: Can the media truly turn everyday folks into violent felons, or do those with criminal tendencies more readily embrace violent forms of media? You be the judge.

Crime 101

When James Perry crept into a dark house in Silver Spring, Maryland, in March 1993, shot two people with a silencer-equipped rifle, and smothered a third, he was following a script of sorts. Every detail had been laid out for him, down to ransacking the house to make the murders look as if they were part of a robbery. The contract killer was so careful in covering his tracks that detectives didn't find any evidence, not a hair or fiber, linking him to the crime scene. It was a textbook case of murder—in every sense of the word.

That's because Perry's crime was lifted chapter and verse from a paperback published by Paladin Press and purportedly written by a professional killer. The book, *Hit Man: A Technical Manual for Independent Contractors,* explains in full detail how to find potential customers, what weapons to use, and how to avoid getting caught. But Perry was caught, and the fact that prosecutors found twenty-two similarities between the advice given in *Hit Man* and the techniques he used in the slayings was not lost on the victims' families. In December 1995, after Perry was convicted on three counts of first-degree murder, the families filed suit in federal court accusing Paladin Press and its owner of aiding and abetting murder.

A number of specialized book publishers have carved out a profitable niche in the booming "self-improvement" category by providing practical tips to aspiring outlaws. They entertain the morbidly curious with such how-to titles as *Making Crime Pay, Home and Recreational Use of High Explosives,* and *The Ancient Art of Strangulation. The Poisoner's Handbook* even spices up deadly recipes with freakish yet folksy comments like, "Botulism is fun and easy to make." But Boulder, Colorado–based Paladin Press, the plaintiffs argued, went too far when it released *Hit Man.* They claimed that the publisher "specifically and maliciously intended, and had actual knowledge that the book would be used by murderers."

Granted, Paladin's do-it-yourself manuals teach readers how to circumvent security alarms, blow up bridges, make silencers, set up a murder-for-hire business, and launder ill-gotten gains. *Hit Man* even gives tips on how to get rid of victims' remains. But according to Paladin's owner, a former soldier with the U.S. Army's Special Forces, the First Amendment gives him same right as everyone else to publish controversial material. Paladin does not advocate that readers use the information for illegal purposes, the owner said; many of its books carry disclaimers warning that they are intended purely for entertainment, academic study, or informational purposes. In fact, some of company's main customers are police departments, security officers, and writers trying to get inside the criminal mind.

The bottom line: More than fifteen thousand people bought *Hit Man* after its release in 1987. Given that only one chose to act on what was written inside, it seems clear the murderer had impulses that preceded the book's influence. So regardless of how provocative *Hit Man* may be, shouldn't responsibility rest with the man who actually chose to pull the trigger?

Outcome Apparently not. In a groundbreaking case, a federal appeals court ruled that *Hit Man* had aided and abetted the triple homicide, and therefore the publisher had no First Amendment protection. Soon after, Paladin agreed to settle the case for an undisclosed sum. The settlement also required the company to stop publishing *Hit Man;* it finally stopped offering the book in 1999.

The Movie Made 'Em Do It

The legal precedent established in the *Hit Man* case is now being cited in a number of other high-profile lawsuits. Take the one filed by a Louisiana convenience store clerk who was shot by a young couple who went on a crime spree after watching the blood-and-guts film *Natural Born Killers*. In 1995, the victim sued Oliver Stone, the film's director and cowriter, as well as Time Warner Entertainment, which distributed the movie. She claimed the 1994 film had inspired her attackers to commit a "copycat crime" and that the filmmakers knew such acts would result from the distribution of a movie "treating individuals who commit such violence as celebrities and heroes."

In the movie, characters played by actors Woody Harrelson and Juliette Lewis drive across the Southwest, slaughtering people and gathering media fame. Stone claimed that the movie was a satire on the media's glorification of violence. But some criticized the movie for not punishing the characters in the end for their crimes and allowing them to live "happily ever after."

Outcome A Louisiana district court judge dismissed the case in April 2001, ruling that the plaintiffs had no proof that Stone or Time Warner had intended to incite violence. He also rejected the claim that the movie had incited acts of violence, pointing out that the shooting happened "three days, five states, and 500 miles away" from where the robbers had watched it. "I think this will . . . set a major example that will discourage looking for some news program or documentary or film every time there is a tragic shooting and try to find someone responsible other than the perpetrator of the violent act," Warner Brothers' attorney told the *Los Angeles Times* after the ruling.

The Music Made 'Em Do It

In another twist on the infamous *Hit Man* case, the parents of a young girl who was brutally murdered in an apparent satanic ritual sued the heavy-metal band Slayer for "inciting" the killing. The fifteen-year-old girl from San Luis Obispo, California, was led into a eucalyptus grove in 1995 by three teenage boys. There she was given marijuana, strangled, and then stabbed to death with a hunting knife. The boys, who are now serving twenty-six years to life in prison for slaying, said they had hoped that by sacrificing a virgin to Satan they would win success for their own rock band, called Hatred.

In 1997, the parents of the murdered girl sued Slayer and its band members; their record label, American Recordings; and various companies of the distributor, Sony. Their lawsuit sought unspecified damages, alleging that the killers "were following specific instructions from obscene lyrics."

Slayer was a pioneer of the so-called death-metal sound with albums that include *Show No Mercy, Hell Awaits,* and *Reign in Blood.* The band's gruesome, misogynistic songs describe torture and satanic sacrifice. Yet even one of the teenage killers admitted that the lyrics had not influenced the murder. "The music is destructive," he told the *Washington Post* in a jailhouse interview. "But that's not why [the girl] was murdered. She was murdered because [one of the other boys] was obsessed with her, and obsessed with killing her."

Outcome In January 2001, a judge dismissed the case, saying the plaintiffs could not prove that Slayer shared responsibility in the killing. The victim's parents, however, filed an amended lawsuit a few weeks later. No news yet on the outcome, but one of the defense attorneys believed that the second case would be thrown out, too. "There's not a legal position that could be taken that would make the band responsible," he said. "Where do you draw the line? You might as well start looking through the library at every book on the shelf."

4

CRIME COSTS: INMATE LAWSUITS II

Make money, fairly make it, if you may,
But, if not fairly, then in any way.

—Horace

Crime pays, but it can sure cost us a pretty penny, too. The National Association of Attorneys General estimates that inmate lawsuits cost the country upward of $81 million per year. That's largely because, in several states, prisoners who are considered in need or "indigent" aren't required to pay filing fees and are granted court-appointed lawyers. Every one of their claims, no matter how crazy, must be considered by the district attorney's office. Fortunately, the bulk of these grievances are tossed out faster than you can say *solitary confinement*. By then, however, the lawsuits have wasted a colossal amount of time and taxpayers' money. In Wisconsin, for example, an inmate filed 117 lawsuits against the state between 1995 and 1998. State officials were forced to fight each one—at a total cost of $1.7 million. And in New York, 20 percent of the entire budget of the attorney general's office is earmarked for inmate claims.

It's worth noting that the number of inmate lawsuits dropped dramatically for two consecutive years after peaking at 68,235 in 1996, the year Congress passed the federal Prisoner Litigation Reform Act. Designed to curb frivolous lawsuits, the law requires inmates to pay fees for all lawsuits they file in federal courts. The number of prisoner lawsuits ticked back up in 1999, however, as soon as inmates discovered a new venue for their complaints: they simply began filing more suits in *state* courts—in states that have yet to enact similar laws.

Yet as the following case shows, that's the way the cookie crumbles . . .

Snack Attack

A death row inmate in California claimed he was denied "proper nutrition" because the cookie in his lunch sack was broken. It took more than a fresh peanut cluster to resolve that lawsuit, one of more than forty the inmate has filed. Taxpayers forked out $4,500 in legal and processing fees— equal to about 2,250 bags of Oreos—before the case was finally thrown out.

Somebody Give This Guy a Tums

Another California felon sued for cruel and unusual punishment after he got a tummyache from eating "an overspiced bowl of chili." That gastrointestinal gripe cost the system only $2,000 before being dismissed.

A Penny Saved . . .

It cost $16,500 to dismiss a claim filed by a California inmate who claimed his photocopying costs had been illegally raised by five cents per copy. His lawsuit demanded a $1.45 refund and thousands of dollars in punitive damages.

Read My Mind

Taxpayers coughed up $18,500 before a judge dismissed a suit filed by a California inmate alleging that prison wardens had implanted electronic monitoring devices in his brain to control his thoughts and broadcast them over the prison's public address system.

Brown Bagger

A cranky convict in California claimed he suffered cruel and unusual punishment during a prison lockdown because he was fed two cold sack lunches and one hot meal rather than the usual two hot meals and one sack lunch. The case cost the state a hefty $20,500 before a judge tossed it out.

Karate Chop

Then there's the jailhouse Jackie Chan who sued for the right to practice martial arts in his California prison. His legal kick to the wallet cost the system $28,000 before a judge decided the inmate should pursue a somewhat milder hobby than hand-to-hand combat.

Stamp Act

It cost $151,000—yes, that's one hundred and fifty-one *thousand* dollars—to dismiss a suit filed by a California con who claimed his constitutional rights were violated when he didn't get five free stamped envelopes from prison officials. The suit was filed in September 1989. It wasn't thrown out until December 1994.

CIVILIAN TARGETS

These costs don't even include all the baseless lawsuits leveled against private businesses and individuals, who are stuck fending for themselves. Here are some cases in point.

Read It and Weep

A former *Los Angeles Times* reporter was sued for a staggering $60 million after he wrote a book, titled *Angel of Darkness,* about convicted serial killer Randy Kraft. Although awaiting execution at San Quentin, Kraft claimed he was innocent in all sixteen murders, so the depiction of him as a killer was not only false and misleading but also "defamed his good name." What's more, he claimed the book caused him to be "shunned by society," rendering him "unable to find decent employment" once he returned to private life.

The case was thrown out in a record forty-six seconds, but only after the author and his publishing company, Warner Books, spent $50,000 in legal fees defending themselves!

The Show Must Go On

A group of death row inmates in Nashville sued Tennessee governor Don Sundquist after he ordered their satellite dish to be removed. They claimed satellite TV eased their tension and created a "more humane atmosphere." What were they watching, Martha Stewart?

Bad to the Last Drop

Two Ohio inmates filed a $20,000 lawsuit against General Foods Corporation, claiming they suffered from caffeine headaches in their cells. The prisoners—one serving time for attempted rape and the other for robbery—accused the company of negligence because it did not warn consumers that its Maxwell House coffee was addictive. "I have been using Maxwell House Instant Coffee for prolong [sic] periods of time," one of the caffeinated convicts wrote. "Upon trying to discontinue use of said product . . . I have suffered painful withdrawal symptoms." The case was dismissed.

Berry Scary

A convicted drug dealer filed a federal lawsuit against the Kellogg Company and J. M. Smucker Company for injuries he supposedly sustained while biting into a Pop-Tart. Demanding $130,000 in damages, he claimed that the toasted treat contained not only a berry filling, but a sliver of glass as well. The jagged shard allegedly cut his mouth, causing him pain, suffering, mental anguish, and emotional trauma, not to mention loss of sleep "due to nightmares in which he was dead in a coffin in prison from eating Pop Tarts." (Talk about a sugar high!) A federal judge ultimately threw the fruity suit out, on the grounds that the inmate had failed to prove his pain and suffering had reached the $50,000 minimum for a federal claim.

Slippery One

A convict in Cumberland, Maryland, sued a food manufacturer for "several thousand dollars" because a ten-ounce bottle of olive oil did not contain 128 tablespoon servings as its label indicated. A superior court judge dismissed the case, ruling that the inmate had deliberately ignored the obvious misprint. "We find this case extremely hard to digest," the judge said.

5

PARDON MY FEELINGS: EMOTIONAL DISTRESS AND MENTAL ANGUISH

Depend on it that if a man talks of his misfortunes, there is something in them that is not disagreeable to him; for where there is nothing but pure misery, there never is any recourse to the mention of it.
—Samuel Johnson

Welcome to the new millennium. The era of hypersensitivity. The age of hurt feelings, emotional exhibitionism, and political correctness. The consequence of an inappropriate opinion or perceived insult these days can be injuries to the victim heretofore rarely seen—injuries that, in the past, were quashed with false bravado. These wounds, which now must be bared in a cathartic show of anguish, are the twenty-first-century version of soft-tissue injuries.

What exactly are these injuries? *Trauma, mental anguish, anxiety, emotional distress, humiliation, embarrassment,* and *stress* are the first buzzwords that come to mind. While it was once considered good form to keep these emotions to yourself, these days it's considered healthier to deal openly with emotional baggage, repressed feelings, and the whole gamut of human foibles. We believe there's nothing wrong with that, but when we start lauding them as a badge of victimhood and a means to a profitable end, they become a hindrance, a barrier to free speech, honest communication, and diverse ideas. In the form of a lawsuit, they can be used as a tool to intimidate, harass, and make money.

Let's pause for a second to distinguish between actual traumatic ordeals and jump-on-the-bandwagon emotional burlesque shows. There are cases of psychological trauma in which the injuries are unquestionably grievous and fair compensation is fully warranted. Just as there are valid physical injuries, there are also legitimate injuries to the psyche. But as with bodily injuries, in which dramatizing and embellishing garner greater awards, so too is the game played with this new, more subjective form of psychological injury.

SHOCKED, OUTRAGED, AND APPALLED

Only the Nose Knows

These days it's not unusual for people to try to improve their physical features with a lift here, a tuck there, a removal or an implant, or even a reduction by suction. Whatever it takes, it can be done, and most people are glad to share their experiences. Carol Burnett displayed her new chin, Ted Danson spoofed his toupee, and Pamela Anderson has her now-you-see-them-now-you-don't . . . well, you get the point.

Despite such makeovers being old hat these days, one Los Angeles woman had no intention of advertising her nose job. In fact, she sued her plastic surgeon because he used "before and after" photos of her to advertise his practice. Without her permission, to boot.

So she may have a point, except for one thing: The photos that were used were taken in 1978, and the newspaper ad appeared in 1995. That's right, the before-and-after photos of her revamped schnozz were taken seventeen years before. Nonetheless, the forty-year-old medical technician claimed that she suffered "serious emotional distress" upon seeing the ad. After all, she had destroyed all photographs taken of her prior to her surgery and had been delighted with her "new face" ever since. But the sight of her presurgery face allegedly opened up "old wounds."

Outcome The jury turned out to be very sympathetic (possibly after viewing presurgery photos of a nose that must have resembled a two-car garage) and awarded the distressed plaintiff $412,500. She can now afford to get a full makeover and spring for nose jobs for her whole neighborhood.

Shop Till You're Caught

To curtail shoplifting, most retail chains these days have sensors installed at their store exits. When an item that hasn't been demagnetized at a checkout counter passes through the doorway, the system beeps. These sensors, however, aren't the only things in stores that are highly sensitive. Apparently some of the customers can go off without warning, too.

Take the California woman and her son who went shopping at a discount department store in August 1997. They picked up some knickknacks and paid for them at the cash register. But as they attempted to leave, a sensor tag that had not been properly deactivated set off the inventory control system. The mother-son duo waited until a salesperson arrived, checked their receipt, deactivated the tag, and wished them on their way. A small inconvenience that could happen to anybody, right? Wrong.

The offended family sued the department store for $110,005. (Why they wanted that extra $5 thrown in, we'll never know.) The mother claimed the store had defamed her family's good name by "publicly accusing" them of having sticky fingers. According to the lawsuit, not only did the shameful display cause the plaintiffs embarrassment and loss of sleep, it also triggered a "change in personality."

Outcome The jurors must have had their baloney sensors on, because it took them just one hour to rule in favor of the department store. The four-day trial, though, cost taxpayers about $24,500 in court fees.

Tit for Tat

A lusty man walked into an Emporium Videos store in Natrona County, Wyoming, and found just what he was looking for: *Belle of the Ball*. The label on the saucy adult video said it starred the well-endowed actress Busty Bell. But when the man popped the cassette tape into his VCR, he was shocked to discover that he had been gypped. According to his calculations, Busty appeared in only eight minutes of the hour-long skin flick.

Did this man do what any red-blooded male would do—rewind the tape and watch it again? No! He sued the video store, demanding $29.95 for the cost of the cassette, $55.79 in medical expenses for the asthma attack he suffered because of the "stress and strain of being ripped off," and $50,000 for "pain and suffering."

Outcome The district court dismissed the boob's complaint, stating that it contained no cause for action. But in March 1993, the Wyoming Supreme Court revived the case on the grounds that the plaintiff should be given a chance to challenge the dismissal. The chief justice, who disagreed with the other supreme court judges, didn't trust the man's lust. "The facts of [this] case simply cannot be forged into a claim," he said. "It is crystal clear that the real culprit was [the plaintiff's] endogenous salaciousness."

Oops, Typo. $40 Million, Please

An Omaha, Nebraska, man sued a CD-ROM maker, its subsidiary publisher, and Best Buy Stores for $40 million in March 1995 for the emotional distress he and his three sons suffered after using *Compton's Interactive Encyclopedia.* You might conclude that the distress suffered must have been of an unparalleled magnitude, in the realm of complete devastation, loss of loved ones, loss of limbs, or a loss of everything near and dear to them. But, no, it's more along the lines of an offensive word.

The grief-stricken father was using the CD-ROM encyclopedia to find information about the African nation of "Niger." The highly sensitive plaintiff accidentally typed in "Nigger," and received entries relating to the racial slur instead. Incidentally, only four references were pulled up. Two were from plays having the word *nigger* in their titles; the other two were references to Joseph Conrad's novel *The Nigger of the Narcissus* (1897) and to a book by black comedian Dick Gregory, *Up From Nigger* (1976).

An important point, we should add, is that the fumble-fingered man's trusty computer was not calling him, or his sons, any names but merely providing the information he had inadvertently requested. But after seeing what the results of his geographical query were, he and his sons became "emotionally damaged"—to the tune of $40 million.

Outcome The case was dismissed by a U.S. district court. Sounds like the plaintiff isn't going to buy Dick Gregory's book.

Tutti-Frutti

Most sports fans are familiar with the colorful National Basketball Association superstar who has created his fair share of problems both on and off the court. Yes, it's none other than Dennis Rodman, the sometimes aggressive, sometimes sensitive, yet always interesting basketball professional renowned for kicking a cameraman in the crotch. And as we all know, the cameraman sued the tattooed, high-flying rebounder and walked away with a small fortune for the indignity.

A less famous lawsuit against Rodman, however, was filed by a Las Vegas craps dealer in October 1997. According to the "embarrassed" Mirage Hotel employee, the basketball player was watching a fellow NBA star at the craps table and decided to bring his friend some luck. Rodman reached over and rubbed the dice on the dealer's bald head, stomach, and groin before rolling them. It turns out, though, that the rebound king's bid for good luck bought him some misfortune instead when the craps dealer sued him for "battery and intentional infliction of emotional distress." According to the lawsuit, Rodman's human lucky charm had suffered "embarrassment, indignity, degradation, and anger."

Outcome As with Rodman's other lawsuits, this one was settled out of court for an undisclosed amount. Maybe the controversial athlete should invest in a rabbit's foot.

Cowabunga!

Believe it or not, a southern California surfer sued a fellow boarder in 1996 for "taking" his wave. According to his lawsuit, the poor dude was traumatized by the sight of an intrusive surf cadet riding off on the wave that was "intended for" him. We can all sympathize with the anguish Murf the Surf must have endured by the sight of some inconsiderate beach bum catching his wave.

Outcome A judge dismissed the case because there was no way to put a price on the "pain and suffering" caused by the ordeal. It seems, though, that the value of the case was accurately determined by the fact that it was dismissed.

TERROR FOR TOTS

Modern Nightmare

Once upon a time there was a nine-year-old girl who was attacked by a vicious "masticating Cabbage Patch doll"—at least that's what her attorneys wanted a jury to believe.

Toy maker Mattel won much unwanted publicity in 1998 when its battery-operated Snacktime Kids doll was dragged into court for chomping on a little girl's golden tresses. Also named as a defendant in the lawsuit was Wal-Mart Stores, which was apparently negligent for having sold the errant doll.

On the technical side, a Snacktime Kids doll gives the impression that it's eating; its teeth go up and down and its mouth takes in pieces of plastic designed to look like food. In this particular case, the little girl's hair got caught in the choppers while she was asleep, resulting in her hair allegedly being consumed to the scalp.

On the dramatic side, the girl's lawyers claimed that the hair tugging caused the child to suffer from nightmares of being surrounded by hungry dolls determined to eat her alive. Therefore, they argued, she would require months of counseling, consoling, and rehabilitation.

On the fantasy side, the attorneys claimed that life would "never be the same" for the plaintiff. Therefore, the little girl should be compensated by both Mattel and Wal-Mart for $25.5 million. If the figure were awarded, the lawyers stood to make $10 million for themselves. But according to them, "When companies choose profits over safety, they should be punished accordingly."

Outcome No news yet on the outcome of this hair-raising case, but we suspect the little girl will be sticking with Barbie from now on.

Goofy Trauma

A fifty-seven-year-old ex-Mouseketeer who had performed at Disneyland's opening in 1955 as well as on the *Mickey Mouse Club* TV show sued Disneyland after she was robbed in the Magic Kingdom's parking lot in 1995. The robbery, though, was just a prelude to the ensuing emotional ordeal her family suffered at the hands of Disney employees.

It all started when the ex-Mouseketeer was held up while attending Disneyland's fortieth anniversary with her daughter and three grandchildren. According to the grand-Mouseketeer, the gun-wielding robbers got away with her money, jewelry, checks, credit cards, and driver's license.

The stickup was immediately reported to Disney's security guards, who escorted the whole family to the security offices located somewhere in the labyrinth of tunnels that crisscross beneath the Magic Kingdom. Here they were interviewed by Anaheim police officers and, for the children, entertained by a Mickey Mouse in full costume. The grandchildren were holding up valiantly, considering that they had just seen their grandmother being robbed at gunpoint. But sadly, they weren't prepared for the shock of seeing some Disney personnel getting out of their costumes.

According to Grandma's lawsuit, the grandchildren were

"traumatized . . . in a backstage area where they were shocked to see the Disney characters taking off their costume heads." The trauma suffered by the gullible children was due to "the reality that the Disney characters were, in fact, make-believe." The family's attorneys believed that the ordeal warranted "punitive damages" for the "negligence and intentional infliction of emotional distress."

Of course grand-Mouseketeer probably lived in Fantasyland anyway, judging by her subsequent performance at trial. During her court testimony, she suffered a "flashback" while describing her ordeal. Shortly after launching into her vivid narrative, she had to stop. "Oh, I'm sorry, I'm dizzy," she gasped. Then, after seemingly struggling for breath and apologizing for making a scene, she abruptly cried, "Oh, God. I can't move my hands!" According to her attorney, "She had a flashback to the whole incident. . . ." She resumed her testimony half an hour later after breathing into a paper bag, applying a cold compress to her throat, and recuperating in an office behind the courtroom.

Outcome The superior court judge who presided over the case apparently wasn't impressed. He dismissed the case halfway through trial, stating, "There is nothing to suggest this incident could have been avoided."

House of Horrors

For nearly a decade, people have flocked by the thousands to pay for a healthy dose of fear at Universal Studios Florida's annual Halloween Horror Nights. The fright festival has it all: bloodcurdling screams, slimy goo, and fiendish creatures jumping out of the shadows. It's scary stuff—too scary, said an Orlando woman who sued Universal Studios in January 2000, claiming that she and her ten-year-old granddaughter were "assaulted" by one of the company's chain-saw-wielding maniacs.

According to her lawsuit, the fifty-seven-year-old plaintiff was escorting her granddaughter through the Hell's High spookhouse at Universal in 1998 when they were set upon by a man waving a loud chain saw, minus the chain. With the maniac in hot pursuit, the terrified duo fled toward the exit door and the safety that surely lay beyond. What they didn't know—and couldn't have known, according to the lawsuit— was that the floor near the door was wet from the mist that Universal was using to cool off customers leaving the den of evil. The two hit the wet patch and crashed to the floor. What made matters worse was that the unsympathetic chain-saw-toting fiend continued his assault—crouching over them and thrusting his weapon, the suit said.

The ordeal apparently left the plaintiff with unspecified physical injuries and inflicted "extreme fear, emotional distress and mental anguish." For that, she demanded that Universal reimburse her $15,000.

Outcome Nothing on the outcome of this legal horror story.

OFFENDING FOOD

The Dirty Dozen

If you're looking for a lawsuit that's in particularly bad taste, how about one filed over pornographic doughnuts? A customer-service representative for Oxford Health Care in Nashua, New Hampshire, stopped at a Dunkin' Donuts shop in January 1996 to buy a few dozen "munchkins" doughnut holes. The fifty-five-year-old woman planned to take them to work to celebrate a group of temporary employees' last day on the job.

But when she got to the office and opened the box, she was appalled to find the fried goodies had been shaped to look like "male sexual organs, complete with testes."

Now, we can imagine her chagrin; can sympathize with her embarrassment; can even share her anger. But who could imagine filing a lawsuit—almost two years later? Apparently, she could. In November 1997, the woman, still shaken by the bawdy breakfast treats, sued Merrimack Donuts, the owner of the Dunkin' Donuts franchise—seeking $150,000 for negligence and emotional distress. Merrimack tried to have the lawsuit thrown out on the grounds that the woman didn't have a legal claim. The company argued that any resemblance of its products to sex organs was coincidental. "The defendant maintains that it is common for several munchkins to stick together during the frying process, and that any shapes that may be formed in the process are entirely accidental," the company's lawyers argued. A trial was scheduled for November 1998.

Outcome The lawsuit never made it to trial. A month before the court date, the plaintiff withdrew her complaint. Apparently she realized that she could have easily returned the illicit doughnuts for a free box of more respectable ones.

Hacking After Hacking

Golfing buddies in Walkersville, Maryland, took a practical joke too far in 1997, when one fed the other a rodent disguised as a hot dog. The two had spent the day at a golf club, where one of them worked as a seasonal maintenance employee. They played a series of jokes on each other between holes, each one-upping the other. But the prankster employee's final gag was enough to make anyone gag. He served his pal what looked like an ordinary hot dog; the hungry golfer took a bite only to discover that it was a mouse wrapped in a bun!

Disgusted, the golfer filed a $500,000 lawsuit against both his rat-fink friend and the Glade Valley Golf Club, which had unknowingly hired a sick prankster as its maintenance man and had inadvertently supplied the mouse.

Outcome No news on the outcome of this one. Chances are, though, that these buddies didn't simply shake hands and make up.

The Tale of the Headless Mouse

An unemployed man in San Luis Obispo, California, filed a lawsuit against McDonald's in 1996 after allegedly finding a mouse in his hot apple pie. According to his stomach-turning tale, the man sank his teeth into the pie and bit off the rodent's head. But he claimed that he didn't immediately know he had done so because he suffered from a previous jaw injury. (That's quite a bite, injury or no injury.) After later finding the unexpected ingredient, he claimed to have suffered from post-traumatic stress disorder, which left him emotionally disabled for more than a year. In other words, he had continued to be unemployed for another twelve months.

McDonald's didn't buy into the man's story. The fast-food giant claimed that he had bought the pie, planted the headless mouse in it, recooked the pie, and then brought it back to the restaurant. Not one to be thwarted, however, the plaintiff then claimed additional emotional distress for being accused of fraud by McDonald's. And his woes were allegedly further aggravated by the media and others also insinuating that he had perpetrated fraud. All this contributed to psychotic episodes, he said.

Outcome A county judge didn't buy the plaintiff's half-baked story. The case was dismissed.

Watch What You Eat

In January 1998, a devout Hindu sued a Taco Bell restaurant in Ventura, California, for serving him the wrong burrito. He claimed that after ordering a bean burrito, he was mistakenly given a beef burrito instead. By biting into it, our faithful fast-food-goer violated his most fundamental religious principle. "Eating a cow, it was really a devastating experience," he lamented.

That single mouthful of ground beef was so traumatizing, in fact, that the plaintiff lost the ability to cope. "I had to go to a psychiatrist. I went to a doctor. I couldn't sleep," he testified. In the end, the only way he could regain inner peace was by traveling to England and India to perform religious purification ceremonies, which included bathing in the Ganges River. His lawsuit demanded compensation for travel costs, medical expenses, loss of wages, and emotional distress all to the tune of $144,000.

Taco Bell obviously didn't take the mix-up too seriously; it offered to exchange the man's beef burrito for a bean one, but refused to refund his money.

Outcome No news on the outcome of this one, but we suspect that the plaintiff should have settled for a new burrito.

Back to the Ganges

In November 1998, a Hindu couple in Lincoln, Nebraska, also demanded that Taco Bell pay for the cost of their religious purification. They apparently were going economy class, because their lawsuit asked for only $4,200 for their trip to the Ganges River.

The Hindu couple's lawsuit stemmed from a piece of meat buried in a fifty-nine-cent cup of rice they had shared at a Taco Bell restaurant. Both husband and wife, who had been vegetarians since birth, unfortunately ate the rice before realizing that it had been contaminated with the meat. As for the required trip to the Ganges, "Those are rituals we need to perform, and finally it boils down to practicing our religious freedom. This kind of thing involves hurting a religious practice," the husband insisted.

Outcome A county judge dismissed the lawsuit a year later, ruling that the plaintiffs had failed to show the rice was tainted or unfit for human consumption.

Here We Go Again

Another vegetarian, this one in Utica, New York, filed a $30-million lawsuit against a Wendy's restaurant in July 1988 when he discovered that a veggie pita he had ordered wasn't all veggie, strictly speaking.

The wayward sandwich wrap apparently contained some gelatin, which is often used to thicken low-fat foods—and also happens to be made from animal tissue. The herbivore accused Wendy's of misrepresenting its Garden Veggie Pita as vegetarian fare, and claimed that he had purchased the delicacy only after being assured by a Wendy's employee that it contained no meat by-products. "It's hard for non-vegetarians to understand," the plaintiff explained, comparing his experience to someone who had unwittingly devoured human flesh. "You feel like you're being tainted."

Outcome Although there is no verdict yet, an executive director of the Vegetarian Awareness Network did succeed in getting the Wendy's chain to stop putting the collagen-laced gelatin into the sauce on its veggie pita.

THE SKY'S THE LIMIT

In-Flight Entertainment

A twenty-seven-year-old computer company owner sued Air France for $12 million in 1997 for being "viciously assaulted and physically attacked by several crew members" during his flight from Paris to New York. It turns out that the young entrepreneur was in the locked lavatory with his pants around his ankles and "in the process of going to the bathroom" when the gung-ho crew members kicked the door open and accused him of smoking a cigarette. Apparently the smoke alarm had gone off, prompting the crew to take swift and merciless action. So swift, in fact, that according to the plaintiff, the flight attendants, while in the course of extending their French hospitality, "pulled him naked outside the bathroom exposing his genitals and other private parts to seated passengers."

The plaintiff said that he was a nonsmoker and, according to his attorney, "It turned out later the alarm was defective."

Outcome No news on the outcome of this lawsuit, but chances are that the plaintiff won't be racking up any frequent-flier miles with Air France.

The Unfriendly Skies

Not to be outdone by Air France, American Airlines provided some live in-flight entertainment of its own when the captain hog-tied a passenger to her seat. Not just any passenger either, but a fifty-year-old Beverly Hills socialite and widow of the founder of the CNA Insurance Company.

The unusual incident started in July 1995 when the woman caught a flight from New York to Los Angeles with her dog, Dom Perignon, stashed in a kennel under her seat. Befitting of a socialite, the widow was traveling first class, but the bubbly Mr. Perignon seemingly didn't appreciate his economy-class accommodations at her feet. According to his owner, Dom Perignon "escaped" from his kennel several times. The flight crew, though, alleged that the woman had refused to keep the canine Houdini in his kennel despite numerous requests that she do so.

Later, the widow claimed that she had been taking a nap when a couple of flight attendants rudely awakened her and demanded that she return her dog to his underseat quarters. According to the crew, the socialite responded by becoming increasingly belligerent and yelling obscenities. She finally threatened to "kick out a window" or "open a door and kill you all." Words not to be taken lightly while cruising at thirty-five thousand feet, as the captain well knew. He decided his first-class passenger needed some steerage-class treatment. Unfortunately, he couldn't find the flex cuffs, which are normally reserved for out-of-control passengers, so he settled for using Dom Perignon's leash to strap the screeching socialite to her seat.

The plaintiff sued American Airlines in 1996, claiming that she was beaten by the captain and suffered a disc herniation in her neck. Further, she said she required psychotherapy for the "post-traumatic stress disorder" of being tied with her own dog leash in an inhumane and humiliating fashion. The crew claimed she was never beaten and that she could not have been hurt because the leash was made of soft leather.

Outcome In March 1999, a Santa Monica, California, jury decided the plaintiff was not entitled to receive any compensation for her flighty ordeal. The Federal Aviation Administration, however, decided that it would award the Beverly Hills socialite something else instead—namely, its new zero-tolerance policy for air rage. The FAA convinced a federal grand jury to criminally indict the woman. With the help of famed Washington lawyer Mark Lane, however, the charges were ultimately dropped in July 1999.

Not surprisingly, the socialite went on to file another lawsuit against American Airlines—a libel suit demanding $5 million in general damages and an undisclosed amount in punitive damages. The suit alleged that the airline had induced the U.S. attorney general to indict her and that the resulting criminal prosecution had caused her to suffer "hatred, contempt, [and] ridicule . . ." as well as "a potential 20 years in prison." She also claimed to have endured the "loss of her reputation, shame, mortification . . . [and] hurt feelings." No news on the outcome of this latest lawsuit.

All Shook Up

Twelve passengers traumatized by twenty-eight seconds of severe turbulence on a flight from Los Angeles to New York filed a lawsuit against American Airlines, arguing that they should be compensated for their "psychological trauma" and emotional distress. In 1995, American Airlines' Flight 58 made an emergency landing in Chicago after running into some severe air pockets over Minnesota. Only one passenger was hurt, but lawyers for plaintiffs argued that their "fear of dying" was so acute that it deserved the kind of large award usually reserved for those with physical injuries. The airline offered to pay the plaintiffs $5,000 to $20,000 each. But the attorneys called the offer "insulting" and proceeded to court.

Outcome In October 1999, a New York jury awarded the plaintiffs $2.2 million—the biggest award ever for emotional distress suffered in an airline incident—for their half minute of fright. Why the airline was responsible for unexpected weather conditions is another question. It's possible the jury was in awe of some of the plaintiffs. After all, Steven Spielberg's sister Nancy, along with her two small children, were on the plane. So were Louis Weiss, the retired chairman of the William Morris Agency, and his wife. Ms. Spielberg and her kids were awarded $540,000 for their white-knuckle ride. The Weiss couple garnered $300,000 of the award.

ON THE ROAD AGAIN

Picking Deep Pockets

A disgruntled Los Angeles bus passenger sued the Metropolitan Transportation Authority in 1992 because he thought he had been pickpocketed by another passenger.

According to the ambiguous victim's lawsuit, he was standing on a crowded bus when he "noticed that his wallet was missing from his left front pants pocket." He then supposedly notified the bus driver that "an adult male passenger" who had been standing next to him might have taken his wallet. The bus driver, however, decided it was more important to pay attention to the road. This didn't sit well with the standing passenger because, according to his suit, "The person who possibly stole his wallet was able to leave the bus before the police could be summoned." The possible thief made a clean getaway with $20 to $30 cash, two ATM cards, and a monthly bus pass.

This called for a lawsuit against the MTA, one that demanded the agency pay the passenger $100 for his wallet and its contents, $49,900 in "general damages," and an unspecified amount in punitive damages. After all, the MTA had breached its "duty of utmost care and diligence for its passenger." The reason? The driver "continued to ignore pleas" to call the police, and instead "in a rude and desultory manner

accused the Plaintiff of misplacing his wallet." The bus operator was allegedly so inconsiderate that he committed "acts of
rudeness and impudence toward Plaintiff without provoca-
tion, with malice and ill will, and with the intent and design to
frighten, oppress and injure Plaintiff." As a result, "Plaintiff
suffered humiliation, indignity, apprehension, anxiety, embarrassment, injured feelings, wounded pride, and other mental
suffering and detriment to his further damage."

Did we miss something? Did the bus driver put him in
stocks somewhere along the way? Obviously the dissatisfied
customer hadn't experienced the amenities offered to Air France
and American Airlines passengers.

Outcome The court dismissed the case a year later. The
piqued plaintiff appealed the decision, but his case was again
thrown out. Fuming, he rode off into the sunset. But not before having picked some pockets of his own: it cost the MTA
more than $14,000 to defend itself against the suit.

Another Wild Ride

In another bus adventure, this one in 1995, a frightened passenger sued the Los Angeles Metropolitan Transportation
Authority after the bus driver was threatened with a knife.
According to the plaintiff, a dissatisfied passenger had waved
a knife in front of the driver's face before bounding off the
bus. He later modified the story, claiming he too had been
threatened, but this was refuted by witnesses and the bus driver.

In any event, the eye-opening scene allegedly caused the
plaintiff "extreme and severe mental and emotional distress,
upset and suffering; fright; inability to sleep; interference with
personal life; and exacerbation of heart condition." And ac-

cording to his attorney, "The fear and anxiety he has suffered may never heal completely." (Just imagine how the bus driver must have felt.)

Outcome A judge managed to do some arm twisting at a mandatory settlement conference, coercing the MTA into paying the "victim" $750. Of course, it cost the MTA more than $11,000 in defense costs just to get in front of the judge so that it could be compelled to pay the paltry extortion.

Cash Crazed

A man grabbed two sacks of cash that had fallen out the back of an armored car. He was caught by the Federal Bureau of Investigation while attempting to skip the country with the $1.2 million in stolen loot. He was tried and eventually found not guilty. Soon after, the thief returned to court—to sue the armored car service in 1991. He claimed that the company was responsible for his crime, because he had been "shocked into a state of insanity" by having found the lost money.

Outcome His case was dismissed. What can we say? It's a mad, mad, mad, mad world!

HUSBANDS AND WIVES

Ride 'em Cowboy!

A former porn star blamed a New York street pothole for the loss of his elderly wife's sexual services. Known by seedy film fans as Jack Wrangler, the fifty-two-year-old star of *Raunch Ranch* sued the city and a paving company for $1 million, claiming that he was left "without conjugal fellowship and sexual fulfillment" after his wife tripped and broke her ankle while crossing Fifty-seventh Street and Sixth Avenue in Manhattan.

According to his lawsuit, Wrangler's seventy-three-year-old wife, a Broadway singer, was waylaid in April 1998 by a "dangerous, hazardous, uneven, defective, depressed and hole-like condition" in the road. In other words, a pothole. Having somehow survived her harrowing fall into the depths of the pothole, the woman was hospital-bound for three weeks and was using a cane and receiving physical therapy at the time the lawsuit was filed in October 1998. Wrangler, who starred in more than ninety gay and straight skin flicks including *Heavy Equipment, Jack and Jill,* and a sequel to *The Devil in Miss Jones,* claimed that he was supportive of his spouse as any good husband would have been—but what about his own needs?

Outcome No news on the outcome of this crazy case. But perhaps it's time for old Wrangler to hang up his spurs.

Low-Down, Good-for-Nothing Mistress

A woman in Utah sued her cheating husband's girlfriend in 1999 under the all-but-forgotten legal theory of "alienation of affection." The eighteenth-century statute regards a woman as her husband's property and can thereby hold a "home-wrecker" responsible for "alienating" a husband's or a wife's "affection" from a spouse. The statute is still on the books in nine states, but has not been used in decades.

The jilted wife and mother of their three children argued, "I felt there should be some accountability and responsibility for luring a husband away from his family." Relying on some explicit love letters that she had found, the plaintiff painted a picture of the "other woman" as an intrusive seductress. Apparently the seminude photos accompanied by verses like, "Reading your letter gave me the desire to have an orgasm. We should have phone sex. It would be fun," bought some sympathy for the plaintiff.

Outcome In February 2000, the jury awarded the dumped wife $500,000 for her bruised ego. No doubt, plenty more folks will be dusting off this statute in the near future.

DO OR DIE

Pooh-Poohed

A California man, an acquaintance of a woman who had been missing for nine months, filed a $10-million lawsuit after a SWAT team raided his house. The man claimed he was "emotionally distressed over the search of his home" and suffered "nightmares and headaches" after the incident. But that's the least of his worries. According to his court filing, the officers also scared his dog, causing it to "poop all over the carpet." Psychological trauma is one thing, but having to get the carpet cleaned—well, it's enough to send a man over the edge.

Outcome Call us presumptuous, but we suspect the plaintiff didn't get his $10 million.

Body Snatchers

People love their pets, and more often than not these furry friends are treated like little people. So it shouldn't be surprising that, when a pet passes away, it would be given the same rites as any other family member. That's just what Ruffian, a ten-year-old New York sheepdog, received.

Ruffian's parents—actually, the New York couple who

owned him—did everything they could to bury him with full dignity. They took him to the Long Island Pet Cemetery, where Ruff was laid to rest complete with a burial and headstone. They also asked that Ruffian's favorite toys, his little pink blanket, and his collar all be buried with him. The caring couple then paid the cemetery $1,100 for its services and undoubtedly visited Ruff regularly thereafter.

But almost two years after the pooch's passing, his parents were shocked to see the owners of the Long Island Pet Cemetery named in connection with charges of mail fraud. Worse yet were allegations that the pet cemetery had disposed of an estimated 250,000 pets in mass graves and cremations. So the dumbstruck couple charged out to the cemetery and tried to exhume Ruff. When the grave came up empty, the cemetery assured them it was a mistake and that employees would look into it. A few weeks later, the cemetery invited the couple back to show them Ruff's burial site again. This time it contained a partly decomposed dog, but no toys, blanket, or collar.

So the shocked and grieving couple sued the pet cemetery in 1991. They alleged severe emotional distress, which required psychological counseling. Further, the "father" suffered from nightmares of the horrible fiasco and actually lost sixty pounds due to his grieving. The case ultimately made it to trial in the New York State Supreme Court.

Outcome Apparently the judge had a couple of pooches of his own, because he awarded the couple a death-defying $1.2 million for their trauma.

Body Snatchers, Part Deux

Okay, if Ruff's owners managed to elicit more than $1 million worth of sympathy for their dead doggy, what are the following families entitled to receive? Compared with the decedents in the following case, Ruff received a burial worthy of a pharaoh.

According to several lawsuits filed against the University of California—Los Angeles in 1996, the university was a bit remiss in its handling of donated cadavers. In fact, if the allegations are to be believed, there were some sick puppies working in the science department at the time. The lawsuits alleged that the battling Bruins took the remains of as many as eighteen thousand donated cadavers, stuffed them with animal remains and fetuses, mixed them with hazardous waste, incinerated them, and then dumped them into either a convenient landfill or the Santa Monica Bay. These caring and decorous practices, referred to as "canoeing," were apparently discovered by a Department of Health investigation in 1993.

Needless to say, the families of the donated cadavers were shocked to discover that their loved ones were being treated as human trash bags rather than serving a higher cause in the name of science. According to the lawsuits, the families had been assured by the university that the cadavers would be treated with dignity.

Outcome In March 1999, a Los Angeles Superior Court commissioner ruled that UCLA had no legal responsibility to the relatives of the deceased and therefore could not be negligent or responsible for damages. The cases were dismissed. (And yet the dead dog's owners got $1.2 million?)

Crying Over Rover

An unfortunate dog passed away in Berlin Heights, Ohio—because of a rancid pizza. The innocent pup's owners, who had purchased the frozen pie, claimed that it looked bad. In fact, it looked so bad that they later described it as "spoiled, rotten, rancid, and moldy." But the expiration date was okay, so they cooked it and ate it.

A short while later, the couple became violently ill and rushed to the hospital. No, they didn't leave the rancid pizza out for the dog, Fluffy, to consume. In fact, the unlucky dog didn't even get so much as a nibble of the pizza. Rather, he was run over by his owners' car in the course of their hasty flight to the hospital. So the dogless couple sued the pizza manufacturer for $125,000 in 1990 for the "emotional distress" of their dog's demise.

Outcome No news on the outcome of this rancid case. (Take it from the top. "They're crying over—the dog they just ran over. . . .")

HAIR-RAISERS

Bad Hair Day

Hair. Beautiful, luxuriant hair. Styled, gelled, braided, weaved, bleached, permed, teased—you name it, just don't mess it up! Especially if you're cutting it for free.

So said the New York woman who went to her friend's house in 1990 and asked to have her pal's husband, an employee of a beauty salon, give her a haircut. The husband agreed. Why not? Nothing fancy, help her out, save her a little money. Unfortunately, the woman didn't like her new look. So almost a year later, she sued her friend's husband for "willfully, intentionally, and maliciously" cutting her hair—without her consent.

The twenty-three-year-old Rutgers University student went on to tell reporters that she suffered "extreme shock" and was "nervous and upset," resulting in an "inability to sleep."

These claims were later verified by a clinical psychologist who stated that the plaintiff had stayed up all night after the haircut, "screaming and hysterical." Further, the traumatized haircut recipient required continued psychological counseling. The plaintiff's attorney claimed that she should be compensated to the tune of $75,000.

Outcome The case was dismissed, giving the plaintiff another disappointment to keep her up nights.

A Hairy Experience

Here's a hair dilemma with a different twist. An Aurora, Illinois, woman in her late twenties filed a lawsuit in 1995 against the Mario Tricoci Company, a salon chain and product manufacturer, for damages to her hair—and career. She didn't claim a bad haircut, but rather that a relaxer that the hairstylist had used during her February 1994 visit caused her tresses to fall out. (If the preceding plaintiff thought she had problems with her bad hairdo, she should try having no hair to do at all.)

Besides the salon, the hairless plaintiff sued the employee who attended to her as well as Avlon Industries, which made the product applied to her hair. Watch out, defendants, this woman has a lawsuit to grind. And if half of what she said is true, who can blame her?

According to her attorney, the plaintiff was a talented and popular pop singer who performed at local clubs. She also had a shot at a recording contract and fame galore. In other words, she coulda been a contender. Unfortunately, after the hair-raising incident, the aspiring starlet never performed again.

She said she went bald shortly after her visit to the salon. Even though the hair grew back, it never did so properly, despite medical assistance. The new "baby hair" may suit punk singers, her attorney argued, but didn't fit his client's classy style. Basically, "it ended her career." After all, "In the industry, the look, if you will, is important."

At this point, some might simply have suggested a wig. But a Mario Tricoci spokesman suggested something else—namely that the lawsuit was frivolous and that the plaintiff was just trying to take advantage of "our quality, high-profile name." Although not denying any of the allegations outright, the spokesman insisted, "There are definitely two sides to this one, especially with the fact that this was filed a day before the statute of limitations ran out. The only thing I can say is that we're definitely going to take this to court."

Outcome No news on the outcome of this case, but the baby-haired crooner may have a tough time proving her case. After all, Sinead O'Connor made it big.

One for the Guys

Hairdo lawsuits are by no means restricted to women. An Orlando, Florida, man sued J. C. Penney and Company's salon in July 1991 because the stylist misunderstood his directions. The disappointed customer had wanted his hair short on the sides and long and curly on top, but ended up with short and not so curly on top and long on the sides.

With an obvious flair for dramatics, the plaintiff claimed the bad haircut drove him to psychiatric treatment and deprived him of his "right to enjoy life." He demanded more than $10,000 in compensation for the hair it had taken him two and a half years to grow.

Outcome The case was dismissed in August 1991. Apparently, the judge figured that Yul Brenner, Kojak, and Mr. Clean had never complained about their rights being deprived.

Little Bitty Haircuts

A three-year-old girl in Los Angeles sued the Yellow Balloon children's hair salon in 1985 because she had to pay $2 more for her cut than did her four-year-old brother for his trim. And due to the magnitude of this injustice, her case called for nothing less than some big-time representation by none other than famed lawyer Gloria Allred.

"This is sex discrimination on its face," said Allred in a press conference in front of the salon. "Girls are charged more even if their haircut takes less time and less expertise." The lawsuit was filed under the Unruh Civil Rights Act, a state antidiscrimination law, and demanded equal prices for equal haircuts, attorney fees, and damages.

Despite conceding that both her children had received "very good haircuts," the concerned mother said she had Allred file the lawsuit because her daughter "is young and has a lot of obstacles facing her, and I want to remove as many of those obstacles as I can."

Outcome The case was settled out of court for an undisclosed sum, and the salon agreed to change its price policy.

CONTEST CASUALTIES

Is That Your Final Lawsuit?

Apparently playing double or nothing, an unsuccessful contestant on the TV game show *Who Wants to Be a Millionaire?* filed a lawsuit for $2 million against the ABC network, Disney, and the show's producers.

The lawsuit, filed in New York in June 2000, claimed that the answer the plaintiff gave while on the show was actually the right one—in zodiacal terms at least—yet he was still disqualified. Host Regis Philbin posed the question: "Beginning in January, which of the following signs of the zodiac comes last: (a) Aquarius, (b) Aries, (c) Leo, or (d) Scorpio?" The plaintiff chose Aquarius and stuck to it even after Philbin hit him with his famous "Is that your final answer?" query. The answer was wrong.

Not so, said the plaintiff. He alleged in his lawsuit that although Aquarius begins in January, the zodiacal calendar begins with Aries, which starts in April. So the question was confusing and ambiguous. And because he was wrongfully disqualified, he added, the show intentionally inflicted severe emotional distress that prevented him from working or sleeping. "It's become my life. I want vindication," he said. "All I think about is that question. I just think about it over and over."

Outcome None yet, but we'll wager he's still thinking about that question—not to mention the $2 million he hopes to win.

Can You Spell O-U-T-R-A-G-E-O-U-S?

It was down to two finalists in the grueling competition. One of them would be the victor and move on to the next round; the other would be disqualified. Twelve-year-old Kent Lose and thirteen-year-old Otto Whin (fictional names to protect the innocent) were duking it out to determine who would represent Los Altos School in the 1987 Ventura County, California, Spelling Bee. A word was drawn and Kent stepped up to the microphone. H-O-R-S-Y. Correct! Then it was Otto's turn. H-O-R-S-E-Y. Sorry, that's incorrect! Contest officials eliminated Otto and advanced Kent to the county finals. Sensing something was amiss, Otto ran home and checked his trusty dictionary. Sure enough, both spellings of *horsy* were acceptable. The officials decided it would only be fair if both boys attended the county finals.

It was there that Otto vanquished the thirteen-year-old defending champion, Junior Poorsport, and moved on to the national bee. Junior's outraged father, Ima Poorsport, let fly a few four-letter words of his own, then sued the Ventura County *Star–Free Press*, which had sponsored the event. He sought $2 million in damages for mental distress, alleging that Otto should not have been allowed to compete. According to the contest's rules, Mr. Poorsport pointed out, each school was allowed only one entrant.

Outcome An appellate court judge didn't go for it. Weighing his words, he ruled that Junior Poorsport lost the spelling bee not because Otto Whin was allowed to participate—nor because the contest had been poorly run—but because he had failed to correctly spell the word *iridescent*. The judge summed up the trial court's ruling by saying, "We'll spell it out: A-F-F-I-R-M-E-D."

Letter of the Law

A twelve-year-old girl who finished third in a spelling bee sued the contest's sponsor, claiming that she was unjustly disqualified when judges failed to follow the letter of the law. The eighth-grader from Notre Dame Catholic School in Vacaville, California, sought a court order declaring her the cochampion or forcing a spell-off among the final four students in the regional contest.

The annual Central Valley Spelling Bee, sponsored by the *Sacramento Bee* newspaper, was won in March 1998 by a thirteen-year-old girl from Citrus Heights. She defeated both the plaintiff and a thirteen-year-old Orangevale boy, who was named the runner-up. Our plaintiff was eliminated after misspelling *impugn*. Under the rules followed by the *Sacramento Bee,* which had sponsored the contest for fifteen years, the two finalists then held a showdown. The Citrus Heights girl was declared the victor after she correctly spelled both a word missed by the Orangevale boy and a follow-up word.

So what happened after our defeated plaintiff walked off the stage? No, her parents didn't urge her to take pride in what she had achieved, nor did they use the event as an opportunity to teach their daughter how to accept life's little disappointments. Rather, they helped her file a lawsuit claiming she would suffer "irreparable injury" due to having "no chance of receiving the prestige, experience, and future benefit that participation in an event as well-known and as respected as the [Scripps Howard] National Spelling Bee would provide."

They argued that regional organizers had violated contest rules set by Scripps Howard, which required all four finalists to remain standing if each one misspelled the same word in a given round. They also alleged that organizers had used words from a list not authorized for regional competitions. In fact, our plaintiffs went so far as to file for a temporary restraining order and injunction blocking the thirteen-year-old regional winner from competing as the sole champion at the Scripps Howard National Spelling Bee in Washington, D.C. "This is not a sour grapes case. They're complaining that the rules for the competition were violated by the grown-ups," argued the plaintiff's lawyer.

Outcome The judge fortunately didn't see it that way. He stated that the suggested rules issued by Scripps Howard to all spellers gave much leeway to regional organizers. Therefore, he ruled, the *Bee* was allowed to design its own list of words, as well as choose which way it wanted to determine a winner.

With that, the case was thrown out—much like a spelling bee contestant who misses a word.

FIELD OF DREAMS

Major-League Pest

A little league dad created a lasting memory when he decided to sue his son's baseball league for $25,000. The legal fracas started when coaches and league officials asked Pop to either stop smoking or move back from the field where the smoke wouldn't bother anyone. The dad didn't take too kindly to the suggestion and, after creating an embarrassing scene, filed a lawsuit claiming that his son had suffered emotional distress because of the commotion.

Not satisfied, the smoker then had the league president served with a subpoena just as he was standing on the pitcher's mound. And to ensure that his peevish antics were recorded for posterity, Pop had junior videotape the process service.

Outcome The judge didn't appreciate the fuming father wasting the court's time. He sanctioned the plaintiff and his attorney $2,500 for "advancing arguments . . . that are frivolous and without any legal foundation."

Shocked Jock

More ballpark mayhem. The coach of a woman's softball team filed a $4-million lawsuit in June 1993 against the city of Roanoke, Virginia, claiming that his constitutional right to the pursuit of happiness was denied. According to the hotheaded coach, an umpire had tossed him out of the game and unjustly prevented his team from playing in an upcoming match by suspending the team's next game. The ultimate sportsman claimed "great mortification, humiliation, shame, vilification, exposure to public infamy, injury to his good reputation, and has been and will forever be hampered in his pursuit of happiness."

Outcome Evidence of real trauma or just an impressive use of five-syllable words? You make the call. Our bet is that the case was dismissed.

A Nonevent

A disgruntled spectator in Japan sued the organizers of the 1998 Nagano Winter Olympics for the mental anguish he allegedly suffered after missing an event due to heavy traffic.

Outcome The court sympathized with his sore feelings and awarded him unspecified damages. If word got around, just imagine all the lawsuits the traumatized commuters in Los Angeles could whip up!

6

CONSTITUTIONAL RIGHT TO WACKINESS: INMATE LAWSUITS III

I have never been more struck by the good sense and the practical judgment of the Americans than in the manner in which they elude the numberless difficulties resulting from their Federal Constitution.

—Alexis de Tocqueville

By now, you might be wondering what a convicted felon has to do to sue the state. The law says that to file a suit in federal court, prisoners must claim either that a federal law has been broken or that their constitutional or civil rights have been violated. Sound tough? You may be surprised.

Inmates—who, by the way, have access to prison libraries stacked with law books—can be quite ingenious when it comes to spotting obscure provisions in the Constitution. Here are some wacky claims made by prisoners who sniffed out some constitutional protections few people know about.

How Gauche!

A group of inmates in Arizona claimed that their constitutional rights were violated when housing units at some prisons were painted light brown. Apparently the muted hue clashed miserably with the iron bars.

A Weighty Case

An Arizona prisoner sued the state when his weight-lifting equipment was removed from his cell. He claimed that prison weights are guaranteed by the First, Fourth, Fifth, Sixth, Eighth, and Fourteenth Amendments.

Broken Record

Another Arizona inmate received a compact disc player in the mail from his family, but due to prison rules was not allowed to keep it. When the device was confiscated, the prisoner penned a flurry of memos to various officials in a futile attempt to get the CD player back.

When that didn't work, he sued the Arizona Department of Corrections, claiming its explanations for forbidding the CD player were "nothing more than a convoluted equivocation based in serving . . . bureaucrats rather than the facts." The loquacious litigant went on to claim he had a constitutional right to have the device, adding in his best legalese, "Defendants have no penological interests in arbitrarily denying the aforementioned Constitutional rights of Plaintiff."

From there, the matter quickly spun out of control. Not only did the inmate insist he would suffer "irreparable injury" unless he got the CD player back, he claimed he couldn't adequately research the constitutional ramifications of the case because he was allowed to visit the prison law library only twenty-seven times in seven weeks—and he wanted to go forty-seven times! His lawsuit argued that there was another fervent filer usurping space in the library, an inmate "who does not do any legal work and has served to impede Plaintiff's access."

Apparently, he wasn't impeded enough. It was only after the plaintiff had filled two legal files with six inches' worth of documents that a U.S. district judge pulled the plug on the CD controversy. The judge dismissed the case, sticking a handwritten note inside the convict's file. "This is a frivolous case over a boom box," the note read. "It does not deserve my further judicial effort."

Don't Open Till X-mas

A Nevada inmate claimed his rights under the First and Fourteenth Amendments were violated when prison officials didn't deliver his mother's Christmas card to him until after Christmas.

Playing Games

A former drifter, serving a life sentence in Arizona for brutally raping and killing a Northeastern University nursing student, sued the state when prison officials took away his Game Boy® video game player. He claimed the boredom he suffered without the device constituted cruel and unusual punishment. The murder victim's mother suggested another way for him to pass the time: "There are other things prisoners can do besides Nintendo. In the old days, they used to make little rocks out of big ones."

Down in the Mouth

An inmate sued the South Bay Detention Center in San Diego, California, for refusing to allow him to use dental floss.

Achy Breaky Law

An inmate alleged that being forced to listen to the jail warden's country-western music constituted cruel and unusual punishment.

Can You Say *Hypochondriac?*

A convicted sex offender in Colorado claimed that he was denied medical care even though he was seen at the prison infirmary 165 times in two years—or once every four days.

To Bee or Not to Bee

A Pennsylvania inmate filed a $3-million lawsuit against Berks County Prison, alleging that he received inadequate medical treatment after being stung by a bee. A judge dismissed the case, ruling that the plaintiff had suffered no adverse reactions and had failed to prove that he needed special treatment.

Rough Passage

Another Pennsylvania prisoner, who claimed to suffer from persistent kidney pain, filed a lawsuit accusing prison officials of showing "deliberate indifference" to his "serious medical needs" and for disciplining him when he sought treatment. As it turned out, the inmate had been examined in the prison infirmary more than 150 times with sophisticated equipment, including CAT scans. He was disciplined for lying to the staff when he handed a doctor two pebbles and claimed they were kidney stones he had just passed.

Proud Papa

A Nebraska inmate doing time in a maximum-security prison filed an "equal protection" lawsuit to have his infant son live with him in his jail cell. He argued that it was only fair that he be allowed to raise his son behind bars because the state's prison for women grants incarcerated mothers time to bond with their newborns.

Bed Abuse

A Pennsylvania inmate sued for cruel and unusual punishment because prison officials deducted $104 from his prison account to replace a mattress he had torn to shreds. In an eleven-page decision, a judge dismissed the case after concluding that prison officials had taken the proper steps—such as holding a disciplinary hearing—before fining the plaintiff.

Coat Abuse

A Brooklyn burglar sued the state of New York for a mere $989 *billion* for the emotional distress he suffered after prison guards "beat up his jacket," which he wasn't wearing at the time. Maybe this crazy con should try on another jacket—one of the "strait" variety.

A Finely Tuned Judgment

The state of New Jersey was named in a $14-million lawsuit filed by an inmate who alleged that the jail wardens had unlawfully injected him in the eye with a "radium electric beam." As a result, he claimed a voice spoke to him from inside his head.

The U.S. District Court dismissed the lawsuit, not because of the irrationality of the case, but because the statute of limitations had run out. What's more, the judge determined the incident could have easily been avoided. As he wrote in his opinion, "Taking the facts as pleaded . . . they show a case of presumably unlicensed radio communications, a matter which comes within the sole jurisdiction of the Federal Communications Commission. . . . And even aside from that, [the plaintiff] could have blocked the broadcast to the antenna in his brain simply by grounding it. . . . [He] might have pinned to the back of his trouser leg a short chain of paper clips so that the end would touch the ground and prevent anyone from talking to him inside his brain." Do you get the impression the judge was having a little fun here?

UNCIVIL RIGHTS

Hundreds more inmates have thrown their caps into the legal ring, alleging these actions by prisons violated their constitutional rights:

- Assigning an inmate to a top bunk
- Banning pornographic books and magazines depicting rape, bestiality, and incest
- Forcing an inmate to work despite a "life-threatening" allergy to insects
- Providing ineffective swamp coolers
- "Allowing" a power outage that damaged an inmate's TV
- Denying an inmate possession of Soap-on-a-Rope
- Assigning a cell too far from the bathroom

- Forcing inmates to shave
- Prohibiting a prisoner from having an accordion
- Confiscating tarot cards
- Letting an inmate's commode explode
- Not having a guard wake an inmate for work
- Improperly removing a prisoner's warts
- Not providing extra pillows

And to top it off . . .

- Prohibiting inmates from filing frivolous lawsuits!

7

NONSENSE AND SENSIBILITY: SEXUAL HARASSMENT AND DISCRIMINATION LAWSUITS

In our quest for nonracist, nonsexist goals, the demand for equal rights can be pushed to silly extremes. The inability to absorb the minor indignities suffered daily by us all without running to court may stop [the law] dead in its tracks.
—U.S. District Judge Patrick Higginbotham

A male employee at the University of Nebraska used to keep a framed photograph of his wife on his desk at work—that is, until a female colleague accused him of sexual harassment. She admitted that the proud hubby had never verbally or physically come on to her in any way. She simply claimed that the five-by-seven-inch photo of his wife in a bikini was offensive and created a hostile work environment. Apparently the nonplussed employee had never experienced the "hostile" environment of a beach or lake.

In this case, the humbled hubby narrowly averted a lawsuit by stashing away his swimsuit shot, pronto. But many others aren't so lucky. Since Anita Hill and Clarence Thomas clashed on national television less than a decade ago, lawsuits charging sexual harassment, racial discrimination, gender bias, and other workplace aberrations have surged. Statistics tell the story: State and federal courts faced some eighteen thousand of these lawsuits in 1990. That number has since climbed by the thousands every year, hitting a staggering 42,354 cases in 1998. And a great many of these legal mountains are nothing more than misconstrued or embellished molehills.

Anyone who doubts that Americans have taken touchiness to new extremes need look no farther than the horror that welled up in an average woman at the mere glimpse of a colleague's swimsuit-clad spouse. What, we ask, made the photo so offensive that it managed to sully the entire office "environment"? Was it the wife's exposed midriff? Or was it the startling revelation that some men actually like looking at their own wives? And what if the photograph looked more like something from a Sears catalog than the swimsuit issue of *Sports Illustrated?* Would the coworker have been allowed to leave it on his desk then? (Probably, but chances are he wouldn't have been so sentimental.) The point is that our tolerance of life's little indignities has become as fragile as Woody Allen's ego. A passing pat on an employee's back these days sends managers scurrying for liability insurance and sensitivity-training videos, while an off-the-cuff compliment or joke told at the water cooler can land even the most well-meaning of folks in court.

These problems are aggravated by the fact that a good many sexual-harassment and discrimination claims are filed purely for revenge or profit. Although few of us are inclined to say so, lest we be accused of being pro-oppression or something just as dastardly, it's common for terminated workers to fire back against employers with trumped-up "afterthought" claims. From Mitsubishi to Texaco to the guy down the hall who put in an age-bias claim after getting laid off, lawyers and threats to sue have been fast supplanting unions and threats to strike as the prime movers of workplace conflict in this country. The shift is reflected at the bookstore, where you can find half a dozen publications aimed at disgruntled workers, with snazzy titles like *The Employee Strikes Back!, The 9 to 5 Guide to Combating Sexual Harassment,* and *Can They Do That? A Guide to Your Rights on the Job.* Attorney E. Richard Larson minces no words in his book *Sue Your Boss.* He tells workers who have been fired, passed over for a promotion, or otherwise aggrieved that newly enacted laws are "very much in your favor" and just "waiting to be used." And if you fall into more than one protected-group category—sex, race, age— Larson advises throwing in a claim for each, whether or not you've seen actual evidence of bias. In other words, assume the worst, because each separate claim gives the employer something to sweat over and pay its lawyers for.

Our first sexual-harassment lawsuit, leveled against a textile manufacturer by an ousted employee, looks suspiciously like a parting shot. You be the judge.

SEXUAL HARASSMENT: PAST AND PRESENT

Oh, Did I Forget to Mention . . . ?

A woman in Chicago had a knack for selling fabric. Within a year of joining Burlington Industries in March 1993, she was promoted to supervisor of the textile company's mattress-fabric sales division. Unfortunately, her interpersonal skills weren't up to par. Two months into her new job, the woman quit when other supervisors told her that coworkers and customers had complained about her. Her letter of resignation criticized her bosses, coworkers, and "whining" customers, and said she had a better offer; it mentioned nothing about sexual harassment.

Three weeks later, however, the former employee sent a second letter fingering her boss as a serial harasser. Her lawsuit against Burlington followed. (Claimants always name the company as a defendant because, as the employer, it's responsible for providing a safe working environment.) She claimed that her boss made sexually suggestive remarks throughout their business relationship, starting with the March 1993 interview that landed the woman her initial sales job. His trespasses were plentiful: apparently, he often stared at her breasts and legs; told lots of dirty jokes; patted her on the knee (twice) and the rear (once, "right in front of her husband" at a holiday party); reduced her to tears by using naughty double entendres in phone conversations between his office in New York and hers in Chicago; and urged her to "loosen up."

It all came to a head during a business trip in the summer of 1993, she claimed. While leaving a hotel bar, the boorish boss allegedly told the plaintiff, "You know, I could make your life very hard or easy at Burlington." In other words: Give me sex or you'll never get promoted. Strangely, she never gave him sex, yet still got promoted to supervisor—with his help, no less—in March 1994. The rest is history.

At trial, the plaintiff said (inconsistently) that she resigned her post because her boss's overtures had become "unbearable"—quite interesting given that they worked in different cities. Even so, she admitted that before quitting she neither complained to supervisors about the predator in their midst nor sought relief under Burlington's strict policy barring sexual harassment.

Both the boss and Burlington argued that the disgruntled plaintiff's tale was an amalgam of complete fabrications and distortions of innocent remarks, and that he never harassed her at all. And her claims that she had told six coworkers that she was being sexually harassed were denied by all six. But under summary judgment rules, the woman was entitled to a jury trial. And so it proceeded.

Outcome A trial judge threw out the case, ruling that Burlington could not be held liable for alleged harassment that it had no way of preventing (since the plaintiff had never reported it). An appeals court, however, reversed the decision in 1998, granting the plaintiff a jury trial. It ruled that the boss's alleged conduct amounted to quid-pro-quo sexual harassment—a type of blackmail in which promotions, raises, et cetera are granted only in return for sexual favors—even though the plaintiff got the "quid" (a promotion) without giving the "quo" (sex). Go figure.

Throw Another Barbie on the Barbie

Two waitresses sued Hoss's Steak & Sea House in Pittsburgh, Pennsylvania, after witnessing a cook skewer a Barbie doll and broil it in a deep-fat fryer. The women, ages thirty-one and thirty-two, alleged that the apparent "satanic ritual" was just one of many bizarre, "sexual" incidents that had taken place at the restaurant, creating a hostile work environment.

But the attorney for Hoss's argued the women were simply out for revenge. He pointed out that the plaintiffs had filed their lawsuit in August 1995, almost a year after being fired for bickering with coworkers. "They want revenge and a little bit more," the lawyer said at trial.

Outcome Apparently, Barbie's brutal murder in boiling oil wasn't enough to make the jurors' hearts melt. After deliberating for two hours, they returned a verdict in favor of Hoss's.

Moonstruck

Some workplaces can be dreary and somber, while others are just a load of laughs. The latter must have been the case at a Los Angeles Pacific Bell office, which became the setting for a particularly revealing case of sexual harassment.

A service technician didn't think it was all that much fun, because he filed a lawsuit in 1997 alleging that his male supervisor had sexually harassed him. Now, it's one thing to be harassed by the opposite sex, but to have a same-sex supervisor do it? That must have been downright annoying. And this cretin of a boss apparently went all out, too. According to the lawsuit, he dropped his pants and exposed his buttocks to the plaintiff.

The supervisor admitted to "mooning" the technician on one occasion. The plaintiff, however, alleged that the dastardly prank had happened on numerous occasions and that Pacific Bell didn't do a thing to stop it or to adequately investigate the matter. So the twenty-eight-year-old technician was left with no choice but to sue both the supervisor and the company.

Outcome The case eventually made it to court, where the trial dragged on for a month. After deliberating for two days, the jury made Pacific Bell pay the moonstruck plaintiff $244,500 for his supervisor's antics.

It's the Size of the Award That Counts

A body-shop estimator filed a sexual-harassment lawsuit against Hi-Tech Painting & Collision in Garden Grove, California, over another workplace prank that went afoul. According to his lawsuit, filed in 1997, the twenty-seven-year-old plaintiff went to the rest room and was urinating when his manager picked the lock and opened the door. In leaped the assistant manager with camera in hand and took a photo of the dumbstruck employee. When the plaintiff later stepped out of the john, he saw his fun-loving managers laughing over the Polaroid as it developed. He asked them for the photo, but the paparazzi wouldn't give it up. Instead, they showed it to other employees, who proceeded to ridicule the plaintiff about the size of his now-not-so-private parts. They took to calling him Shorty, Splinter, Rod, Tiny, and Pee Wee. The comedy troupe even made a point of staring at his crotch whenever he walked into a room.

The plaintiff eventually transferred to another office in Santa Anita, California. But three months later, when he had all but forgotten about the incident, the damnable photo reemerged. Apparently, the two Garden Grove managers had kindly decided to forward the snap to the Santa Anita shop. The manager there immediately showed it to his employees. Once again the guffawing began, and so did the witty nicknames—Splinter, Pee Wee, and Moby Dick.

Knowing of no other way to regain his parts' privacy, the embarrassed estimator sued the two managers of the Garden Grove shop, as well as the company. The case eventually made it to trial, where the plaintiff claimed he had suffered humiliation, embarrassment, and emotional distress, and was "not the same" after the incident. The defendants argued that their actions were just good-natured "horseplay" among employees. In fact, they said, the plaintiff had laughed when he saw the photo and had actually shown it to some of the employees himself.

Outcome After a nine-day trial and nine hours of deliberation, the jury returned with a verdict. They awarded the emasculated plaintiff $1.5 million! Well, if nothing else, "Pee Wee" has a big *verdict* to brag about.

Watch Your Sein Language

The TV comedy *Seinfeld* is no laughing matter—at least not for one Milwaukee, Wisconsin, man. The former executive at Miller Brewing Company was fired after nineteen years of service for recounting a gag from the sitcom at work.

The hullabaloo began in 1993 when the executive naively repeated to a female coworker some rather risqué lines from the TV show, which he had watched the night before. In the episode, Jerry Seinfeld, the main character, can't seem to recall his girlfriend's name, but does remember that it "rhymes with a female body part." He spends the next thirty minutes trying to figure out her name, with his sidekick George proffering such unlikely possibilities as "Mulva" and "Gipple." At the end of the show, Seinfeld finally remembers the woman's name—Dolores—which indeed rhymes with an intimate part of the female anatomy.

The executive thought the episode was so hysterical that he couldn't keep from sharing some of its finer points with his coworker, even though she didn't care to hear them. In his great enthusiasm, he challenged her to think of a word that rhymed with *Dolores,* and even photocopied a page from his dictionary with the word in question to show her. She wasn't amused. In fact, she was appalled. So appalled that she complained to her boss, who, fearing a lawsuit, fired the executive that week and had him escorted out of the building by security guards. With that black mark on his employment record, the dismissed executive was unable to find another job for nearly two years.

But every dog has its day—and his came at trial. In 1997, the fired executive sued Miller Brewing for wrongful termination, arguing that his behavior didn't amount to sexual harassment.

Outcome Agreeing that silly Seinfeld banter failed to constitute a threat, a jury of ten women and two men awarded the plaintiff $26.5 million in damages, the largest award in Wisconsin's history. Although the award was later overturned by an appeals court, the jurors' decision sent a loud-and-clear message to America's workforce: Lighten up!

Victor Victoria

A sexual-harassment lawsuit was filed in 1996 by a high-priced call girl—or call guy, as the case may be. At least that's what the sheriff's deputies in San Francisco were trying to figure out when they arrested the transsexual for prostitution. It seems they had a difficult time determining whether to place "Victoria" with the men or the women. Although she had been arrested as a man, she insisted she was a woman and claimed she feared for her safety if she was dumped into a cell with a bunch of guys.

So the deputy in charge decided to make things simple and ordered a strip search to determine if Victoria might not actually be a Victor. According to Victoria's subsequent lawsuit, she begged the deputies not to make her strip and asked that they check their records, since she had been booked in the same jail three years earlier. Those records, she claimed, would show she was female. But the deputies figured they could make the determination more quickly and accurately by having the modest transsexual prove her point.

According to Victoria's lawyers, prostitution arrests are not the kind of offenses that warrant strip searches. Rather, the old strip routine is reserved for those whom the officers believe may be hiding contraband (as opposed to something else, that is). They claimed Victoria suffered "emotional pain and suffering" due to the deputies peeking into her panties.

Outcome A jury decided to compensate the plaintiff handsomely by awarding her $755,000 for doing something she probably would have done for $100, given different circumstances. Victoria was so ecstatic after the award, she gushed that it was "life transforming" that the jury believed her.

SEXUAL HARASSMENT: THE FUTURE

With women suing men, men suing women, men suing other men, and everyone suing their companies, what could possibly be next in the evolution of sexual-harassment lawsuits? Well, how about women suing dogs or robots? After all, no one said the unwelcome groper need be human. Here are a couple of cases that may well foreshadow the twisted avenues workplace harassment suits will take in the not-too-distant future.

Heel, Rover!

A woman in Danbury, Connecticut, had to make regular trips to the local courthouse to examine documents related to pending litigation. On each visit, however, she felt sexually harassed—not by an ogling court employee, but by a canine. The woman claimed that Kodak, a golden retriever owned by one of the judges, would sneak up behind her, lift up her skirt with its snout, and sniff around her crotch while she researched files. Certain that she saw the judge smirking as his dog inspected her, the woman filed a federal lawsuit in September 1996. She claimed the judge knew that his furry friend preferred women in skirts and intended to sexually harass her. She also alleged that the actions of judge and his dog had caused her emotional distress and had deprived her of her constitutionally guaranteed right of free access to the courts.

Outcome Despite the plaintiff's dogged pleas, a federal appeals court dismissed the case in January 1998. The fact that the woman never claimed to have cut short her visits as a result of Kodak's overtures may have helped put her case in the doghouse.

When Mail Carriers Attack

A woman in California sued her former employer, Pacific Bell, for injuries she sustained when "Zippy," the office's mail-delivering robot, went postal. The woman alleged that on December 22, 1997, the day before her last day at work, the five-hundred-pound self-propelled robot "went out of control" when she attempted to reach for some mail it had brought to her desk. Zippy is essentially a pair of motorized carts linked by a coupling. The lead cart follows a guide path of magnetic strips under the hallway carpet and stops at predetermined locations.

According to the plaintiff's lawsuit, when she hit Zippy's stop switch, the frisky droid "began to move without warning and pinned [her] against a filing cabinet or other furniture." The accosted employee sought $200,000 for lost wages, medical bills, and loss of earning capacity.

Outcome Minutes before trial, Pacific Bell settled out of court for $80,000. It seems Zippy didn't benefit much from all those mandatory sexual-harassment videos.

PREPUBESCENT PERPETRATORS

Our hypersensitivity to sexual affronts has so saturated the workplace that it's quickly flowing over into our schools. Soccer moms, now fearful that their six-year-olds will be kissed by real-life Georgie Porgies, are invoking—of all things—Title IX of the 1972 Education Amendments Act. Title IX was designed to prevent sexual discrimination by schools receiving public money. The original enforcers of the law dreamed that by tearing down the barriers of traditional gender roles, the law would create a hardy new species—boys who learned to sew in home-ec class and girls who rebuilt hot rods in auto shop. But today's Title IX enforcers envision helpless girls being victimized by naughty boys—and are resorting to legal intervention.

Playground Harassers

There's a new craze hitting elementary schools across the country. No, it's not Pokémon or N'Sync. It's sexual-harassment lawsuits—and one of them recently made it from the playground all the way to the Supreme Court.

A Forsyth, Georgia, woman claimed her ten-year-old daughter suffered from a five-month "barrage of sexual harassment and abuse" from a fifth-grade classmate. The pint-sized predator allegedly tried to grab his quarry's breasts (that's assuming she had any), rubbed up against her in the hallways, and whispered that he wanted to "get in bed" with her. When school officials failed to stop the situation, Mom and daughter sued the school board for $1 million, claiming that it had failed to protect the girl's civil rights as guaranteed under Title IX.

Outcome Not persuaded by this broad interpretation of the law, a federal district court judge threw the case out, reminding the plaintiffs that neither the school board nor any of its employees "had any role in the harassment."

Undaunted, the plaintiffs' attorney then took the case to an appeals court, where it was again thrown out. Still not satisfied with the reception she was receiving to her reinvention of the 1972 statute, the lawyer appealed once more and ended up in the Supreme Court.

Here, the attorney's persistence finally paid off. In May 1999, the court ruled in a narrow 5–4 vote that schools can indeed be held liable for failing to prevent student-on-student sexual harassment. But in a biting dissent, the minority court predicted that the ruling would both set off "runaway litigation" by parents who mistake childish conduct for harassment and unduly burden schools with new costs and policing obligations. The four dissenters chided the majority, saying it was "oblivious to the fact that almost every child, at some point, has trouble in school because he or she is being teased by his or her peers. . . . After today, Johnny will find that the routine problems of adolescence are to be resolved by invoking a federal right to demand assignment to a desk two rows away."

GENDER BIAS: THE WOMEN'S SIDE

Despite Susan B. Anthony's best efforts, gender bias is alive and well—and playing out in courtrooms near you.

Spoiled Rotten

In 1996, a Japanese man sued his former wife for $38,000, claiming she had broken their prenuptial agreement because she refused to do all the household chores, cook him rice and miso soup for breakfast each morning, and give him a monthly allowance of $850—all while she held down a full-time job. (In Japan, the woman usually takes the man's paycheck, pays the bills, and then gives her husband a sum he can spend on lunch, drinks, and entertainment.)

Outcome The Tokyo District Court ruled for the wife in August 1997, but only after it noted that she had been willing to fulfill all her husband's household requirements as long as he lived up to his end of the marriage arrangement: The wife had stipulated from the outset that if she was to take care of the house and her job, they needed to live near her place of employment. He had refused.

The judge denied the husband's demand for damages, but did require the wife to return her wedding ring and a cash gift of $8,000.

Little did the wife know that she may have launched a cultural—and legal—revolution in her homeland. A Japanese women's group, noting that many of the country's men expect their working wives to not only do all the housework but also draw their baths, applauded and predicted more lawsuits. One told the *Washington Post,* "If she can win this suit, it's going to give all these other women who are tortured by housework the idea to sue. They will realize that they can go to court and win." Or they could simply apply an oversized frying pan to their husbands' thick heads.

Striking Out

A college softball coach in Oregon was fired in 1993 for finishing the season with a less-than-impressive 0–24 Pac-10 record. Unfortunately, this losing streak was consistent with her previous six years of coaching, in which she had amassed a sad 9–112 record. But that didn't mean she was going to retire her title quietly. After school officials fired her, she sued Oregon State University, claiming the losses weren't her fault. Rather, they were all due to gender discrimination.

She alleged the university didn't pay her enough and that the males coaching in similar positions received significantly more. Further, the university didn't spend enough money on her softball team and provided the players with inadequate facilities. (Never mind the fact that she couldn't coach her way out of a paper bag.)

Outcome Her arguments were ultimately presented to an eight-woman federal jury, which apparently took up her cause. After a sixteen-day trial, the jurors awarded her a hefty $1.3 million, despite the fact that the two sports committees that had decided to replace the coach were also comprised mostly of women.

Oregon State University appealed the award in 1998, arguing that it was excessive and "disproportionate to any damage conceivably sustained by the plaintiff." A district court judge cut the award to $724,000.

Dressed for Success

A woman in Tennessee who said wearing slacks violated her religion filed a lawsuit in 1998 after she was fired for donning a dress to work. "We believe you have to dress holy and look holy and walk daily with God," said the woman, a member of the Pentecostal Holiness denomination. "We believe [wearing pants] is a sin. The Bible says it's an abomination."

Claiming that her dismissal violated her freedom of religion as guaranteed under the Civil Rights Act of 1964, the woman demanded that she be reinstated and receive back pay as well as unspecified damages. Seems fair, right? After all, businesswomen wear skirts on the job all the time, so why not her? There's just one detail that's been left out: The plaintiff didn't work in a store or office building or hospital. She ran the machines at an automotive factory.

According to the lawsuit filed in Nashville federal court in June 1998, the Pentecostal plaintiff was working for TAD

Staffing Services employment agency in April 1996 when she was sent to work as a machine operator at a Robert Bosch Corporation plant. A few days into the assignment, however, her supervisor sent the woman home, saying her long, loose-fitting dress posed a safety hazard. If the material got caught in the whirring machinery, he claimed, she risked being dragged into the cogs and seriously injured. The plant's personnel director informed the staffing agency that the woman would have to be taken off the assignment if she refused to wear the appropriate clothing—a jumpsuit or pants. So instead of slipping on some slacks, she sued.

Outcome No news on the verdict. But as a personal aside, we think that, given the circumstances, the great employer in the sky would waive the skirt requirement just this once.

GENDER BIAS: THE MEN'S SIDE

Seeing how easily women can reduce their bosses and others to quivering wrecks and often win large awards to boot, it wasn't long before aggrieved males began trying their luck with gender-bias claims, too. Their resounding battle cry: "Two can play at this game!"

But She's Not Wearing One

In 1996, a man was denied entrance into the formal dining room of a posh California hotel because he was not wearing a necktie. The maître d' offered to lend him one. But the man, perhaps already sensing a lucrative opportunity, refused and left.

Soon afterward, the rebuffed diner filed a gender-discrimination suit against the hotel, claiming he was treated unfairly because of his gender. His argument? If women weren't required to wear ties, he shouldn't have to wear one either.

Outcome The judge decided the case had merit and awarded the guy $18,000! Now maybe he can buy a tie.

Party Pooper

While consumers still seem to tolerate discounts offered to select patrons such as senior citizens or college students, the practice of offering a deal to one gender and not the other has rubbed some people the wrong way.

Take the lawyer who sued three South Florida nightclubs in April 1999, hoping to put an end to the common weekend practice known as ladies' night. The Fort Lauderdale attorney claimed the pubs were guilty of unlawful discrimination because they charged men full price for admission on Friday and Saturday nights while allowing unescorted women in at a reduced rate or for free. Nightclubs have long used ladies' nights not only to attract more female customers, but also to lure more male customers with the prospect of meeting single women.

Outcome No news on the outcome of this lawsuit. A similar case, however, was won in October 1985 by a man who sued eight nightclubs and nine car washes in California that offered special rates to woman on certain days. In that case, the state supreme court deemed ladies' days discriminatory.

For Her Eyes Only

A man sued Chippendales for gender discrimination after being barred from viewing an all-male strip show at the Los Angeles nightclub. The plaintiff said that when he tried to attend the show on May 20, 1987, he was told no men were allowed. (Chippendales is generally patronized by women attending bachelorette parties.) His lawsuit demanded unspecified general damages, attorney fees, and a permanent injunction to stop Chippendales from keeping men out of its strip shows.

Outcome Chippendales settled the case out of court in 1990. It gave the plaintiff a letter of apology, an undisclosed amount of money, and a promise that men would be allowed into the show.

Pumped Up

Another angry lawyer slapped a Texaco service station in Escondido, California, with a $2-million sex-discrimination lawsuit in August 1992. He claimed that the practice of having station attendants pump gas at self-service pumps for female motorists was unfair to men, who had to pump their own gas. "[The plaintiff] has suffered unequal treatment, humiliation, and monetary loss as a result of paying the same price as women but receiving less service," his lawsuit alleged.

Outcome The suit was settled out of court, with the gas station agreeing to cease its chivalrous activities and force women to fill their own cars. It's good to know someone's out there policing the petroleum industry for such heinous civil rights violations.

What, No Women?

A male inmate in Arizona took the concept of sex discrimination to new heights when he sued the state for not assigning any female guards to his prison unit. Apparently, the cheeky con believed that having only male guards—while fellow prisoners were given female deputies to ogle—constituted discrimination against him. (No doubt, he'd prefer his prison guards sporting the latest in Victoria's Secret apparel as well.)

Outcome The case was dismissed.

RACIAL UPRISINGS AND RELIGIOUS WARS

Gender discrimination has some ugly twin sisters—racial and religious discrimination. And unfortunately, these serious issues are being exploited by plaintiffs and attorneys looking to cash in on civil rights laws.

Splitting Hairs

For more than a year, an Atlanta firefighter was relegated to doing paperwork, emptying the trash, and collecting donations from fire stations for Georgia hospitals. Why wasn't he out fighting fires? Because he refused to shave his beard.

The fire station where the eleven-year veteran worked had banned facial hair on its firefighters in 1988, citing safety standards. Beards, Atlanta Fire Bureau officials said, prevented firemen's air-filtering masks to seal properly, potentially allowing deadly smoke to seep in.

But the reassigned firefighter, who is black, would hear nothing of it. In 1990, he joined with eleven other African American firemen who had been reassigned to sue the Fire Bureau for racial discrimination. The plaintiffs argued that they suffered from pseudofolliculitis barbae, ingrown facial hair that can result in scarring if shaved. African American men are more susceptible to the skin condition because their facial hair tends to grow out curly, causing more ingrown hairs. As such, the plaintiffs claimed that the no-beard policy was simply a smokescreen for discriminating "against black males as a class." They sought reinstatement of their old jobs and payment for missing out on the potential overtime they could have worked.

Outcome In 1992, a federal appeals court decided that the plaintiffs' complaints didn't have a whisker of a chance. The court dismissed the case, ruling that the city's regulations mandating shaves were appropriate because facial hair did indeed interfere with the respirator seals on firefighters' masks.

Animal House?

In August 1998, the *New York Jewish Week* newpaper prominently displayed a photo of a Yale University sophomore and Orthodox Jew in a front-page article. But to many a rabbi's chagrin, the devout student wasn't being honored for community service or lauded by an impressed professor. Instead, he had gained media fame because of the federal lawsuit he and three other Orthodox Jewish undergraduates had filed against Yale. Their grievance? The university had forced them to live amid the sexual shenanigans of campus life.

Yale, a secular, private university, has long prided itself on the Oxford-like setting of its twelve colleges, where students and faculty members live, eat, and learn together in a community of scholars. Because Yale believes this shared environment is an integral part of undergraduate education, it requires all freshmen and sophomores to live on campus. According to the plaintiffs, however, this housing policy created a religious and moral dilemma. It forced the teens to reside in an atmosphere that was "contrary to the fundamental principles of Judaism [as] lived according to the Torah and 3,000-year-old rabbinic teachings." More specifically, the on-campus rule required them to live in co-ed dorms, dorms in which men and women can and sometimes do share bathrooms. Such intermingling between the sexes didn't square with their interpretation of Jewish rules concerning modesty and privacy. And though none of the students had spent a single night in a Yale dorm, the group argued that the potential presence of alcohol, condoms, and immodest dress in the dorms was "symbolic of a moral looseness that doesn't fit in a Jewish scheme."

So to avoid engaging in that moral looseness, the students hired a Washington attorney and filed a discrimination lawsuit against Yale, its president, and its deans. They demanded repayment of their dormitory fees and unspecified monetary damages, as well as a court order allowing them to live off campus. "Yale is denying rights that these students should have," said their attorney. "Yale offered no on-campus housing that was acceptable." The university provides some sixty other Orthodox students a kosher meal plan and alternatives for those who can't use electronic keys or turn on lights on Shabbat and holidays. The campus Jewish organization also holds a minyan every morning, a Monday-night Talmud class, and a Tuesday-night individual study program. But apparently that wasn't "acceptable" enough. (Just imagine if the university had to bend over backward to accommodate every student's choice of lifestyle. Then, between all the school-funded keg parties and campus wet-T-shirt contests, the Yale Four would really have something to worry about.)

Outcome In January 2001, after several years of legal wrangling, an appeals court rejected the plaintiffs' claims that Yale discriminated against them by requiring unmarried freshmen and sophomores to live on campus. "Plaintiffs insist that there is no substitute for a Yale education, and in a collegiate sense that is undoubtedly so," the court ruled. But it noted that students knowingly expose themselves to a secular environment by choosing to attend Yale. "If some of them, including the plaintiffs, were dissatisfied with the Yale parietal rules, they could matriculate elsewhere."

Unpatriotic Complaint

A self-avowed atheist in Topeka, Kansas, sued Shawnsee County treasurer Rita Cline in August 2000 because the treasurer had hung a poster proclaiming IN GOD WE TRUST in her office. The American Civil Liberties Union took up the plaintiff's cause in court, arguing that Cline had overstepped the boundaries between church and state and that the poster represented an attempt by the treasurer to promote her religious views in violation of the First Amendment. Cline's lawyer, however, had a simple defense: "In God We Trust" is the national motto. As such, displaying the motto was no different than flying the American flag.

Outcome A federal judge dismissed the complaint in December 2000, calling it "patently frivolous." She ruled that the plaintiff had failed to show she had suffered any direct injuries from the poster and hadn't proved that her ability to exercise free speech was hindered in any way. In fact, the judge decided that the lawsuit was "so lacking in foundation" that she ordered the plaintiff to pay the treasurer's legal fees. "The court has no hesitation in finding that this claim is meritless," the judge wrote in her ruling.

What's a Gal Gotta Do to Get a Raise Around Here?

A woman in Panama City, Florida, sued her former employer in July 1998, claiming that the audio lab where she had worked fired her for not embracing its religious rituals. The perturbed plaintiff began to figure something was awry when the firm forced her to be baptized and to attend office prayer meetings. Then, one morning, she arrived at work only to find her colleagues, presumably overcome by the Holy Spirit, lying prostrate on the floor and speaking in tongues. She claimed the eerie experience caused her, among other things, to "compulsively read the Bible" and refuse to have sex with her husband.

Outcome No word yet. Maybe they will hire her back now.

Bring on the Lions

Religious wars seem to be flaring up everywhere. The latest skirmish took place at Foodmaker Incorporated, the parent company of the fast-food chain Jack in the Box. Fortunately, this holy fracas didn't involve any weapons or bombs, but it did end up with somebody getting fired. Namely, a thirty-six-year-old store manager who then sued Foodmaker, claiming that he was canned due to "dual discrimination."

The fast-food chain claimed that it gave the plaintiff the boot after he lied during a company investigation of missing funds. But the fired filer had a different take: He believed he was being discriminated against because he was a Christian and his ex-boss was a Muslim. Further, the zealous plaintiff claimed that since he was also an alcoholic, his termination constituted "disability discrimination."

The store manager wanted $300,000 prior to trial. The company offered to supersize his next purchase of fries for free. (Actually, they offered him nothing.)

Outcome The jury agreed with the defendant, basically telling the Christian tippler to try practicing some basic virtues.

Bible Thumping

A man in Jackson, Mississippi, sued the Oxford University Press for $45 million in September 1994. He claimed that the Bible, which Oxford publishes, is based on hearsay and oppresses African Americans and homosexuals. His lawsuit also demanded that Oxford omit all references to racism against black people and discrimination against gays "as soon as possible."

Outcome The plaintiff dropped the lawsuit one month later, because of threats and lack of money. He told reporters that "Christians with shotguns" were threatening his life. He went on to add, "I think their defense is as strong as O. J. Simpson's defense. They reach all the way back to England where they wrote the Bible. I don't have the funds to fight."

WHAT'S YOUR HANDICAP?

How exactly did alcoholism emerge as a protected category in the American workplace, akin to race, sex, and religion? The most powerful force pushing in that direction has been the rise of the disability rights movement, which culminated in Congress's passage of the 1990 Americans With Disabilities Act. The language of the law is so broad that it defines *disability* simply as something that "substantially limits" a major life activity. Walking, hearing, and seeing are clearly covered. But so are a plethora of less obvious "disabilities," such as mental and emotional impairment. Now, it seems, almost anyone facing disciplinary action or termination can save his or her hide—and win a little cash—by conjuring up a disability-discrimination suit.

No-Win Situation

Sometimes you're damned if you do, damned if you don't. At least that was Exxon Corporation's experience when it tried to comply with the law. After the Exxon *Valdez* tanker ran aground in March 1989 and dumped eleven million gallons of oil into Alaska's Prince William Sound, the petroleum company restricted any employee with a history of drug or alcohol abuse from fifteen hundred safety-sensitive jobs. (Alcohol use was linked to the *Valdez* oil spill, although the ship's captain, a recovering alcoholic, was later cleared by a jury of charges that he was drunk on the job.) Exxon said the policy was a "business necessity" based on the urgent need to promote safety, further environmental protection, and prevent future liability.

Both the U.S. Department of Justice and the Environmental Protection Agency applauded Exxon for its new policy. But does that mean it's now in the government's good graces? Apparently not, because the Equal Employment Opportunity Commission sued the company in June 1994, claiming that its policy violated the Americans With Disabilities Act by discriminating against substance abusers! One attorney pointed out the contradiction: "The same U.S. government that exacted a huge fine for the 'crime' of placing Captain Hazelwood in charge of the Exxon *Valdez* is now suing Exxon, claiming that the [Disabilities Act] requires the company to permit future Captain Hazelwoods to assume similar positions."

Outcome Both parties petitioned the court to determine whether Exxon could defend its policy as a business necessity. A judge found against Exxon, ruling that the company would have to prove that each individual affected by its policy posed a "direct threat" to safety.

But Exxon appealed, and the lower court's decision was overturned. In 2000, an appellate court ruled that the company need not provide direct-threat evidence for each individual when it has developed a standard applicable to all employees. "The court should take into account the magnitude of possible harm, as well as the possibility of occurrence," it wrote. "A probability that might be tolerable in an ordinary job might be intolerable for a position involving atomic reactors, for example."

Slam Drunk

A high school student was suspended from his varsity basketball team in the spring of 1999 after being caught driving under the influence. It was his second alcohol-related offense. But rather than sit out his time on the bench, the seventeen-year-old athlete sued Warren Township High School in Gurnee, Illinois—under the Disabilities Act. He claimed that his suspension amounted to discrimination because he suffered from alcoholism, a federally protected disability. He sought $100,000 in compensation and reinstatement to the team.

Outcome A federal judge threw out the case in November 1999, ruling that school officials could not have discriminated against the plaintiff because they hadn't known he was an alcoholic at the time they suspended him. And even if the school had known of his alcoholism prior to the suspension, the judge added, federal law permits schools to punish disabled students for using alcohol. Excusing the plaintiff's breaches of the athletic ethic code would "create a double standard: one for alcoholics and one for everyone else," he said in his decision.

Accident-Prone

In 1996, a former truck driver for Ryder Systems in Miami sued the company under the Disabilities Act, claiming that he had been unfairly removed from his position. Apparently, after the plaintiff suffered an epileptic seizure on the job, Ryder decided his health condition presented a safety hazard. The company transferred him to another division, which did not require driving or handling heavy equipment.

Outcome A jury awarded the plaintiff $5.5 million. Ryder has since appealed the verdict, and for good reason. After being transferred, the disgruntled driver took a job at another trucking company, had a seizure behind the wheel, and crashed into a tree!

See No Evil

United Parcel Service was sued in March 1997 by the Equal Employment Opportunity Commission over the delivery company's "discriminatory" policy of refusing to hire truck drivers who are blind in one eye. For its part, UPS claimed it was only following good business practice. The Department of Transportation forbids one-eyed drivers from operating big rigs; UPS applies the same policy to drivers of its delivery trucks. "We have tens of thousands of our ubiquitous brown trucks on the road each day," said a UPS spokesman. "We don't think there's anything more important than safety." (Except perhaps avoiding the lawsuits it would surely face if a half-blind driver ran someone over.)

Outcome A federal district court judge in San Francisco ruled against UPS in December 2000, declaring that one-eyed drivers could be just as safe as drivers with vision in both eyes and, therefore, could not be automatically rejected as job applicants. However, the judge added that UPS was entitled to consider vision limitations as a safety factor and could require one-eyed applicants to take extra driving tests, showing that they could avoid a darting pedestrian or cyclist.

Double Trouble

Two nearsighted sisters from Spokane, Washington, sued United Airlines in 1992, claiming that the airline had violated the Disabilities Act by requiring its pilots to have at least 20/100 vision without glasses or contact lenses. The sisters had applied to fly for United but were rejected when the airline discovered that they had 20/200 vision in their right eyes and 20/400 vision in their left.

In court, the sisters' lawyer argued that contacts, which corrected their vision to 20/20, should make them qualified pilots. "I don't think the ADA means that if you're able to correct your disability, then you're again fair game for discrimination," he said. United, however, argued that the plaintiffs had simply "failed to meet its visual acuity standards" and that correctable nearsightedness was not a legally recognized disability. "If it were," the company said, "then the nearly 100 million Americans who have nearsightedness that is correctable by ordinary glasses or contact lenses would be covered by the ADA."

Outcome The Supreme Court sided with United in 1999, ruling that protections under the Disabilities Act are generally limited to people whose conditions are not readily correctable with common devices like glasses and contacts. In her 7–2 majority opinion, Justice Sandra Day O'Connor noted that the law counts forty-three million Americans as being disabled. "Had Congress intended to include all persons with corrected physical limitations among those covered by the act, it undoubtedly would have cited a much higher number of disabled persons in the findings," she wrote.

Getting His Wires Crossed

In June 2001, a man who made his living installing traffic lights sued the county of Palm Beach, Florida, claiming that his firing violated the Disabilities Act. The fifty-four-year-old man contended that he was color blind. The county said that was the point. He couldn't distinguish between the nineteen different colored wires used in traffic lights and kept mixing them up! The Equal Employment Opportunity Commission, which chose to represent the plaintiff, argued that color blindness was a disability protected under the law and that the county should have, therefore, accommodated the man's little problem.

Outcome No news on this case yet, but we assume the court will give this case the red light.

Hypertension Hype

A truck mechanic in Manhattan, Kansas, was fired by United Parcel Service in 1994 because his high blood pressure exceeded federal standards for driving commercial trucks. The man sued UPS under the Disabilities Act, claiming that his hypertension constituted a federally protected handicap.

In an unmedicated condition, the plaintiff's blood pressure was 250/160, a level so high that it limited him in several major life activities. But as long as he took medication, his only limitation was that he couldn't hold a job requiring repetitive lifting of two hundred pounds. UPS drivers, however, must meet Department of Transportation regulations, which require workers to maintain a blood pressure lower than or equal to 160/90. The plaintiff's doctor testified that, even with medication, his blood pressure would always be higher than 160/90. As a result, UPS discharged him. "The mere fact you can't meet a standard doesn't mean you're disabled," UPS's lawyer argued. "It simply means you're not qualified for a particular job."

Outcome A federal district court in Kansas rejected the plaintiff's discrimination claims in 1996, ruling that workers with remediable conditions, such as high blood pressure, are not disabled. The U.S. Supreme Court upheld the decision in 1999. In her 7–2 majority opinion, Justice Sandra Day O'Connor wrote, "If the impairment is corrected, it does not substantially limit a major life activity."

Going Off Track

Is staying conscious an essential job function for a train dispatcher? Consolidated Rail thought so when it denied a dispatcher's job—which involves directing trains and taking emergency action to prevent crashes—to an employee with a heart condition that caused him to black out.

The employee had worked for Conrail from 1977 until 1994, mostly as a train conductor. In 1994, he underwent heart surgery during which a cardiac defibrillator was implanted in his chest to control an irregular heartbeat. Despite warnings from his physician about not working on or around moving trains, the man returned to work as a conductor, only to pass out three days later. At that point, Conrail told him that, for safety reasons, he could no longer work as a conductor and that he needed to find another job within the company. Unfortunately, the only position available was the dispatcher position. However, because the man's fainting episodes created a "significant risk," Conrail decided that he was not eligible for the position.

The man sued the railway company under the Disabilities Act, but a federal judge threw out the case. So in March 2000, the Equal Employment Opportunity Commission took up his cause in a Philadelphia federal appeals court. The agency argued that the man's ability to lose consciousness presented no "direct threat" to other people and that Conrail could have accommodated him. "While consciousness is obviously necessary to perform" train-dispatcher tasks, "it is not itself a job function," the agency's lawyer said.

Outcome The appellate court ruled against the plaintiff, saying that his heart condition could indeed threaten people's safety. "No reasonable jury could fail to find that . . . employing (the plaintiff) as a train dispatcher would have presented a significant risk to others."

Let Me Out of This Ambulance!

A medical emergency technician in Michigan was fired in 1994 for insulting and ridiculing patients while driving them to the hospital. Mecosta County, which had employed the man, said he had demonstrated "conduct unbecoming of a paramedic and a history of rudeness to patients and colleagues." The man, however, sued Mecosta County under the Disabilities Act, claiming that his obnoxiousness was the result of fluctuating blood pressure caused by his untreated diabetes. He contended that his employer should have accommodated his disability by reassigning him to a less hectic service area.

Outcome A district court threw out the case, but a panel of appellate judges reversed the dismissal in December 1997.

They ruled that, although the plaintiff could have controlled his blood pressure with medication and exercise, his diabetes could still be considered a disability.

Off Balance

In 1994, a high-level computer programmer in Florida admitted that he broke into parked cars on his way to work, stole thousands of dollars from coworkers' desks and purses, and kept a loaded handgun in his briefcase, which he sometimes used to threaten fellow employees. GTE Data Services ultimately fired the executive, reasoning that there was more than adequate cause. But the man filed a lawsuit under the Disabilities Act, claiming that he had a chemical imbalance that caused him to have a short temper and engage in irrational behavior. The gun, he further claimed, was a by-product of this chemical dysfunction.

Outcome A district court judge ruled that a jury should decide whether or not the plaintiff had a mental disability that might require accommodation under the Disabilities Act. But when the case went to a jury trial, the judge there summarily dismissed the case and upheld the firing. "We're talking about a gun, and that made everything else meaningless," said GTE's lawyer. "It would be an undue hardship to have to accommodate that."

Heaping It On

A garbage-truck driver in Denver took off for Mexico on a Sunday in 1997 upon learning that a niece there had died after a long illness. When he returned on Wednesday, he was told that his employer, USA Waste, had fired him for skipping work without notifying a supervisor. The man quickly hired a lawyer, who proceeded to sue the company under—can you guess which statute? Not the Family and Medical Leave Act, but the Americans With Disabilities Act, on the grounds that USA Waste's action was a mere pretext to discriminate against him for having a back injury that prevented him from doing heavy lifting in his sanitation rounds. The company denied the charge and argued that the former employee had displayed a "poor work attitude" aside from the absenteeism incident.

Outcome In February 2000, a Colorado jury sided with the plaintiff and awarded him $250,000. The man's lawyer said, "It is this kind of case the ADA is written for."

Green Thumb

While lawn mowing may not top the list of favorite activities for many people, a DeForest, Wisconsin, woman made a federal case out of it. The woman was ticketed by the town in 1998 because she didn't mow the foot-high grass in front of her home. She challenged the town's weed ordinance in Dane County Circuit Court, claiming she was protecting exotic prairie plants growing in her yard. She lost that battle when the court ruled that her exotic plants were just nuisance weeds.

The woman didn't give up. In July 1999 she sued DeForest officials in federal court, claiming that she couldn't mow her lawn because of chronic back problems, which she said exempted her from the ordinance under the Americans With Disabilities Act. She sought a temporary injunction to prevent the town from carrying out its mandatory mow order, even though the town had offered to cut her grass for free. "Those are thistles and other weeds growing there," said one of the town's trustees, who was named in the suit. The plaintiff "tried and failed in one attempt against the village, and now she's trying something else."

Outcome Apparently, the judge thought so, too. She dismissed the case, ruling that the plaintiff could have easily hired someone to mow her lawn.

No Smarts Required

Just because you're not the sharpest tool in the shed doesn't mean you can't be a brain surgeon or nuclear physicist. Take a lesson from the aspiring attorney in New York who flunked the bar exam five times, then sued the American Bar Association for not accommodating her learning disability. The fifty-year-old woman claimed that she had a reading disorder, although an independent expert found nothing to substantiate her claim. And it's no wonder. The plaintiff already had a Ph.D from the University of New York and taught at a Long Island college.

Outcome In September 1998, a federal appeals court in Manhattan ruled in the plaintiff's favor, granting her double test-taking time and the privilege of taking the test in a private room with an assistant to record her answers. Ironically, the woman later took the bar exam again—with these new privileges—and flunked anyway.

Watch Your Tongue

A supermarket bagger with a neurological disorder was fired in 1996 when his involuntary outbursts of profanity and racial slurs offended women and African American customers. The twenty-two-year-old sued his former employer, Farmer Jack Market, for wrongful termination, claiming that it should have accommodated his coprophilia, a symptom of Tourette's syndrome that causes people to uncontrollably blurt obscenities.

In trial, Farmer Jack's attorney argued that even if the plaintiff's verbal outbursts were involuntary, they clearly violated the company's "critical work rules" barring abusive language or rudeness to customers. "The job at issue here is 'courtesy clerk.' In summary, they are to extend courtesy to customers," he told the judges. "The language is directly related to the plaintiff's ability to do the job."

Outcome A Michigan appeals court agreed in July 2000, ruling that the supermarket chain did have the right to fire the plaintiff. The judges concluded: "We find it ridiculous to expect a business . . . to tolerate this type of language in the presence of its customers."

Sleeping on the Job

A man who worked at a nuclear power plant in Aiken, South Carolina, was fired in November 1996 after sleeping at work several times. He sued his employer for wrongful termination, arguing that he suffered from narcolepsy—a sleep disorder that he alleged was protected under the Disabilities Act. He claimed that the power plant had not accommodated his condition by allowing him to take occasional naps on the job.

Outcome A district court judge tossed out the plaintiff's claim in January 2000, ruling that his condition "did not constitute a disability for the purposes of the Americans With Disabilities Act."

Sex Ed

A college English professor, who was fired in 1989 for kissing and sexually harassing several students, sued the school under the Disabilities Act to get his job back. The man, who taught at a technical college in Auburn, Maine, claimed that he was a sex addict and that his dismissal, therefore, constituted illegal discrimination against a disabled person. He even got two doctors to testify in court that he suffered from a permanent mental disorder known as sex addiction.

Outcome A state supreme court judge threw out the case in May 1994, ruling that allowing the plaintiff to claim protection from firing would be nothing short of excusing sexual misconduct.

Doctor Strangelove

A gynecologist in Paducah, Kentucky, sued his insurance company in October 1999 for refusing to cover his "sex addiction." As it happened, the doctor had to surrender his medical license in 1994 after having "inappropriate contact with the female patients." The licensing board later let him resume practicing general medicine, but only if he worked in the state corrections department and never saw female patients.

Frustrated by his predicament, the gynecologist called his insurer, Provident Life & Accident Insurance, and demanded $8,700 a month in disability payments. He claimed that he suffered from a sex addiction that prevented him from practicing his specialty. Provident refused to make the payments, arguing that the doctor couldn't pursue his specialty not because of a disability but because of a licensing problem with the medical board. Hence the doctor's lawsuit.

Outcome No news on the outcome, but we're betting it wasn't good.

Down in the Mouth

In September 1995, a man who was working for a temporary employment agency was assigned to a telemarketing job at Apland & Associates, a Chicago publishing company. The job involved phoning businesses to see if Apland could produce their publications. During three days of training and evaluation, the new hire made mock sales calls and read scripts. Ironically, one of the Apland publications he promoted in one exercise was a book on the Americans With Disabilities Act. At the end of training, an Apland supervisor rejected him, telling the temping agency that he was not "a good fit" for the job because he "mumbled."

The rebuffed employee immediately sued Apland, claiming that the company had not accommodated his disability—which, in this case, happened to be some missing teeth. He argued that he was forced to shape his mouth in unusual ways when he spoke in order to compensate for not having any front teeth. His lawyer further claimed that Apland officials fired him not because he mumbled but because of the way he looked when he talked. "The ADA is supposed to protect cosmetic disfigurements," she said.

Outcome The plaintiff lost in federal district court, but a federal appeals judge sent the case back to the lower court. "Unlike the plaintiff, the Americans With Disabilities Act has teeth," the judge wrote. After that ruling, Apland settled for an undisclosed amount. "Most [antidiscrimination] laws are noble efforts to right wrongs in the workplace," Apland's lawyer said. The plaintiff's claims, though, "are a classic example of abuse of those laws."

8

FOOD FIGHTS: INMATE LAWSUITS IV

The hand that feeds should be heavily gloved.
—Paul Eldridge

While prisoners' grievances run the gamut, one particular bone of contention seems to be food. Finicky inmates' mealtime antics are enough to put old Morris the Cat to shame. Feast your eyes on these examples.

I Scream, You Scream, We All Scream For . . .

Ice cream was the basis of a lawsuit filed by one convicted criminal in Syracuse, New York. The icy inmate demanded that the state pay him $1 million for civil rights violations because his rocky road melted when a guard wouldn't put it in the freezer. The judge coolly dismissed the case, ruling that the "right to eat ice cream was clearly not within the contemplation" of our nation's forefathers.

Guilty Gourmet

An Oklahoma inmate, who was at one time a chef, sued because he felt the prison food was bad . . . and he wanted bigger portions.

Loafers

Three Washington inmates claimed the Clark County Jail had subjected them to cruel and unusual punishment by serving them Nutra-loaf, a mixture of ground vegetables, beef, chicken, eggs, apples, potatoes, and other dietary staples.

Let Them Eat Cake

A New York prisoner sued after falling victim to a vindictive act of dessert vandalism. According to the inmate's filing, the slice of cake on his dinner tray had been "hacked up."

Let Them Eat More Cake

A Florida inmate convicted of murdering his business partner and sealing the body in a cement tomb sued prison officials because the piece of cake he got for dessert "was not big enough."

Cake and Eat It Too

A New York inmate filed a lawsuit after being locked in his cell for stealing an extra piece of cake from the mess hall. A judge awarded the dessert snatcher $200 in damages.

Too Spicy

Some out-of-state convicts banded together to claim their rights were violated because they were served too much Mexican food while incarcerated in a Texas prison.

Not Spicy Enough

A group of Minnesota inmates sued for damages because they weren't provided with enough salsa.

Holy Frijoles!

Several Minnesota inmates filed lawsuits claiming cruel and unusual punishment because the prison menu featured an "improper variety" of beans and excess bologna.

Everything in Its Place

An Indiana inmate sued because the meat and vegetables on his dinner plate were "somewhat mixed together" one night. Imagine if his cake had been hacked up!

You Must Be Yolking

A New York felon filed a federal lawsuit because his scrambled eggs were cooked too hard.

Stacked Against Him

A Florida inmate serving a life sentence for attempted murder and aggravated assault sued in an effort to force prison officials to serve him fruit juice with his meals and three pancakes instead of two for breakfast.

Nutty Lawsuit

A convicted robber in Nevada sued for civil and property rights violations in U.S. district court because he was gypped out of a jar of peanut butter. He claimed that while imprisoned in Carson City, he ordered a jar of chunky peanut butter from the prison store but was delivered a jar of the creamy kind instead. When he refused the creamy, he was told the store was temporarily out of chunky but would receive more soon. Unfortunately, while waiting for the shipment, the inmate was transferred to a new state prison in Ely, and his jar of crunchy peanut butter was never forwarded.

The judge didn't look too kindly on the nutty suit. After pointing out that the case had cost several hundred dollars in court time and attorney fees, he ruled, "Plaintiff is out one jar of crunchy peanut butter worth $2.50 and should seek relief through the prison grievance system of the Nevada small-claims court."

Sounds Contagious

A Pennsylvania prisoner filed a lawsuit alleging he had contracted "cancer incubus" from a cheeseburger, and that a prison nurse served him a cup of water laced with "hepatitis incubus."

Citrus Suit

A convicted drug dealer in New York sued for $2.5 million, claiming his throat hurt after eating a prison-issued orange.

Kool It

A suit filed by Missouri inmates claimed that a limit on Kool-Aid refills constituted cruel and unusual punishment.

Get a Grip

A frequent filer in Florida sued because cooked and raw cabbage were served at the same meal. He also objected to the size of his spoon and complained that prison officials had served French toast when the menu had promised pancakes.

Midnight Munchies

Three inmates in Idaho filed a $10.7-million lawsuit claiming cruel and unusual punishment because guards failed to feed them late-night snacks.

Fine Diner

An inmate who suffered from ulcers sued the Shawangunk Correctional Facility in New York because he was not served lamb, oysters, and veal for his meals. These foods were approved but not prescribed by his doctor.

Festive Feaster

A convicted rapist, robber, and kidnapper filed a $129-million lawsuit while doing time in Missouri. He claimed prisoners were entitled to a salad bar and brunches on weekends and holidays. The case was dismissed.

Gobble Gobble

A Florida prisoner filed a federal lawsuit because his turkey leg contained gristle. The case was dismissed.

Nothing But the Best

Another Florida inmate, who has filed more than four hundred prison lawsuits, sued for the right to have his meals served on fine china instead of paper plates.

Don't Strain Yourself

A Nebraska inmate sued because he was ordered to pick up a hamburger bun he had dropped. The messy prisoner claimed the order was a "work assignment" and that he was prevented from working due to a medical condition.

9

FUNNY BUSINESS: CONTRACT, TRADEMARK, AND OTHER CORPORATE LAWSUITS

A corporation is just like any natural person, except that it has no pants to kick or soul to damn, and by God, it ought to have both.

—Anonymous

To be sure, megacorporations make quite a target for the sue-happy masses. Our nation's largest companies face mountains of lawsuits alleging everything from breach of contract to unfair payment practices. But rest assured, corporations aren't the innocent patsies that they may have you believe. Most keep hordes of attorneys on their payrolls, lawyers who spend as much time filing lawsuits as defending their clients against them. Witness just a few statistics released by the Consumer Attorneys Association of Los Angeles:

- Corporations file ten times as many lawsuits as injured consumers.
- Corporations sue each other at the rate of one lawsuit every 12.5 minutes of the business day.

- One-third of all cases that clog federal courts for more than three years are business disputes.

DON'T TREAD ON ME

Corporations can be especially touchy when it comes to copyrights and trademarks. Just ask Harley Davidson, which patented the sound of its V-twin motorcycle engine, then sued Honda for duplicating the distinctive rumble. And there are plenty of other raw-nerve companies that are taking their nit-picking to the courts. Take a peek at these.

Nay to Pony Boy

A couple in Pennsylvania decided to get their son something special for his twelfth birthday—his own Internet Web site. The parents had no problem picking a domain name; their son's nickname was Pokey, so they chose "www.Pokey.org." The happy sixth-grader immediately began constructing the site, which featured photos of his Australian shepherd puppy.

Needless to say, the boy's Web site was not overrun with visitors. But then, in December 1997, something happened that made Pokey.org very famous: Pokey received a certified letter from a Philadelphia trademark attorney. "We represent Prema Toy Co., Inc., which is the owner of the famous trademark 'POKEY,' " the letter began. It said U.S. trademark law gave Prema—the Marin County, California, toy maker that owns the rights to the cartoon characters Gumby and Pokey— sole authority to use the word *Pokey*. The boy was ordered to transfer his domain name, Pokey.org, to the toy company immediately or face a trademark-infringement lawsuit.

The boy was upset and decided to write about his problem

on his Web site. Within days, his story was all over the Internet. "It was amazing how overnight it spread," Pokey told reporters. "People from China and Finland and other places were e-mailing me in different languages." Almost all the messages were the same: Don't give up.

Outcome It looked like a legal battle was about to rage. But in April 1998, while Prema was readying its lawsuit, the boy received a letter from Art Clokey, the man who had originally created the Gumby and Pokey characters. Clokey said he felt bad that Pokey had been "caught in the workings of an adult world. In the spirit of Gumby, I want [the boy] to have the domain name Pokey.org. I am sorry for the whole misunderstanding. I am giving instructions that Pokey.org be returned immediately." With that, Prema had no choice but to scrap its lawsuit.

Kimba and the Muppets

Hormel Foods, the maker of the luncheon meat Spam, sued Jim Henson Productions to stop the creator of the Muppets from calling an animated character in a new movie "Spa'am." Hormel claimed that the Spa'am character was an "unclean, grotesque boar," and "an unsavory-appearing feral pig" that called into question the purity and quality of its meats.

Outcome In 1995, after a three-day trial before U.S. District Judge Kimba Woods (the famed former candidate for U.S. attorney general), the Muppets emerged victorious. Judge Woods ruled that Spa'am was basically an honest, decent boar who makes friends with Miss Piggy and all the good Muppets. "Spam is a luncheon meat. Spa'am is the character of a wild boar in a Muppet motion picture. One might think that more need not be said."

Don't Mess with Purple People

Barney, the much-loved purple dinosaur, star of his own children's TV show, videotapes, and live performances, is not one to be messed with. Just ask the Famous Chicken of San Diego, California.

The Famous Chicken was a mascot for more than 150 professional sporting events throughout the United States each year. He made a habit of physically abusing Barney as part of his entertainment at baseball parks, hockey rinks, and basketball courts.

But in a counterpunch, Barney fired off a lawsuit against the aggressive bird. That's right. Barney claimed that the big fowl "would punch, flip, stand on, and otherwise assault" him, and it wasn't going to happen anymore. Not as long as Barney's lawyers could do something about it.

Actually, Lyons Partnership, the Dallas company that owns the rights to Barney, couldn't care less about the dinosaur's pain and suffering; it sued for copyright and trademark infringement. Apparently, the Famous Chicken had never obtained permission to use a facsimile of Barney to kick around. So Lyons Partnership demanded that he pay the company several hundred thousand dollars for the bad publicity. Its lawsuit alleged that it didn't do children any good to see their much-adored purple dinosaur get body-slammed or have the tar beaten out of him.

The Famous Chicken, on the other hand, felt his routine "was a harmless joke which makes the fans laugh."

Outcome Apparently the federal judge who heard the case in July 1998 agreed with the Famous Chicken. Not only did he dismiss the case, but he also ordered Lyons Partnership to pay more than $180,000 to the Famous Chicken for costs incurred in defending himself. In his ruling, the judge said nobody was likely to confuse the counterfeit Barney with the "kind, gentle, and loving version." Need any more be said?

Shacked Up

Radio Shack didn't want good-natured gadget geeks confusing its stores with a den of debauchery. That's why the retail electronics chain filed a lawsuit against Bianca's Smut Shack, a small Internet Web site, for giving its stores a bad name.

Tandy Corporation, which owns Radio Shack, claimed that the kinky on-line chat room tarnished the "goodwill" associated with its trademarked name. The Fort Worth, Texas, conglomerate holds the rights not only to the term *Radio Shack* but also to *The Shack* and *Shack*. It began sending Bianca's cease-and-desist letters in 1995 stating, "These marks represent valuable assets and any unauthorized use dilutes their value to the corporation." It also blocked Bianca's application for a trademark of its own.

The name *Bianca's Smut Shack* was dreamed up in 1994 by three friends who wanted to attract a lot of traffic to their eclectic site—an on-line community where people talk mostly about sex, but also exchange HTML tips and post unique recipes for such things as chocolate-chip hamburgers. *Bianca* was the name of a Bohemian friend who used to stay with the men in Chicago. *Smut Shack* was their homage to her free spirit.

It's hard to imagine even the most naive on-line shopper logging on to www.bianca.com in the hope of finding a hi-fi or answering machine. As one of the sexy Web site's founders put it: "We don't sell electronic equipment, we sell a good time." But Tandy planned to take advantage of a then-new federal law that broadened trademark protection. To prevent a competitor from using a trademarked word, a company used to have to prove consumers were confusing the two brands. Now the plaintiff need simply show that unauthorized use of the word "dilutes" the brand. The new law allows Ringling Brothers, which bills itself as the "Greatest Show on Earth," to prevent, say, a ski resort from having the "Greatest Snow on Earth."

Bianca's Smut Shack faced an uphill battle. After all, this wasn't the first time Tandy had thrown its weight around on the Internet. The Software Shak, a Dallas firm that sells software on-line, had to drop the *c* in its name after threats from the electronics bigwig. So what did the tiny Internet company do? It rallied its fifty thousand Web visitors with a missive reading, "If you'd like to drop Tandy a note telling them you think Radio Shack should sponsor, rather than suppress [sic] the Smut Shack, that'd be keen."

Outcome Whatever the Smut Shack supporters wrote to Tandy must have worked. In June 1997, the companies reached an out-of-court settlement allowing Bianca's to stay in business. After all the hoopla, some might wonder why Tandy bothered going after the Smut Shack in the first place. Chances are Bianca would bring in a lot more customers than a sale on batteries.

Smutty Barbie

Toy giant Mattel didn't enjoy the idea of its famed Barbie doll being associated with a Web sex site either. It filed a lawsuit against the porn site BarbiesPlaypen.com in 1999 under a new U.S. anti-cyber-squatting law that prevents Web sites from using names that are "confusingly similar" to well-known trademark names. Mattel argued that the Web site, which featured a live chat "with our sexy girls" and promised "the hottest, filthiest, nastiest smut" on the Net, could confuse consumers into thinking the toy company was somehow condoning or sponsoring the site.

Outcome In July 2000, a federal court judge found in favor of Mattel, agreeing with the company's contention that the porn site would "adversely color the public's impressions." He ruled that Internet Dimensions of Florida was clearly attempting to use the fame of Mattel's doll to promote its Web site's business in pornographic photos. "The Barbie dolls, with their long blonde hair and anatomically improbable dimensions are ostensibly intended to portray wholesomeness to young girls," the judge wrote in his decision. "The 'models' on the BarbiesPlaypen.com site—although many have long blonde hair and anatomically improbable dimensions—can in no way be described as engaging in 'wholesome' activities." The defendant was ordered to pay attorney fees and unspecified damages.

Fondue à la Barbie

A Utah artist and real estate appraiser who also managed to raise Barbie's ire ended up with a federal lawsuit being delivered to his doorstep by county sheriffs—compliments of Mattel. The lawsuit claimed that the artist was guilty of trademark and copyright infringement. "Little did I know that Mattel, chief purveyor of images that degrade and silence young women, would turn the full force of its multibillion-dollar power on me," quipped the defendant.

Apparently, Mattel wasn't pleased with the man's artistic renderings of its wholesome doll. It saw his creations—which included a naked Barbie wrapped in a tortilla, smothered in enchilada sauce, and about to be cooked in the oven—as "using our trademarked work for commercial benefit." His other artistic interpretations—such as *Malted Barbie,* who was about to be pulverized by a mixer, and *Fondue à la Barbie,* which featured a fondue pot stuffed with smiling Barbie heads skewered on sticks—were viewed no more favorably by the toy maker.

The artist, backed by the American Civil Liberties Union, argued that Mattel had no right to use trademark law to trample his free expression. After all, he was simply conveying his thoughts on "mindless consumerism" via his artistic creations. "I considered the many products in our world that would best represent the brainwashed consumer," he stated under oath, "and I immediately thought of the Barbie doll."

Outcome In 2000, a federal judge turned down Mattel's request for a preliminary injunction, saying it did not appear that the lawsuit would succeed. Mattel has appealed the ruling.

Those Blasted Colonies

The Times, a London-based newspaper with a daily worldwide circulation of 780,000, threatened in January 1998 to file a trademark-infringement suit against a 5,000-circulation weekly paper in Smithfield, Massachusetts, because it also happened to be named *The Times.* After using the name for thirteen years, the tiny weekly publication received a letter from a Connecticut law firm representing the British newspaper. The formal notice said that continued use of *The Times* name would "divert trade from our client, and will tend to confuse and deceive purchasers."

Outcome Rather than wage a costly court battle, the publisher of the Massachusetts paper immediately changed its name to the *Smithfield Times.*

A Knight Hawked a Watch, You Say?

Knightwatch versus Night Hawk. Or how about Knight Hawk, or Night Watch? It can get pretty confusing, especially when you're requesting phone numbers from directory assistance. That's why Knightwatch Security Systems, a security service in St. Louis, Missouri, sued its crosstown rival Night Hawk Security Systems when the 1997 yellow pages came out.

In the 1996 phone number guide, each company had one listing. But in the following year's edition, Night Hawk added listings for Knight Hawk and Night Watch. The phone number for each listing was Night Hawk's. Knightwatch was infuriated, claiming that the listings were deceptive and designed purely to lure away its customers. But Night Hawk disagreed. The real problem, it squawked, was the name Knightwatch had chosen for itself. Night Hawk had already been in business for twenty years when Knightwatch opened its doors.

Outcome It's tough to remedy a problem with yellow pages listings. You can't recall the guides once they're distributed, and the book is used for an entire year. The courts, however, came up with a solution. The judge required Night Hawk to order an "intercept referral greeting" from the phone company. For one year, an automated recording would tell callers to press 2 to reach Night Hawk or 3 to reach Knightwatch.

The companies also reached an out-of-court settlement. Night Hawk agreed not to use any name that included *watch,* but could use *Knighthawk* or any other version of *hawk.* For its part, Knightwatch agreed to not use a name that included *hawk,* but could use *Night Watch* or other combinations of *watch.* Not a bad solution, but we may have a better one. Why don't the two companies simply merge? Then they could call themselves The Knight Watched a Hawk Last Night, or any variation thereof.

AROUND AND AROUND WE GO

Another extremely touchy subject for corporations is patent infringement. Just witness the seemingly endless barrage of lawsuits being launched over products that appear too similar to someone else's.

That's the Way the Cookie Crumbles

In September 1989, PepsiCo, RJR Nabisco, and United Biscuits of Britain agreed to pay rival Procter & Gamble a tasty $125 million to settle a lawsuit filed against them in 1984. "This is the largest payment ever reported as a settlement in a patent litigation," crowed P&G's elated attorney.

The lawsuit claimed that the three defendants had violated P&G's patent on "crisp and chewy cookies." P&G had introduced its Duncan Hines ready-to-eat cookies in 1983 only to see the three defendants follow with the same type of cookies in 1984. PepsiCo sold them under the Frito-Lay name; United Biscuits sold them under the Keebler name; and RJR sold the crisp and chewy cookies under the Nabisco name.

Apparently, after years of litigation, the three defendants agreed to call it quits before incurring any more costs trying the case. "Even though the case was on cookies, it was a very complex case that involved 200 expert witnesses and some 100,000 pages of pretrial testimony over about 872 days," said P&G's lawyer. By the time the case was eventually set for trial in October 1989, it had already evolved into somewhat of a Cookie Monster. The ten thousand exhibits marked for trial took up so much room that the removal of half the spectator seats was required. The remaining half of spectator seats was set aside for the thirty-six trial attorneys representing the four corporations.

Round Two

Perhaps trying to recoup some of its earlier losses, PepsiCo's Frito-Lay snacks division sued Procter & Gamble in November 1995 for claiming that its Pringle's Right Crisp potato chips were "more nutritious" than Frito-Lay's chips. A claim that P&G insisted was accurate until "Frito-Lay reformulated their product and reduced the sodium level."

Outcome P&G agreed to settle the case by changing its Right Crisp claims. "Customarily manufacturers inform one another when product changes are made that affect commercial claims," said a P&G spokesman in a news release. "The ads are changed and that's the end of it." In other words, sneaky PepsiCo had pulled a fast one by making its chips more nutritious while the Pringles clan was busy tooting its own horn.

We'll Show Them

Procter & Gamble went back on the offensive in October 2000, this time suing PepsiCo's Frito-Lay division for infringing on its patent on "low-fat fried snacks." According to the lawsuit, Frito-Lay "did not have a salted snack chip product . . . that competed directly with P&G's enormously popular Pringles." But eventually Frito-Lay decided to get a foot in the multimillion-dollar tubular canister chips market by launching its own stacked chips called Stax. In the process, the company allegedly trampled on P&G's Pringles processing patent.

Outcome No news on the outcome of this latest food fight. Chances are, though, that the two corporate titans have been busy removing spectator seats in the courtroom to accommodate their chip exhibits and attorneys.

Throwing in the Towel

Procter & Gamble, on the defensive this time, was sued by Scott Paper's Canadian division in 1995. Scott Paper claimed that P&G had misled consumers about the absorptive power of its Bounty paper towels by calling them the "quicker-picker-upper" in commercials.

According to Scott Paper, the catchphrase implied that Bounty paper towels were superior to other towels in their absorbing abilities. But in actuality, Bounty towels were simply eleven inches long compared with the industry average of nine inches. Therefore they were not better, just bigger.

Outcome No news on the outcome, but we suspect P&G's marketing execs were working overtime to come up with a replacement phrase. "Ours is bigger"? "The quickie-pickie-upper," perhaps?

TOO CLOSE FOR COMFORT

Individuals can be just as litigious as corporations when it comes to protecting their names or ideas. The following cases offer just a meager sampling of the great lengths people will go to in order to secure their "intellectual property" rights.

Mistaken Identity

A man in Long Island, New York, sued Jerry Seinfeld and his TV producers for $100 million for allegedly using his "name, likeness and persona" to create the balding, bespectacled character on the hit comedy *Seinfeld*. According to Michael Costanza's lawsuit, his privacy rights had been violated by the character George Costanza, whom he alleged was essentially a spin-off of himself. The plaintiff claimed that he and Seinfeld had been friends at Queens College and that he and the character, played by Jason Alexander, share physical and personality traits and even held some of the same jobs. But the publicists of *Seinfeld* said that the lovable, neurotic George Costanza was actually based on the show's chief producer, Larry David.

Outcome In June 2000, a trial judge ruled, "While a program about nothing can be successful, a lawsuit must have more substance." He dismissed the case and ordered the plaintiff to pay $2,500 for filing a "frivolous" lawsuit.

True to character, the real Costanza filed an appeal. A Manhattan appeals court upheld the dismissal but let the plaintiff get off without paying the $2,500 sanction.

Birdbrains

What came first, Don Henley or the egg? Members of the Eagles rock band claim it was the former—so much so that they sued the National Foundation to Protect America's Eagles in 1998. The band alleged the conservation group was unlawfully using its name to help sell its own music and videos. The trademark-infringement lawsuit, filed in federal court in Knoxville, Tennessee, also objected to the foundation's phone number, (800) 2-EAGLES, and Web site address, www.eagles.org. (Ironically, Henley, a founding member of the rock group, has donated money to the foundation.)

Outcome In June 2001, one day before the trial, the Eagles' attorney dropped the lawsuit, stating, "Our witnesses are not available." Don Henley and the band were on tour in Europe.

In a parting shot, the lawyer for the newly renamed American Eagle Foundation offered, "Don Henley and the band . . . are champions of the little guy only when it is convenient to them."

Butting Heads

A Dallas street artist peddled a pretty exclusive style of art, or so he thought. Working under the trade name Butt Sketch, he earned his living sketching people's buttocks. But in 1992, another street artist took to drawing tushes, too. He aptly named his business Fanny Sketch.

Our butt sketcher, however, wasn't about to take this indignity sitting down; he filed a federal lawsuit accusing the posterior impostor of cutting into his bottom line.

Outcome In the end, the fanny sketcher decided to turn the other cheek and promised to stop doing patuty portraits that might cause people to confuse his work with that of the original butthead.

It's Mine. No Mine. No . . .

Talk about semantics. In January 1997, a man in Cincinnati, Ohio, filed a lawsuit against former House speaker Newt Gingrich and the entire Republican National Committee, claiming that the "Contract With America" infringed on a phrase he had coined years before. The possessive plaintiff claimed that although the harm done to him could "not be fully calculated or adequately compensated in money damages," he would be willing to settle for a mere $50,000.

As it happened, the fifty-five-year-old wordsmith ran in the 1994 elections as an independent write-in candidate in Ohio's Eighth District. In August that year, he published an advertisement titled "Covenant with the Citizens," aimed primarily at banning abortion. The phrase never appeared in the actual ad, but the politician had claimed rights to the phrase since July 1994. Gingrich and the other Republicans, he alleged, infringed on his rights of ownership when they promulgated a "Contract With America" in September 1994, making it the focus of congressional races nationwide. He said he complained repeatedly to them, but got no response. "They stonewalled me from the get-go," he told reporters. "The arrogance of power."

The defendants argued that the phrase didn't simply happen overnight. It was the result of a process that lasted more than a year, with "input from Republicans all across the country." The plaintiff, however, insisted that his suit wasn't frivolous. Still, he had to file it himself because no lawyer would represent him.

Outcome No news on the outcome, but we suspect that the plaintiff wasn't happy with it.

What's in a Name?

Don't call him mister. A Republican nominee for California attorney general sued the secretary of state in an effort to be listed on the November 1998 ballot as "chief deputy attorney general." He contested the policy that limits ballot designations to three words. The Third District Court of Appeals devised a quick solution to the man's identity crisis: It settled the issue by turning *attorney general* into one word by placing a hyphen between the two.

Outcome Despite his snazzy designation, the plaintiff lost the race by a 52–42 margin. His title has since been simplified to ex–chief deputy attorney-general.

Don't Confuse Him with Uncle Fester

It's been said that good actors have the ability to "become" their characters. But how many retain that role after they retire? At least one: Former "Munsters" television star Al Lewis sued the New York State Board of Elections in an effort to be listed as "Grandpa" on the nominee ballot for state governor. Renowned for his role as the smart-alecky grand-vampire of the ghoulish Munster family, the actor claimed that by not listing him on the ballot as "Grandpa Al Lewis," voters would be confused and fail to cast an informed vote. The outspoken Lewis—known for referring to New York governor George Pataki as "Potato Head Pataki," New York mayor Rudolph Giuliani as "Benito," and former New York lieutenant governor Betsy McCaughey Ross as a "moron"—was on the 1998 ballot as a Green Party candidate.

Outcome A state supreme court justice dismissed the case in October 1998. He ruled that granting Lewis's request would lead to unrelenting attempts by candidates to highlight their given name by a nickname, street name, stage name, title, degree, or any other name created by the fertile imagination. The judge added that it was Lewis's "duty to educate the voters as to who Al Lewis is."

CRAZY BUSINESS DEALINGS

Let's face it. There's a war being waged in the corporate world. And in the trenches march legions of lawyers, both on the offense and defense, churning up the soil with their Gucci shoes and cartloads of transcripts, briefs, and legal lunacies. They're helping employees sue employers, consumers sue companies, and corporations sue other corporations. Basically, everybody and anybody can sue whomever they please. Some even end up suing themselves.

Be Your Own Boss

Here's a guy whom, for our purposes, we'll call Joe Slick. This hardworking Chino, California, man did the work of two men—literally. He owned a chemical manufacturing firm, and was also on the payroll as a worker. In other words, Slick was both the employer and an employee. This working relationship was just fine, until one day when Slick, the employee, got pulled into a mixing machine and was severely injured. Slick, the employee, hired a lawyer and sued Slick, the employer, for negligence. Slick, the employer, hired his own attorney to defend the company. Strangely, both Slicks decided to settle their dispute out of court. They decided that Slick, the employer, would reimburse Slick, the employee, $122,500 for his injuries.

Needless to say, when the Internal Revenue Service got wind of the deal, it wasn't pleased. The IRS demanded that Slick, the employee, pay $64,185 of the settlement in income tax. It also insisted that Slick, the employer, forfeit $58,500 for trying to pass off the payment to Slick, the employee, as a business expense. Slick was outraged—and so was Slick. Both Slicks and their respective lawyers appealed the IRS's decision to the U.S. Tax Court.

Outcome In 1990, the judge ruled that Slick, the employer, could deduct the $58,500 as a business expense and that Slick, the employee, could keep the settlement tax-free. Now that's slick!

Business Assets

A buxom exotic dancer also stuck it out against the Internal Revenue Service when she sued for the right to claim her breasts as a tax deduction. The Indiana native, who went by the stage name Chesty Love, had undergone "multiple medical procedures" to enlarge her bosoms to an eye-popping 56 FF. She considered her breasts—which weighed ten pounds each—business "assets": by doubling her bra size, she also nearly doubled her weekly income, from $416 to $750. And since the surgery was done to "augment" her earnings, the full-figured entrepreneur naturally deducted the costs from her gross income. The IRS, though, rejected the $2,088 write-off, stating that enhancements to appearance are personal and, therefore, could not be considered work-related expenses.

Outcome A special trial judge ultimately reversed the IRS's decision in March 1993, after Chesty filed suit. The judge determined that the bosoms in question were "detrimental to [the plaintiff's] health and contorted her body into a grotesque appearance, all for the purpose of money." The judge added, "Even though the implants were surgically made a part of her body, we are convinced that they are not inherently personal in nature." In other words, the IRS had to back off Chesty's breasts.

Herpes on the High Seas

A southern California man used his forty-two-foot yacht for romancing women on the high seas. Unfortunately, he gave his former girlfriend herpes during a Thanksgiving Day trip to Catalina Island, which he described as a "sex-filled sailing adventure." The adventure was only starting, he soon found out, because the woman then sued him for "knowingly and negligently" sharing his genital ailment with her while aboard his personal love boat.

The good captain settled the suit out of court for $140,000 but didn't want to be stuck with the loss. So he filed a claim with the Firemen's Fund, which insured his boat, insisting that it should have defended him under the conditions of his policy.

The insurer, however, decided that it had nothing to do with the man's nautical entanglement and politely turned him down. The skipper then sued the insurer, claiming that the company was obligated to defend him. His reason: Seagoing sex "was part of the boat's use contemplated in the insurance policy." And since the sex had taken place in the yacht's stateroom, the insurer was obligated to cover the herpes mishap under the "bodily injury" clause of its policy.

Outcome This presumptuous argument was ultimately heard in Los Angeles County Superior Court, where the judge dismissed the suit. The plaintiff appealed. In 1998, an appeals court upheld the dismissal, calling the yachtsman's theories "outlandish" and "absurd." In his published opinion, the presiding judge wrote, "This is not the type of boat 'use' contemplated by [the plaintiff's] yacht policy. The presence of a boat in this instance is incidental, not essential."

BLAME IT ON THE BIG BOYS

Bold, Brash, and Miffed

Two U.S. West phone company employees, whom we'll call Bold and Brash, had a good thing going. Due to an administrative error, they began receiving a $70-per-day allowance for working outside their home territory. But the fact was that the duo were working where they had always worked—near their homes. This easy money kept rolling in for more than two years until the phone company eventually discovered its mistake and immediately cut off the unwarranted payments.

But Bold and Brash would have none of that. After all, they were accustomed to receiving the undeserved payments and now had to drastically alter their budgets. So, in 1996, they sued both the phone company, challenging the cutoff, and their union for not helping them with their inane claim.

Outcome A federal court judge—we'll call him Miffed—threw the case out.

Actress in Distress, Jury to the Rescue

Has it occurred to anybody that actors may be getting paid a bit too much these days? After all, a sitcom star can turn down $100 million for a year of work, while other big names collect tens of millions for a single movie. Even a guy who's more famous for his facial contortions than acting abilities gets $20 million per flick.

It shouldn't be a surprise, then, that a celebrity-struck jury would be willing to dole out big bucks to an actress who didn't even act. That's exactly what happened with this thirty-five-year-old actress who signed a contract to portray a new character on the once-popular TV show *Melrose Place*. The lucky starlet's deal with Spelling Entertainment Group in February 1996 guaranteed her eight episodes for the 1996–1997 season. The contract also included a series of options that, if the Spelling company decided to exercise them, would extend the contract up to four years.

Filming for the new hire was to start in early July 1996. Unfortunately, she never made it that far, because forty-two days after signing the contract her manager notified the executive producer that his client was almost six weeks pregnant. It's not clear what the actress and her manager expected Spelling to do after that announcement—perhaps rewrite every episode to fit her new status or delay shooting the series for six or seven months. But two weeks later, they received a letter from Spelling terminating the contract. In response, the actress sued the company, claiming that she would lose income over the four-year period of the contract. (She must have forgotten that the four years were an option.)

With her shrewd attorneys leading the charge, the spurned actress then claimed that she was terminated because of her pregnancy, a violation of the Fair Employment and Housing Act. She also alleged that the Spelling company had breached the implied covenant of good faith and fair dealing.

The defendants argued that they had to fire the actress because of the inevitable change in her appearance resulting from the pregnancy. The contract specifically provided for termination in the event of "any material change in Artist's appearance which extends beyond five consecutive days." Additionally, to smooth things out, the production company offered the pregnant starlet a role on *Melrose Place* beginning the following season, at a slightly higher rate of pay. The plaintiff, however, preferred to take the case to trial, which ultimately lasted nineteen days.

Outcome The jury deliberated for four more days, clearly leaving their common sense in front of their TV sets, and came up with a fat figure for their expectant actress. They awarded her $4.9 million.

A Real Couple

Every marriage has its ups and downs, its squabbles, its embarrassing incidents. Some couples give up when the going gets tough, but others seem to tough it out under the most trying of circumstances, as did the following pair.

In 1992, the love-struck couple in Pennsylvania didn't resort to marriage counselors when they had a falling out; they filed twin lawsuits against those they felt contributed to their problems. The husband's lawsuit claimed that an American Legion hall had served him so much liquor that it made him break into his estranged wife's workplace, Binney & Smith, shoot at her coworker and lover, then ram a police car during his foiled getaway attempt.

The wife's lawsuit, directed at Binney & Smith, claimed that her employer should have prevented her coworker from befriending her, seducing her, and convincing her to begin a consensual sexual relationship.

It all makes sense to us. As the employer, it was Binney & Smith's duty to tell its employees to knock off being friends because it could very easily lead to an affair. Imagine the welcome reception the employer would have received to that piece of advice. The Legion hall, on the other hand, apparently should have told the husband that it wouldn't serve him any more drinks because there was a good chance he would zoom to his estranged wife's workplace and use her coworker for target practice. Voilà. No disruptions, no gunplay, no ramming police cars, and no lawsuits.

Outcome Both lawsuits were eventually dropped.

You Play, You Pay. Not!

The World Wide Web has brought a lot of conveniences and, yes, some vices into homes all over the planet. One Marin County, California, Web surfer happened to discover gambling on the Internet. It seems she really enjoyed herself, too, but got in a little over her head, racking up more than $70,000 in debt.

The Internet gambler owed a dozen banks and credit-card companies for her losses in craps, blackjack, and other games. Because she decided not to pay, one of the banks, Providian National Bank, sued her for nonpayment. So in July 1998, the gambler filed her own lawsuit against Providian, Visa International, MasterCard International, and fifty on-line gambling services. Her contention: Because gambling is illegal in California and the United States, she didn't owe anyone the money she had borrowed and lost.

Outcome If a good defense is a strong offense, then this woman must have written the playbook. She managed to reach an out-of-court settlement with the credit-card companies in which her debt was wiped out—and they paid her $225,000 legal bill as well. Since then, Providian Bank has stopped processing Internet gambling transactions.

Losing Streak

A twenty-seven-year-old student at Indiana University School of Medicine sued Ameritrade, an on-line brokerage service, in 1999 after losing $40,000 in self-service Internet trading. Yes, the whiz kid had figured he'd strike it rich by using his medical school nest egg to buy stocks on margin. *(On margin* essentially means that the brokerage firm loaned him money to buy shares in a number of technology companies.) Unfortunately, he did so just before the stock market plunge of August 1998.

His lawsuit demanded that Ameritrade pay him $225,000 in damages. Why? Although the intrepid investor admitted to never having read Ameritrade's special margin-trading instructions prior to his on-line antics, he argued, "[I] never dreamt I had any possibility of losing all my money."

Outcome Amazingly, the regulatory arm of the National Association of Securities Dealers sided with the plaintiff in January 2000. It awarded the medical student $22,670 to compensate for his loss and $17,844 for attorney fees.

Nice Rebate

In 1995, a woman in Alabama paid $1,100 to buy a home satellite system from a Gulf Coast Electronics independent retailer. With the 21 percent finance charge she agreed to pay, her purchase would eventually cost a total of $1,800. But it seems the woman was pleased with her investment, because she subsequently convinced her parents to buy the same system from the same company for the same price. Unfortunately, the family was later shocked to discover that the stores had been selling similar dish systems for around $200. So they sued the stores and the company that financed their purchases, Whirlpool Financial National Bank, a unit of Whirlpool Corporation. They claimed that they had been overcharged and misled about their financing terms.

At trial in May 2000, the plaintiffs testified that neither of the three had graduated from high school and that only the daughter could read and write. Their attorney told the jury that Whirlpool, the largest maker and marketer of home appliances, with $10.5 billion in sales, was preying on the poor, elderly, and uneducated. He asked the jury to award his clients punitive damages.

Outcome The Greensboro court complied with the attorney's request and probably floored him in the process. They awarded his clients $975,000 in compensatory damages plus $580 million in punitive damages! The judge later reduced this outrageous amount to a "more sensible" $300 million. But even this judgment jarred the local business community. It pressured the Alabama legislature to pass a tort-reform measure that caps punitive-damage awards at no more than three times compensatory damages if the award is greater than $500,000 for noninjury cases and $1.5 million for physical injury cases.

Where'd That Gas Station Come From?

Buying a house is often one of the biggest decisions people make in their lives. Usually the process entails a good amount of head scratching, hemming and hawing, and deliberation. Naturally, among all the other considerations, the immediate neighborhood and surrounding areas are also important factors in whether to pass or buy.

So when a woman in Los Angeles bought a house located near a gas station—one that had been in business for more than thirty-six years—the odds were that she knew the station was there. It's not as though it could have been hidden and needed mentioning in any disclosures. But the woman felt otherwise. She sued an oil company—one that didn't even own the gas station—claiming that it diminished the value of her property by $167,000. She also demanded an additional $50,000 for "pain and suffering" and $1,000 in medical expenses.

Outcome After a one-day trial, the judge dismissed the case in 1996.

Don't Mess with Tardy Plant Employees

A Volvo GM truck plant in Virginia decided that it could use a mascot. The company figured that a big obnoxious critter could be used to discourage tardiness by employees. So it hired an actor dressed as a giant rooster to heckle the employees who were running late.

With the clever scheme in full swing, Mr. Rooster was performing his duty by sneaking up behind tardy employees and crowing. Not exactly the best greeting for people who may not have had their morning cup of coffee. Sure enough, the rooster eventually picked the wrong guy to henpeck. A fifty-year-old worker, who was already grumpy from back pain, turned around and jumped on top of the rooster and began choking it. Accounts of the incident state that it took two people to pull the peeved employee off the noisy bird. The truck plant suspended the rooster-battering employee for three months.

The eighteen-year employee applied for unemployment benefits but was denied. So, in 1998, he sued the truck plant for suspending him. He argued that he was justified in attacking the rooster that had sneaked up behind him and verbally goosed him.

Outcome The judge also seemed to think so, because he ruled in the worker's favor, stating, "The bird had it coming." The employee was compensated for the time he lost from work due to the suspension. And it probably wasn't chicken feed, either.

10

PRISON PRIMA DONNAS: INMATE LAWSUITS V

The fashion wears out more apparel than the man.
—Shakespeare

You might think prison is the last place anyone would care to make a fashion statement. Not so for a good many image-conscious cons, who have sued for everything from passé prison garb to the types of towels they have to dry off with. Here are just some of the lame lawsuits these jailhouse trend-setters have filed in the name of style.

Feet First

An Arizona felon failed to put his best foot first when he sued the Department of Corrections, demanding that he be allowed to wear Reebok Pumps or LA Gear sports shoes instead of prison-issued Converse.

Cool Shades

An Ohio car thief claimed his constitutional rights were violated because he wasn't allowed to wear sunglasses in jail.

Tighty Whiteys

A convict in Minnesota demanded damages because his prison-issued briefs were too tight. He claimed the snug undies constituted cruel and unusual punishment.

Below the Belt

Another inmate, who was serving a life sentence in Oklahoma's Joseph Harp Correctional Center, filed a lawsuit because prison officials made him wear regulation white cotton underwear. Talk about setting yourself up for cruel and unusual punishment: he wanted the right to wear women's nylon bikini panties.

Throwing in the Towel

A convicted felon from New York filed a lawsuit after being "forced" to use "improper" white towels instead of beige ones.

Pretty in Pink

Another inmate from the Big Apple sued for his constitutional right to use pink towels instead of prison-issued white ones. (What's everybody got against white towels?)

Switcheroo

Two prisoners in Pennsylvania filed a lawsuit in an effort to force the state to pay for their sex-change operations while they were incarcerated.

Dressed to Kill

Another Pennsylanvia inmate sued for damages because he was not allowed to grow his hair long, wear make-up, and sport women's clothes while doing time for murder.

Smile Pretty

A Nebraska inmate convicted of murdering his wife sued prison officials after they refused to pay for braces for his teeth. An independent dental examination determined that no orthodontic work was necessary.

Try a Toupee

A Utah inmate filed a $1-million lawsuit for the emotional suffering he had to endure after the state suspended a program that provided free hair transplants for prisoners.

Inadequate Coif

A convicted New York rapist sued the state, claiming he suffered from insomnia, headaches, and chest pains after a prison barber gave him a "defective haircut." (And what, pray tell, constitutes an effective one?)

11

JUMPING ON THE BANDWAGON: CLASS-ACTION LAWSUITS

A Mob's a Monster; Heads enough, but no Brains.
—Benjamin Franklin

If you lose money gambling, do you sue the casino? If you don't like the way Fight Night pans out, do you make the boxer foot your pay-per-view bill? No? Well, millions of Americans already have. And know it or not, you may be one of them.

They're called class-action lawsuits, and unwitting consumers are getting roped into them every day. In a class action, a lawyer takes on a client who feels wronged, then identifies a group, or class, of other people who have suffered in a similar way and asks the court for permission to represent them, too. If the case goes well, the class—whose members are often unaware they are even plaintiffs—wins money. The lawyer takes a percentage.

Don't get too excited, though. Most people only win enough money to take their family to dinner and a movie, and that's if they're lucky. In many cases, it's only their attorneys who end up coming out ahead. Take the following examples.

Small Matter, Big Award

In the tradition of finding a flaw and then building a lawsuit around it, ten California lawyers created a class action in 1997 over computer monitors that supposedly had screens half an inch smaller than advertised. Although computer owners, by and large, didn't complain, the lawyers needed only one plaintiff to file a lawsuit on behalf of all consumers around the nation who had bought the wayward monitor. The monitor owners weren't notified that a lawsuit had been filed on their behalf.

Outcome Recognizing the futility of trying to fight such a suit, the monitor manufacturer, Dell Computer of Austin, Texas, settled out of court by sending its customers a $6 cash refund or a coupon for $13 off their next purchase of a monitor. Meanwhile, the lawyers split more than $16 million—an amazing one hundred thousand times more than each computer owner's cash settlement!

Don't Spend It All in One Place

In a similar case, a credit-card issuer was slammed with a class-action suit in 1995 over wording on its monthly bills. It all started with one man who consulted a lawyer regarding his confusion about the meaning of the term *grace period* on his monthly statement. The lawyer quickly sued the bank that had issued the credit card—on behalf of all its thousands of customers. These credit-card holders had not been overcharged, cheated, or subjected to any other negligent or malicious conduct by the bank. The lawsuit simply alleged that the bank had confused them by using ambiguous wording.

Outcome The credit-card company ultimately settled out of court because it was cheaper than going to trial. Its customers were reimbursed a whopping 93¢ each, while the lawyer walked away with $140,000. Keep in mind that, although the customers ended up with some extra change to blow, chances are they didn't come out ahead: The bank had to cover its legal fees, not to mention the cost of issuing thousands of ninety-three-cent checks. And what better way for it to do so than to pass the costs on to its customers?

House Call

Is there something wrong with this picture? In July 1996, an apartment owner in Orange County, California, settled a group housing-discrimination lawsuit for $775,000. More than two dozen people claimed that they had been denied apartments or overcharged because they had children. Several other plaintiffs accused the owner of racial discrimination.

The hefty settlement seems quite a victory on the surface. But we're forced to wonder just how vindicated the aggrieved parties really felt when the lawyer who represented them got to keep $645,000, or 83 percent of the award. The tenants who had suffered the discrimination and the Fair Housing Council of Orange County, a nonprofit group that led their charge, were left to divide up the remaining 17 percent.

The plaintiffs' law firm claimed it had earned its weighty fee by working on the case for three years and more than five thousand hours. It's hard to see why so much time was needed on a case that hardly seems to be a groundbreaker. The law firm, however, said the apartment owner's "failure to settle sooner" kept the meter running. Maybe they should have twisted his arm a little harder.

Deductive Reasoning

A real estate broker in Portland, Maine, never wants to win another class-action lawsuit again—at least not when it costs him more than he wins. In 1995, the broker was surprised to discover that he was among the winners of a class action against his mortgage bank. He learned of his victory only when he spotted a $91.33 "miscellaneous deduction" from his escrow account, where a portion of his mortgage payments were set aside to pay his property taxes and insurance. The charge turned out to be his payment for lawyers he never knew he had hired. His winnings were just $2.19 in back interest.

The lawsuit, which accused the bank of keeping excessive amounts of its customers' money in escrow accounts, involved a nationwide class of 715,000 then-current and former mortgage holders. The three hundred thousand current holders wound up paying the lawyers' bill of $8.5 million. Only after the case was settled in 1994 did some members of that group realize they had ended up with a loss.

The broker, however, fought back in a particularly ironic way: He filed a new class action against the original plaintiffs' lawyers, accusing them of defrauding the thousands of mortgage owners who, like himself, lost more than they had gained.

Dozens of lawsuits over escrow accounts were filed in the early 1990s before federal regulations more strictly limited the excess money that mortgage banks could hold in their accounts. This case, however, stands out as a blatant example of how class-action lawsuits are ripe for abuse. Not only did the lawyers' take dwarf the plaintiffs' meager share; but apart from a few dollars in back interest, the "awards" were refunds of the plaintiffs' own money, which would have been returned sooner or later even without the lawsuit. The broker and others who had no excessive money in their accounts were hit hardest, because they received no refund but still had to pay legal fees. What's more, critics say, the fees were larger than they should have been, because they were based not on the current value of the refunds but on unrealistic projections of their future worth. "There is evidence from around the country," said one Maine politician, "that in many instances class actions are benefiting lawyers to a much greater extent than their clients."

You don't say.

CLASS-ACTION SWEEPSTAKES

If you haven't been involved in a class action or received one of those intriguing letters informing you that someone you've never met has been negotiating on your behalf, you probably know someone who has. In the 1970s, class-action lawsuits were somewhat of a novelty. Not anymore. Thanks to a sequence of legal decisions since the mid-1980s and increasingly aggressive tactics by lawyers, class actions involving thousands, even hundreds of thousands, of claimants are becoming commonplace.

So how do lawyers find so many plaintiffs to represent? Simple. If you're an investor or customer of a firm targeted for a class-action suit, you'll usually find a notice in your mailbox informing you that you've automatically been included among a long list of plaintiffs. Like those Publisher's Clearinghouse mailings that seem to promise easy money, eye-catching numbers are often sprinkled amid the legalese. But here's the clincher: Originally, you had to sign the document and send it back if you agreed to take part in the suit. Now, more times than not, you have to sign the document and send it back if you don't care to join. Since it takes more effort to opt out than it does to stay in, most people simply go with the flow. Voilà, an instant class.

To be sure, class-action lawsuits have compensated people sickened by asbestos, won refunds from corporations that fixed prices, and driven unsafe medical devices from the market. But cornball class actions can tie up the courts, stifle innovation, raise insurance rates, and jack up the cost of doing business. In many cases, consumers see their legal rights bargained away without their consent. And companies have been run into the ground by the threat of a massive payout, sometimes for the slightest affront or infraction. Witness the following case.

Return to Sender

Two enterprising attorneys in Missouri filed a class-action lawsuit against a TV station and a mom-and-pop facsimile company called BMIS. Their complaint? The station had sent their law firm an unwanted fax.

BMIS was hired by Channel 2 in St. Louis to fax community calendars, announcing such things as boccie ball contests and weather updates, to local residents. In an unfortunate turn of events, however, the company faxed a Channel 2 flyer to a law firm in June 1995. The lawyers there were immediately outraged; apparently their office had only one fax machine, and they didn't want it tied up. But rather than politely asking the TV station or BMIS to stop faxing the notices, they sued.

In 1991, Congress passed the Telephone Consumer Protection Act, which allows people who receive unsolicited advertising faxes to sue and collect up to $500. But the lawyers didn't want to trek all the way to court for a measly $500. So instead, they filed a class-action lawsuit on behalf of every single person who had received the offending facsimile from BMIS, enabling them to collect legal fees from thousands of individuals.

Outcome No news on the final outcome of this crazy case. We do know, however, that the lawsuit not only left BMIS with a $14,000 legal bill, but also scared away all of its customers. Under that financial strain, the tiny company was ultimately forced to close down. "What was most disheartening to me was that an attorney could use the system so freely at virtually no cost to himself," BMIS's former owner said. "It was up to me to bear all the expenses to defend myself, and it cost him nothing."

What a Hoot

In a similar case, Hooters of America, a restaurant chain known for its scantily clad waitresses, was slammed with a class-action suit in 1995 for "willfully and knowingly" faxing unsolicited lunch coupons to residents in Augusta, Georgia. The lawsuit, filed on behalf of 1,321 people who had apparently been inconvenienced by finding a free coupon on their fax machine, alleged that Hooters had violated the infamous Telephone Consumer Protection Act of 1991.

Outcome In May 2001, a Richmond County Superior Court judge fined Hooters $11.9 million for its illegal faxing activities. Each of the plaintiffs represented in the class action received about $3,000. Meanwhile, their attorney pocketed $4 million, or 33 percent of the award. "We are very grateful and pleased with . . . the decision the judge has entered, and we think it is supported by the evidence," the lawyer said. Sure, but whether unwanted faxes, formerly balled up and tossed in the trash, now merit full-scale lawsuits remains another question.

STRENGTH IN NUMBERS

It's not hard to see why class actions continue to thrive. For one thing, they are an easy way for lawyers to extort large settlements. Faced with legions of plaintiffs, most companies will pay up rather than risk going to trial and chancing an "all-or-nothing" verdict. It doesn't take a genius to see how a massive class can magnify a claim (whether valid or not), make it more likely for the defendant to be found guilty, and result in much higher damage awards. That's why attorneys are so eager to recruit as many plaintiffs as possible. The more people they can claim to represent, the greater their leverage at the bargaining table. And the more plaintiffs there are to reimburse, the higher the out-of-court settlement—and the larger the lawyers' cut. It's the old "strength in numbers" strategy. Take the next case.

Ex Post Facto

Should attorneys make millions suing a company that 'fessed up to a product error and fixed it for free even though none of its customers had ever noticed? Apparently some California lawyers thought it was fair game.

The attorneys filed a class-action lawsuit in 1995 against the computer-chip maker Intel on behalf of every person who had ever purchased a particular Intel Pentium microprocessor. They got the idea after reading Intel's voluntary announcement that it had incorrectly reported benchmark speed tests for two of its chips, and that it had since corrected the problem.

Outcome Intel settled the lawsuit out of court. As part of the settlement, it issued its customers $50 rebates on their next purchase of an Intel processor. Meanwhile, the lawyers walked away with $1.5 million. Not bad, given that the case involved little if any harm to consumers, no illegal conduct by Intel, and no meaningful recovery for anyone except the lawyers themselves.

Hijacked

In 1991, lawyers in Atlanta, Georgia, filed a class-action lawsuit against nine of the nation's largest airlines, accusing them of price fixing. They claimed that the airlines had used a computerized reservations system to mutually raise ticket prices. The suit was filed on behalf of some four million passengers who had bought tickets within a specified four-year period.

Outcome Without admitting any wrongdoing, the airlines settled out of court for $450 million. The lawyers received $50 million of the settlement. The rest was distributed to the millions of class members in the form of coupons that gave them $25 off their next round-trip ticket!

To Your Health

Blue Cross and Blue Shield of Missouri, the state's largest health insurer, was hit with a class-action lawsuit in June 1994 for allegedly overcharging patients. A cadre of seven law firms claimed that the St. Louis–based company had not passed on discounts from hospitals and doctors to seventy-five thousand members of its health plans. Instead, these members unknowingly paid larger-than-necessary shares of their health bills through copayments. For its part, Blue Cross contended that it had done nothing wrong and that its subscribers had benefited from the discounts through lower insurance premiums.

Outcome In October 1995, Blue Cross decided to cut its losses and settle out of court for $5 million. "We have watched the experience of other health insurers subject to similar suits and we decided that a settlement, rather than long and costly litigation, was in the best interest of our customers and our companies," said Blue Cross's president.

The funny thing is that the company's subscribers—the ones who were allegedly defrauded—were reimbursed roughly $44 apiece, while the seven law firms divvied up $1.7 million in legal fees. And chances are that Blue Cross had to boost its premiums to compensate for the settlement. So who really won out?

Derailed Justice

It was a sight for a class-action lawyer's sore eyes. A leaky railroad car filled with a petroleum by-product had burst into flames, forcing eight thousand residents in New Orleans to evacuate their homes overnight. Within twenty-four hours, attorneys filed a blanket class-action lawsuit against nine companies, several of which were only tangentially involved. Although no one was hurt in the 1987 incident, the lawyers decided to represent ninety-eight hundred area residents who had allegedly suffered "mental anguish."

Outcome After a two-month trial in 1997, a jury awarded the plaintiffs $3.4 billion. One company, CSX Transportation, was ordered to pay $2.4 billion of the total—despite the fact that it did not own, repair, or load the railroad car. The company simply owned the track that, other than being under the tank car at the time, played no role in the accident. The attorneys received almost 50 percent of the award. CSX's president and chief executive put it lightly when he said the verdict was "clearly inconsistent with the facts." The company, along with two others, has appealed.

STRIKING STRIKE SUITS

One particularly nasty type of class-action litigation is the "strike suit." In class-action securities lawsuits, as strike suits are formally known, trial lawyers sue companies when their stock price drops for one reason or another. The lawyers usually charge company executives with defrauding investors for not telling them in advance that the price of the stock would fall. All it takes is one shareholder with one share to file on behalf of every investor. But rarely do such lawsuits go to court. The potential cost of fighting such a claim—the securities equivalent of whiplash—is so large that most companies will pay up simply to make the lawyers go away. That's why 90 percent of strike suits are settled out of court at an average cost of $11 million.

The practice is particularly devastating to high-tech and biotechnology firms. That's because these companies operate in a highly volatile industry, making them especially susceptible to stock-price swings. At last count, one out of every four Silicon Valley firms—including such respected names as Intel, Apple Computers, and Hewlett-Packard—has been slapped with a strike suit at some point. And although lawyers assert that they are acting not out of self-interest but on behalf of small and powerless shareholders, in most settlements investors get a measly fifteen cents per dollar. The lawyers pocket the rest.

Between 1988 and 1998, the number of strike-suit filings rose by 338 percent in federal courts and by more than 1,000 percent in state courts. San Diego, California, trial lawyer Bill Lerach, known as the Darth Vader of securities litigation, boasts about having filed at least four hundred securities class actions, resulting in more than $4 billion in corporate settlements. According to a February 1991 speech he gave at a legal conference in Orange County, whenever he sees a stock price take a dive, he turns to his secretary and asks for that company's press releases, analyst reports, and record of insider selling. Then he gets to work to see if he "might have a case." Lerach's critics point to the uncanny similarity in the verbiage of many of his claims. It's true that this mechanical approach to litigation has caused an embarrassing gaffe or two. For example, a 1993 complaint referred to tobacco and food giant Philip Morris's standing in "the toy industry." And that's nothing. Feast your eyes on the following strike suits.

Price War

For six consecutive quarters, the high-tech company Silicon Graphics grew rapidly. But in March 1991, Desert Storm diverted defense spending away from the company's software and into military hardware. As a result, the company reported lower quarterly revenue, and its stock price dropped from $42.50 to $38. Three law firms, including Bill Lerach's, immediately filed a strike suit—presumably because Silicon Graphics had failed to anticipate Saddam Hussein's invasion of Kuwait. Strangely, the named plaintiff in the suit, who represented the entire class, happened to be the eighteen-year-old daughter of one of the attorney's stockbrokers. She held just two hundred shares of the stock.

Outcome When outside counsel confirmed that it had done nothing wrong, Silicon Graphics decided to fight. After a year of haggling, a judge dismissed the suit. Lerach's firm dropped out, but the other two tried again. Another year of wrangling passed; finally Silicon Graphics settled, paying about $1 million, plus $500,000 in legal fees. "It just made more sense to pay than to fight," said the company's chief executive officer. "We're not happy about it. The suit made us curtail [research-and-development] spending, it was a colossal waste of time, and it's a stain on what I consider a great company."

A Minor Slipup

Adaptec, the leader in the small computer systems interface market, boasted thirty-six consecutive quarters or almost nine years of rising profitability. But in December 1990, it held a meeting with securities analysts to let them know that, due to a combination of business events, the company's revenue for the quarter would be about 15 percent lower than expected—but that it would still post a significant profit. The next day, the Milpitas, California, company's stock dropped from $15 to $10.

Within four days, Bill Lerach's firm filed a strike suit against Adaptec, accusing its executives of knowing of a "lack of future viability." The lawsuit alleged broad financial wrongdoing that supposedly stemmed back fourteen months before the filing.

Outcome To kill the proceeding, Adaptec came to court with fifteen hundred boxes of paperwork, which cost the company about three years and $5 million to compile. Meanwhile, the suit cost the plaintiffs' lawyer just $120 to file. In the end, Adaptec settled out of court for $4.3 million.

This Calls for Some Clarification

Pyxis, a San Diego–based maker of machines that dispense drugs, had a run-in with Bill Lerach in early 1994, after an influential stock analyst published a report questioning the company's accounting practices. The analyst said Pyxis chose an overly aggressive method that inflated the value of its contracts, a claim that Pyxis denied. An advance copy of a *Business Week* article about the dispute was released that March. The same day, Lerach's law firm filed a class-action suit against the company, alleging that its management misled shareholders for personal gain. Among other things, the suit cited the April 1994 article, which hadn't even hit newsstands. Pyxis scrambled to do damage control, placing an advertisement in *Investor's Business Daily* to reassure wary investors. A few weeks later, the analyst who had written the damning report issued a "clarification" in which he said Pyxis had used appropriate accounting methods.

Outcome The lawsuit was dismissed by a federal district court in July 1994. By then, however, Pyxis's stock price had plunged to $22 a share from $33.

On and On and On

Glendale Federal Bank has been fighting the same shareholder lawsuits for almost a decade, even though the case has never advanced beyond the initial pleading stage before a judge. Like many other lending institutions, the Glendale, California, bank's loan portfolio was battered by the recession of the early 1990s, and the company posted a quarterly loss of $141 million in 1991. Within forty-eight hours, GlenFed was hit with six suits filed on behalf of investors who were allegedly misled by the company's annual reports that referred to "superior" asset quality and "stringent" credit procedures.

Outcome The case was dismissed by a federal judge, appealed by plaintiffs, dismissed by a three-judge panel, then appealed again. Most recently, an eleven-judge panel chastised the plaintiffs in a twenty-seven-page ruling. The judges wrote that the plaintiffs "seem to have done little more than copy verbatim language from Glendale Federal's public filings, and then proclaim . . . the statements were false." Nevertheless, the panel concluded that "despite its many deficiencies," the suit could not be dismissed for the reasons cited by the three-judge panel. The case was returned to that lower panel, which was directed to find other grounds for dismissal or allow the case to proceed. "When companies have to pay hundreds of thousands of dollars to defend cases that have no basis in fact and very little merit," said GlenFed's attorney, "it is not in the best interests of society."

IN A CLASS OF THEIR OWN

Sometimes, class-action lawsuits are so off the wall that they defy common logic. Witness the following case in which the most benign of household objects—your average toothbrush—becomes the center of an industrywide conspiracy.

Long in the Tooth

An Illinois man who had a brush with tragedy while cleaning his teeth filed a class-action lawsuit in March 1999 against the American Dental Association, Colgate-Palmolive Company, and several other makers of toothbrushes. He claimed to suffer from what he termed "a disease known as toothbrush abrasion." He also identified the abrasion as "an injury" and "a distinct clinical entity caused by toothbrushes of the following bristle types: firm, medium and soft, both natural and synthetic." Basically, all of them.

His lawsuit, filed on behalf of "all others similarly situated," claimed that consumers were not properly informed or warned about the dangers of this self-inflicted injury: "It was the duty of the defendant manufacturers to furnish a product, i.e., toothbrush, which was in reasonably safe condition when put to a use in a manner that was reasonably foreseeable considering the nature and intended function of the product." But toothbrushes, the plaintiff soon discovered, "were unsafe and unreasonably dangerous for their intended use in that the packaging contained no warning as to the risks of toothbrush abrasion or instructions on how to brush to avoid toothbrush abrasion." (A warning? Instructions? How about, "Hold toothbrush in hand. Insert bristled end into mouth. Move brush up and down. Stop before teeth and/or gums wear out.")

The plaintiff charged the defendants with negligence but alluded to something far more sinister—an industry conspiracy much like the one tainting the tobacco trade. Seemingly, manufacturers knew about the disease/injury/clinical entity since "at least 1949" but nonetheless continued to produce toothbrushes that were "likely" to cause abrasion. (Likely? Like ones with bristles?) He fingered the American Dental Association as well, because the organization gave its seal of approval to the hazardous hygienic tools.

Our plaintiff went so far as to create a Web site where those who felt wrongly abraded could learn more about their affliction. If you logged on to www.toothbrushlawsuit.com, you would have learned that toothbrush abrasion is "progressive." In other words, it gets worse if you keep making it worse. You also would have discovered that the disease "is most prevalent in those with good oral hygiene"—that is, people who brush their teeth. In fact, "there are studies that show that people who do not brush their teeth, never develop" symptoms of toothbrush abrasion. Consider yourself warned.

Outcome In July 2000, a judge ruled that the toothbrush-injury lawsuit had no bite. He dismissed the case, saying the plaintiff had failed to substantiate his litany of allegations.

Sucker Munch

It just might be possible for some people to make a silk purse out of a boxer's ear. In 1998, a disappointed fight fan filed a class-action lawsuit against heavyweight boxer Mike Tyson, his promoters, and several cable companies, demanding that they pick up the pay-per-view bills of up to two million boxing enthusiasts.

The complaint stems back to a July 1997 boxing match during which Tyson bit his competitor, Evander Holyfield, on the ears. The plaintiff's suit called the "cannibalistic" episode "one of the most despicable and one of the most unexpected acts in the history of professional boxing." It went on to claim that Tyson, after receiving a warning about the first bite, went after Holyfield's other ear "possibly because the reduced surface area of Holyfield's right ear after [the] first attack made it a more difficult biting target than the still intact left ear."

Despite the plaintiff's seemingly silly allegations, nine law firms banded together to champion his cause in New York Supreme Court. Their lawsuit alleged that because Tyson was disqualified during the third round of the title match, the fight ended early and, therefore, shortchanged all the folks who had shelled out money for the privilege of viewing the match on TV. It named Tyson, Mike Tyson Productions, promoter Don King, Don King Productions, KingVision Pay-Per-View, Viacom International, Showtime Networks, and SET Pay Per View as defendants that were "unjustly enriched" by the shortened fight.

Outcome No verdict yet on this below-the-belt jab at justice.

The Unhappiest Place on Earth

Mickey Mouse, a bigot? You be the judge. In August 1997, a woman in northern California and a man from Texas filed a class-action discrimination lawsuit against Disneyland when they failed to qualify for a $10 discount on their entry fees. The suit was based on the fact that for several months out of the year, the Magic Kingdom offers a "Resident Salute" discount to customers with southern California zip codes in an effort to attract local residents during the off season. But to the offended out-of-towners, the discount was more than a mere promotion; it was dire proof that Disney was playing favorites.

It all started in May 1997, when the plaintiffs were charged $36 each to enter the Anaheim, California, theme park. It wasn't the actual price that angered them so much as the fact that other park visitors who resided within the designated area were allowed to buy the same adult one-day passes for $26. Their lawsuit contended that "as a result of the defendants' discrimination, every non–Southern California visitor to the park whose residence address falls outside of 90000 through 93599 has been damaged by paying approximately $10 more for a passport into the park than those persons whose residence addresses fall within the applicable promotional zip codes."

The plaintiffs sued on behalf of every U.S. tourist who had paid the standard admission price during promotional months. The lawsuit was based on an obscure 1995 federal court decision that dubbed Disneyland a "common carrier." In a previous case, judges determined that the Pirates of the Caribbean boat ride qualified the theme park as a common carrier, or anyone "who offers to the public to carry persons, property or messages." And according to state law, a common carrier cannot give preferential pricing to one person over another.

The plaintiffs demanded general damages and legal fees. They also insisted on a change of venue because they believed they couldn't get a fair trial within Disney's domain. "Disneyland has been overcharging the rest of the country for entry into their park for the past three years in the millions of dollars," argued the plaintiffs' lawyer. People save for a trip to the Happiest Place on Earth, he added, "only to find that Mickey Mouse doesn't treat all people equally."

Outcome No news on the outcome of this case. However, a similar lawsuit, filed by a Palm Springs, California, man who claimed that Disneyland's discount policy was discriminatory, was thrown out in 1992.

A Beef with Ronald

In 2001, outraged Hindu vegetarians slapped McDonald's with two class-action lawsuits, one in Washington and one in Texas, accusing the fast-food chain of using beef flavoring in its french fries. The plaintiffs sought unspecified damages on behalf of every vegetarian who ate McDonald's fries after 1990 believing that they contained no meat. The legal hoopla hinged on a 1990 marketing campaign in which McDonald's proclaimed that it had switched from using beef fat to vegetable oil to cook its fries. The company, however, continued to add beef flavoring to its fries before they were frozen.

For its part, McDonald's argued that it was just a terrible misunderstanding. Its switch to vegetable oil was "all about healthy hearts and eliminating cholesterol," said the company's spokesman. "We certainly don't market ourselves as vegetarian." But that argument didn't fly with the vegetarian plaintiffs. They claimed that, for them, eating the meat of cows, which are deemed sacred in Hindu belief, was akin to a cowboy in Montana eating his own horse. They alleged that munching on the offending fries had caused them extreme "mental anguish." As one plaintiff put it, "I feel sick in the morning every day, like I want to vomit. Now it is always there in my mind that I have done this sin."

Outcome No verdict yet. News of the lawsuits, however, ricocheted to India, where windows at McDonald's restaurants were smashed and effigies of Ronald McDonald were smeared with cow dung. Hindu nationalists have since demanded that the country's prime minister close down the Golden Arches' twenty-seven Indian branches.

Houston, We Have a Legal Problem

Sometimes, when it comes to group grievances, not even the sky is the limit. Take the group of men in the Middle Eastern country of Yemen who claimed they inherited Mars from an ancestor some three thousand years ago. They filed a class-action lawsuit against NASA for landing on the red planet without their permission.

According to the lawsuit, the National Aeronautics and Space Administration committed trespass on July 4, 1997, when its Pathfinder spacecraft landed on Mars and its Sojourner rover began roaming the planet to send back photos and data for analysis. U.S. scientists "began exploring . . . without informing us or seeking our approval," the plaintiffs complained. They demanded that NASA immediately suspend all operations and refrain from disclosing any information about the planet's surface, atmosphere, or gravity.

Outcome The plaintiffs presented documents supporting their claim to Yemen's prosecutor general and asked him to order that David Newton, the U.S. ambassador to their country, be brought to court. The prosecutor general, however, described the men as "abnormal" and said they were only seeking fame and publicity. "I threatened them with arrest if they failed to withdraw the case, and they did," he said.

Virtual Stalker

A woman in Tarrant County, Texas, filed an individual lawsuit against Yahoo!, accusing the Internet search portal of violating the state's antistalking law by placing "cookies" on her computer and observing where she surfed the Web. (Cookies are small text files that allow Internet companies to recognize a user each time he or she accesses a Web site.) The suit, filed in Dallas County District Court in February 2000, also claimed that Yahoo! trespassed on personal property and committed civil theft.

The "stalking" claim sounds crazy enough on its own. But it was taken to new heights when the woman's lawyer decided to seek class-action status for the case, a move that allowed him to sue on behalf of Yahoo!'s fifty million users. The suit pointed out that Yahoo! acknowledges in its privacy policy that it uses cookies to research its users' demographics, interests, and behaviors on its site. "Such uses allow the defendants to watch, to spy, to conduct surveillance, to analyze the habits, inclinations, preferences, and tastes, and otherwise to follow and stalk those who visit the defendants' sites," the suit alleged.

For its part, Yahoo! said it did not follow its users around the Web and that it used cookies only to anonymously aggregate user behavior. "The case presents a very creative legal theory but is completely off base and in some ways flat-out wrong," said the company's associate general counsel. "There's no question that privacy is an important issue, but the case is unfortunate because in our view it needlessly scares people."

Outcome No outcome yet, but it seems these class-action lawyers are doing some stalking of their own.

Bon Voyage

Sixteen Colorado prison inmates filed a class-action lawsuit in 1996 when they were transferred to jails in other states due to overcrowding. The convicts demanded to be released immediately, claiming they had been "kidnapped and transported across state lines" against their will. One clever burglar who was shipped to Texas argued that authorities did not have the power to "take the petitioner hostage at gunpoint, while he was merely disembarking the 737 airliner which had just conveyed him to the San Antonio International Airport on July 16, 1996." (He makes it sound like he was a waylaid tourist!)

Outcome The case was dismissed. No charge for the flight, either.

Jailhouse Lawyers

Then there's the gang of Arizona inmates who banded together to file a class-action lawsuit in 1996. The group, twenty-two in all, decided they didn't have adequate access to legal books that they needed to draft lawsuits—so they sued. Interestingly, though, the plaintiffs did have enough legal material to pursue their case all the way to U.S. Supreme Court.

Outcome There, in an opinion filed by Justice Antonin Scalia, the court ruled that prisons should indeed supply enough legal material to let inmates contest their sentences and confinement conditions. But prisons were not obligated to provide inmates with enough material "to transform themselves into litigating engines capable of filing everything from shareholder derivative actions to slip-and-fall claims," Scalia wrote in his majority opinion. In other words, the "litigating engines" didn't need a complete law school library in every cell block.

Card Shark

Parents, thank your lucky stars that one upstanding citizen in our legal community has set out to rescue little Bobby and Sue from the seedy underworld of bettors and bookies. This Los Angeles trial lawyer filed no less than three class-action lawsuits in 1998 accusing the makers of baseball trading cards of insidiously inducing children to gamble.

Manufacturers such as the Upper Deck Company and Pacific Trading Card Incorporated print limited quantities of certain "chase" cards—usually with pictures of the most popular athletes—and randomly insert them into packs. Our legal avenger contended that by printing the odds of getting one of these rare and valuable cards on the outside of packs, these companies "encourage speculation." (Which leads us to ask, isn't that part of the fun? Why else would kids bother collecting scraps of cardboard?) The lawsuit claimed that the card companies had created "the functional equivalent of a lottery" and should be forced to pay damages to all kids who were lured into buying the cards over the past four years. "It's just like Joe Camel," the lawyer argued. "They're selling a dangerous product to kids."

Outcome A federal judge dismissed the lawsuit against Upper Deck. He ruled that baseball trading cards were as benign as church raffles where senior citizens buy tickets in hopes of winning free toasters and trips to Florida. The cases against the other card manufacturers are still pending.

MAKING MY MOLEHILL INTO YOUR MOUNTAIN

Sometimes, individuals dream up class-action lawsuits simply to dodge personal responsibility and blame their own missteps on entities with money. Try following the bouncing ball of blame with the following finger-pointers.

Fool's Gold

After a bad stint at the poker tables, a New Mexico man tried to cash in on a bigger jackpot—a lawsuit against the casino. The compulsive gambler had nothing to lose—literally. He had already hawked his truck, trailer, boat, motorcycles, two horses (Rocket and Mora), income tax refund, guitars, even his rain gutter and fence. According to his wife, he would sometimes stay at the casino for four days straight without sleep. Other times he would go in drunk. "I kept thinking, 'I'm gonna win. I'm gonna win. There's all these big jackpots, and I'm gonna get one,'" he told reporters in 1996.

After running out of things to pawn, our witless wagerer found something else to get him out of his financial mess: a legal loophole. He sued the Isleta Gaming Palace, citing a 140-year-old New Mexico law that reads, "Any person who shall lose any money or property at any game at cards, or at any gambling device, may recover the same." The forty-seven-year-old plaintiff sought to recoup the $56,685.70 he squandered between January 1995, when the casino opened, and November 1995, when he filed the lawsuit. He also asked for $1 million in punitive damages, attorney fees, and an additional unspecified sum for severe suffering. "I would say, to some extent, that it was my own fault," the gambler admitted. "But I'm protected under state law from my addiction."

This argument was apparently so flawless in its naïveté that the plaintiff's attorney decided to make a class action out of it. He sued on behalf of every pitiful gambler in the state who had lost money at the Isleta Gaming Palace over the prior nine months.

For its part, the casino contended that it faced no liability.

The booming business was on Isleta Pueblo, twenty miles south of Albuquerque. Because it was on Indian land, owners argued, it was sovereign and exempt from state laws. Besides, they added, the plaintiff could have just walked out. "We didn't chain him in the chairs," said the casino's operations manager. "We didn't serve him alcohol all night and get him drunk. He has free will like everyone else."

Undeterred, the plaintiff and his lawyer decided to sue New Mexico governor Gary Johnson, too, citing a ruling by the state supreme court that the gambling pacts that Johnson had signed with Native American tribes were illegal. They also set out to sue the banks, credit-card companies, and ATM networks that "facilitated" gambling at the casino. Asked if he was blaming the right people for his problems, the plaintiff responded, "You're right. Governor Johnson caused a lot of the problems in the first place by signing the [gambling] compacts."

Now, let's get this straight. These people gamble, lose, then sue for repayment. What's wrong with this picture? Isn't risking a loss precisely what gambling means? But then again, why play fair when you can find a loophole, right? The plaintiff's wife summed it up nicely when she described the arcane statute as the Lemon Law of gambling: "If you spend your money and you're not pleased with the way things are working out, you can get it back."

Outcome No news on this crap shoot, but we'd wager on a dismissal.

Tricks Up Their Sleeves

A group of card-counting blackjack players filed a class-action lawsuit against several casinos in Atlantic City, claiming that their efforts to beat the odds were being thwarted by illegal "countermeasures," namely the frequent reshuffling of decks by dealers.

Card counting is an unsanctioned memory technique that can improve players' odds of beating the house as the number of remaining undealt cards declines. The plaintiffs, which included sixty individual gamblers and several card-counting schools, argued that the casinos had interfered with their ability to win by allowing dealers to reshuffle the decks whenever they suspected patrons of counting cards. They also alleged that the casinos violated the "cheating games" section of the New Jersey Casino Control Act by using video surveillance equipment to identify card counters and informing dealers of their participation in a blackjack game so that the dealers could take countermeasures against them.

Outcome A three-judge panel in New Jersey dismissed the case in November 2000, saying it "bordered on the frivolous." The judges unanimously found that all of the "countermeasures" used by the casinos had been specifically approved by the New Jersey Casino Control Commission. One judge added that blackjack players "can avoid any injury simply by walking away from the alleged wrongdoers, the casinos, and by not playing blackjack in casinos. In fact, that is what the casinos apparently want them to do, at least as long as they count cards." And although staying out of casinos would deprive them of chances for winning money, the judges noted that "surely it would be difficult to characterize that lost speculative opportunity as an injury to business or property."

What a Racket

A California lawyer resented getting hit with three speeding tickets over two years on the same stretch of highway in Huntington Beach. But rather than simply slowing down, he filed a class-action lawsuit against the city and its police force in 1990, accusing them of racketeering.

The lawyer had been caught each time for racing his Porsche—with the vanity plate TP GUN—at eighty-five miles per hour down a particularly dangerous one-mile stretch of the Pacific Coast Highway, which had a forty-mile-per-hour speed limit. But he claimed that the police, by using radar to enforce the speed limit, had created an illegal "speed trap." He based his argument on the fact that the city had not justified the speed limit by conducting a traffic survey within the prior five years. The enterprising attorney demanded that the city reverse the speeding convictions of every driver ticketed in that area over the past nine years. He estimated that Huntington Beach had earned $20 million in ticket fines during that period, but under the Racketeer Influenced and Corrupt Organizations Act—originally intended by Congress to combat organized crime—it would be liable for up to triple that amount in damages, or $60 million.

Outcome In preliminary proceedings, the lawyer's crafty claims seemed to sway a Los Angeles federal court judge, who noted, "It's a troublesome [argument], but it appears to be clever and that presents a problem." In September 1991, however, the judge slammed the brakes on the plaintiff's case, ruling that there was no basis for his arguments. "Police officers acted within the scope of their authority.... A speeding charge was squarely warranted," he wrote in his opinion.

Big Dreams for Small Minds

A Texas man was stuck with a $450,000 legal bill in 1997 after hiring a lawyer to help him get a $17.90 refund from a rental-car agency!

The lawyer racked up the whopping fee in a futile effort to win class-action status for the otherwise small-potatoes case against Hertz Corporation. Going on the notion that Hertz had violated Texas law by selling supplemental liability insurance without a license, the ambitious attorney had hoped to sue on behalf of every customer who had bought the extra coverage.

When the courts ultimately rejected his request for class-action status, the lawyer went ahead and represented his client in an individual lawsuit against Hertz. Once again, the duo struck out. A Texas district court jury dismissed the case after deliberating for less than an hour.

The lawyer, however, wasn't about to forgo payment for all his efforts. Who else was there to bill but the original client? And perhaps it serves him right, said Hertz's lawyer: people "ought to at least pick up the phone and try to resolve their differences before running down to the courthouse to sue."

12

HOLY SMOKES:
INMATE LAWSUITS VI

*"Faith" has been at all times . . . only a cloak, a
pretext, a screen, behind which the instincts played
their games.*

—Friedrich Nietzsche

When prison officials refuse to provide the special food, fash-
ions, and whatnot that inmates demand, many tireless criminals simply appeal to a higher power: they invoke the
Religious Freedom Restoration Act.

The law, passed in 1993, states that government officials at
all levels have to bend their rules and make special exemptions
for people whose actions are based on their religion. The idea
was to prevent the rights of minority faiths from getting lost in
the shuffle. But for all its good intentions, the law has essentially forced corrections officials to jump through every legal
hoop that troublemaking felons can dream up.

After the law took effect, legions of inmates quickly con-
verted to strange new religions that required wardens to serve
them special food, let them wear strange symbols and clothes,

and even allow them outside at night to celebrate lunar eclipses. In one Illinois prison, inmates have professed to more than three hundred unique religions, most of which haven't applied for membership in the National Council of Churches. The state prison has everything from the Church of Jesus Christ Christian, a white-supremacist sect, to practitioners of witchcraft, and each of them seems to need something special. The result has been a mass pilgrimage to the courts and a wave of nuisance lawsuits filed under the guise of religion.

Standing on Ceremony

A group of Native American inmates claimed their rights were violated when prison officials in New Mexico refused to build them ceremonial sweat lodges in their cells.

What a Turkey

An inmate in Ohio polished off a helping of turkey stuffing on Thanksgiving, then claimed eating turkey violated his beliefs as a devout Muslim. He sued prison officials for $40,000 and demanded the right to return to his Islamic homeland to have the stuffing purged from his system in a ceremonial cleansing ritual.

Hey, Keep It Down!

A Pennsylvania inmate claimed that prison officials violated his religious freedom when they refused to allow him to call his Islamic brothers to prayer by chanting loudly enough to be heard throughout the cellblock—at four o'clock in the morning! A judge dismissed the case, ruling that the prison's need to maintain order took precedence over the inmate's need to chant.

Not Kosher

A group of Muslim inmates in New Mexico filed a lawsuit complaining that they were not given a pork-free diet or allowed to wear kufi caps, and that they had to pay for their scented oils and prayer rugs.

Altar Ego

Some "religious" lawsuits don't have even a modicum of merit. Take the former priest who was excommunicated after his conviction for child molestation. He sued the Arizona Department of Corrections because wardens wouldn't allow him to buy altar bread for use in his cell.

Feelin' Irie

A death row inmate sued a Florida prison, claiming that as a Rastafarian he had the religious right to dreadlocks, a cassette player, reggae cassettes, a Casio mini portable keyboard for composing spiritual songs, and a poster of his spiritual mentor, the late reggae star Bob Marley.

Naked Faith

An inmate in Illinois sued because he was not allowed to practice his religion in the buff. Perhaps he was planning to donate his prison clothes to charity.

Sacrificial Lamb

An Arizona inmate sued because he wasn't allowed animal parts to burn in a religious service. Well, at least he didn't demand the warden's firstborn.

Devilish Fun

A group of Satan-worshiping convicts in Nebraska sued prison officials because they weren't given unbaptized baby fat for their candles.

Holy Porterhouse!

A Missouri felon filed a lawsuit stating that he was entitled to be served a fancy cut of steak once a week in accordance with his religious obligations. Throw in some of the ex-priest's bread and wine, and he's got a pretty tasty dinner.

It's a Guy Thing

A Texas inmate filed a lawsuit claiming that his prison-issued clothes violated his religious freedom. As a member of a group called the Lost-Found Nation of Islam, he argued that his religion forbade him to wear the same clothing as women. Apparently the unisex no-fly, no-pocket pants he was forced to wear violated that ordinance.

It's a Girl Thing

A Nebraska prisoner filed a lawsuit claiming that he was really a woman trapped in a man's body and, thereby, strip searches by male guards were not allowed by his religion.

Nothing's Free

A Texas inmate claimed his religious freedom was denied because state prison officials refused to give him free Christmas cards to send to his family and friends.

Can't You Just Take My Word for It?

A smooth-talking inmate in Oklahoma argued that his religious freedom had been violated but that he couldn't say precisely how, because the main tenet of his faith was that all its practices were secret.

13

MAIM AND BLAME: MALPRACTICE LAWSUITS

Q: *Doctor, before you performed the autopsy, did you check for a pulse?*
A: No.

Q: *Did you check for blood pressure?*
A: No.

Q: *Did you check for breathing?*
A: No.

Q: *So then it is possible that the patient was alive when you began the autopsy?*
A: No.

Q: *How can you be so sure, Doctor?*
A: Because his brain was sitting on my desk in a jar.

Q: *But could the patient have been alive nevertheless?*
A: It is possible that he could have been alive and practicing law somewhere.

—Transcript of actual testimony

Physicians, psychiatrists, attorneys, and other degree-toting professionals have earned the dubious honor of determining our physical, emotional, and financial health. Yet for all the good they do, these well-educated—and well-paid—social servants are finding themselves on dangerous ground. Like sitting ducks in a shooting gallery, they're easy targets for anyone itching to fire off a lawsuit. One false move, and they're toast.

Those perhaps most often caught in the crossfire are physicians. The fact is that the quality of medicine has improved to such an extent that people scarcely believe in happenstance anymore. Take obstetrics. When doctors deliver babies today, they are expected to deliver perfect babies. Unfortunately, it doesn't always turn out that way. Twenty years ago, birth defects were considered acts of God. Today, there are no acts of God. Someone, namely the obstetrician, is always at fault.

Sure, there are legitimate cases of malpractice in which doctors have botched procedures out of carelessness or a lack of experience, cases where the patient clearly deserves fair compensation. Take the guy who had the wrong leg amputated. His cross-eyed surgeon made a serious error; no argument there. But not all cases are that simple. Too often, competent doctors are hauled into court by patients embittered by the hand they've been dealt, "victims" who would rather blame someone else for their medical misfortunes than admit to themselves that heart attacks, hernias, and hemorrhoids happen. It's human nature to point fingers, and doctors—saddled with the imperfect nature of medicine—make perfect scapegoats. Thus, malpractice lawsuits.

What's the harm, you might wonder? The doctors' insurance companies cover their expenses, and the plaintiff gets a nice chunk of change to salve his wounds, right? Not exactly. The vast sums insurers spend covering defense costs, not to mention any damages, are largely why U.S. doctors pay an average of $16,000 a year for malpractice insurance—ten times more than in Europe. The result has been a slow exodus from the medical field, with more established practitioners bowing out early and fewer new ones entering high-risk specialties. Since 1987, 12 percent of U.S. obstetricians have quit delivering babies in favor of early retirement, the "safer" practice of gynecology, or some entirely different pursuit—for fear of being sued.

There is another, more subtle threat to baseless malpractice suits: They compromise the quality of our medical care by putting doctors on the defensive. Nowadays, physicians can't simply be physicians. Surgeons can't simply be surgeons. To duck potentially career-ending malpractice claims, doctors must also don the hat of legal experts. And this medical moonlighting has serious repercussions. Consider the bizarre case of the man who lopped off his own hand, and then cried "malpractice" after refusing to let surgeons sew it back on.

Handing It Off

The thirty-year-old man—let's call him Johnny—had just started his first day of work at a North Carolina construction site in 1995 when he hallucinated seeing the numbers "666" on his right hand. Believing this meant he was possessed by Satan, Johnny brandished the nearest power saw and, as any good God-fearing paranoid would, severed his hand cleanly at the wrist. Horrified coworkers immediately put a tourniquet on his arm, packed the hand in ice, and called 911. Johnny was transported by helicopter to a nearby hospital.

Now, at this point, no one could have known that Johnny had a history of alcoholism and mental illness and that a year earlier he had quit taking his antipsychotic medication, allegedly worried about mixing the pills with booze. But most people (no medical degree required) would figure that a man who deliberately amputates an appendage in a fit of religious paranoia has some problems. Certainly, hallucinations are symptoms of psychosis. A red flag should have gone up about Johnny's mental state.

And it did. A psychiatric resident extensively interviewed Johnny, diagnosing him with manic depression, slight psychosis, and alcohol dependence. She secured his consent for surgery, then gave him two drugs, including a major tranquilizer. From there, the doctor scheduled hand-reattachment surgery. But two hours later, on his way to the operating room, Johnny changed his mind and refused to let the doctor proceed. According to a court statement, he warned, "If you sew it back on, I'll cut it off again." Now the consent was invalid.

Panicked, the doctor consulted the hospital's psychiatric department and was told that a resident had earlier deemed Johnny competent to consent to surgery. Needless to say, those weren't the words the doctor had hoped to hear. If Johnny was considered competent to consent to medical care, that meant he was also competent to decline it.

With visions of lawsuits dancing in his head, the doctor then contacted the hospital's risk management department, which in turn suggested that he call a circuit court judge to get an emergency court order to allow the surgery. The judge, however, advised the doctor that if he reattached the hand against the patient's wishes, he might be held liable for assault and battery. The result? With the threat of litigation looming over him, the nervous surgeon decided not to reattach the hand and stitched up the wound instead.

A year later, Johnny sued the doctor, the hospital, a psychiatrist, and two psychiatric residents for $23 million. The medical experts, he claimed, should have known he was psychotic and therefore incapable of making an informed decision, and they should have obtained a court order to reattach his hand.

Outcome Johnny dropped the suit against the residents before trial and settled the case against the psychiatrist for an unknown sum. The hospital was dropped as a defendant in midtrial after the judge disqualified the plaintiff's expert witness. That left just the doctor. Was he guilty of malpractice?

Fortunately, the jurors decided no. The doctor, they said, did everything he was legally required to do when he inquired about Johnny's mental capacity. Technically, mental illness does not equal legal incompetence; and although hallucinating, Johnny was determined by a psychiatrist to be able to weigh the risks and benefits of surgery. Once the patient was declared competent, the doctor had no choice but to honor his request, however strange, not to reattach the hand. After all, it's not up to a doctor to decide what patients shouldn't do in the name of their religions.

But there is another, more serious question at issue here: The doctor did what was legal, but did he do what was right? Common sense and compassion tell us he should have erred on the side of helping the patient. The bottom line is that a young man was permanently maimed, and he didn't have to be. And therein lies the biggest threat of rashly filed malpractice lawsuits: They make good doctors trounce their better judgment and practice "defensive medicine" in order to protect themselves from liability claims. And in the end, it's the patients who lose.

ON THE DEFENSIVE

Defensive medicine is a two-sided coin, with each side as tarnished as the other. On one hand (excuse the pun), doctors may try to shield themselves from liability by withholding the best treatment, as in Johnny's case. Complex surgery and new, experimental treatments, which present the most risk, are often the first to go. More often, however, gun-shy doctors will attempt to practice "flawless" medicine, as if each case were going to court. They cover their tracks, in essence, with a cornucopia of preventive measures—a barrage of costly and often superfluous tests, more consultations, more referrals, and more hospital admissions. These days, it's common practice for someone who suffers from headaches to fork out $3,500 for a CAT scan and a neurologist's reassurance that there is no brain tumor or other serious disease. At this rate, a sprained ankle may soon require a CAT scan, too—to make sure it wasn't a brain tumor that caused the patient to trip and sprain his ankle. Yet for all the precautions that doctors may take, costly, cockeyed malpractice claims keep finding their way into our courts. And far too many of them are based on nothing more than emotional heat or, worse, greed.

So how can we distinguish a worthy claim from an unworthy one? Invariably, malpractice cases start treading on frivolous turf when they lack one or more of three hard, cold fundamentals: a wrongdoer; a serious, permanent injury; and causation, or a crystal-clear link between the two—between what the bungling doctor did and what the patient suffered. Think of it as a three-legged stool. With all three legs, you've got a pretty solid case. Take one leg away, however, and the suit falls flat.

Chilly Reception

A Los Angeles woman was taken to the emergency room in 1996 after fracturing her ankle in a Jet Ski accident. A doctor treated the injury, then sent her home with instructions to apply ice to the dressing intermittently for pain relief. Weeks later, the woman sued her doctors—for frostbite. She claimed she was told to apply ice directly to the wound *twenty-four hours a day for ten days straight*. And she did!

Outcome The jury gave the plaintiff the cold shoulder to go with her frozen foot. It dismissed the case, deciding that even if the physician had given her such improper instructions (which we find a tad hard to believe), only an egghead would strap ice cubes to her ankle until the joint turned blue.

Fat Chance

A 205-pound man in Virginia Beach, Florida, knew he had to do something about his weight. So in August 1984, he underwent a gastric-stapling operation, in which doctors stapled his stomach into a smaller size to limit how much he could eat. The surgery was a success, and after implanting more than seventy tiny stainless-steel staples in his stomach, doctors sent the twenty-three-year-old patient back to his hospital room to recuperate.

Unfortunately, all that surgery must have made the patient pretty hungry. Two days after the procedure, he walked down a hospital hallway, spotted a refrigerator, and ate so much that he popped his newly implanted staples. The man was forced to undergo emergency surgery and six weeks of intensive care.

After recovering, the patient sued Humana Hospital— Bayside in June 1987 for its insensitivity in leaving an unmonitored fridge within his reach. He sought $250,000 for "enduring extreme pain and suffering and emotional distress." The hospital argued that his own negligence was to blame. The plaintiff knew his prescribed food intake after the operation and should have known the consequences of exceeding it, the hospital's lawyer said.

Outcome Realizing the heavy burden of proof he needed to win his case, the plaintiff ultimately dropped his suit.

Nip and Tuck and Tuck and Tuck

A serial plastic surgery patient who had undergone twelve operations in seven years sued her doctor for malpractice in July 2000, despite having consented to all the procedures. There's nothing unusual about patients being unhappy with the results of a procedure and then suing their doctors; plastic surgeons, in fact, pay among the highest malpractice insurance premiums of all specialists. But the fifty-three-year-old New York native blamed her doctor for performing the surgery at all, claiming that he should have known she had an obsession with her body image that made her incompetent to give real consent. (Ironically, plastic surgeons who were asked to comment on the case in the *New York Observer* wondered whether any of their patients were totally free of the disorder.)

Over the prior twenty-nine years, the plaintiff had gotten a nose job, several eyelid surgeries, three liposuctions to the chin, tattoos on her eyebrows, several injections of fat and Botox to smooth out wrinkles, removal of skin growths, liposuction of the abdomen, flanks, thighs, and knees, a breast-lift, a liposuction of the inner thighs, and a tummy tuck, among a number of other plastic surgery procedures. But her real problems were inside her head, her lawsuit alleged. And the doctor should have known it.

Outcome No news on the outcome of this cobbled-together case. But if the plaintiff ultimately wins, Park Avenue's notoriously body-obsessed plastic surgery aficionados may soon be obligated to get their heads shrunk before they can get their faces lifted.

Sick in North Carolina

A law student in Chapel Hill, North Carolina, went ballistic with an M-1 rifle in January 1995. He killed two people on a busy street not far from the university. One of the victims was shot once while riding his bicycle, then was pursued by the relentless gunman until the dirty deed was completed.

At trial, the gunman's attorney managed to persuade a jury that his plaintiff had suffered from paranoid schizophrenia and basically was just having a bad day. The jurors found the killer not guilty by reason of insanity and, rather than sending him to prison, had him committed to a state psychiatric ward.

Here the loose-cannon law student seems to have regained his senses, becoming coherent enough to file a lawsuit against the psychiatrist who had treated him eight months prior to the shootings. He claimed that the psychiatrist had failed to make a correct diagnosis and hadn't explained the seriousness of his illness to him. Further, the shrink should have referred him to another doctor after their half a dozen sessions ended. "The murders would not have happened if the doctor had done his job properly," he alleged. (Now that's a sincere show of remorse.)

Outcome In April 1999, a twelve-person jury bought the argument set forth by this certified madman. (Apparently, when he's killing people he's insane, but when he's suing doctors he's quite sensible, believable, and sympathetic.) The jurors awarded him $500,000—essentially because the doctor who had treated him nearly a year before the rampage fell short in his divining abilities and neglected to forecast the killing spree. Apparently, insanity is contagious.

As a side note, the plaintiff cashed in on his killing spree even further when he published an autobiography, titled *Nightmare: A Schizophrenic Narrative,* in February 2001. A month after advertising the book and selling several copies, however, the publisher terminated its contract with the author over liability concerns.

Acne Attack

A Chicago medical student suffered from a bad case of acne. So in May 1986, his dermatologist prescribed him the popular acne medication Accutane. Four months into his treatment, though, the thirty-six-year-old man walked into a local forest preserve, spotted a fifteen-year-old boy, shoved him to the ground, and shocked him with a stun gun. The following week, he went back into the reserve, shocked a twenty-five-year-old man, and sexually assaulted him.

The medical student was arrested and charged with battery, sexual assault, unlawful restraint, and armed violence. But because he had no criminal record, he was able to strike a deal with prosecutors. He pled guilty to just two counts of battery and was sentenced to one year of probation. The governor of Illinois ultimately pardoned him after his doctor wrote letters on his behalf.

The case took on an even stranger complexion when the medical student sued his dermatologist. He claimed that the acne medication he was taking had caused his crimes by making him unusually aggressive. And he blamed his doctor for failing to properly monitor his condition.

Outcome A judge threw out the plaintiff's case, ruling that he had already taken full responsibility for the crimes by pleading guilty. But the Illinois Supreme Court overturned the dismissal in September 1997 and ordered the case to go to trial. The justices ruled that, just because the plaintiff had accepted an attractive plea bargain offered by prosecutors, he should not automatically have to forfeit his rights to a civil trial. The court's sole dissenting judge said the ruling "invited the rancor of the community toward the legal profession and the justice system."

Hit or Miss

While recovering from a hysterectomy at a hospital in Mesa, Arizona, a seventy-one-year-old woman pulled a .38-caliber revolver from her husband's briefcase and opened fire. She intended to shoot her spouse, but when the dust had settled, he wasn't the one injured; a nurse and a paramedic had been hit instead.

In January 1997, the quick-drawing patient decided that she was a victim of her own crime. She sued Valley Lutheran Hospital, claiming it was negligent in allowing a gun into the ward. What's more, the shooting that resulted from such negligence caused her "extreme anxiety, mental anguish, and other emotional suffering."

Outcome We haven't heard the outcome of this case, but we think Ma Barker doesn't stand a chance.

IT'S HIS FAULT

In each of the previous cases, there was indeed a wrongdoer; it simply happened to be the patient instead of the doctor or hospital. Often, however, there is no wrongdoer. Questionable malpractice suits often assume that just because there is a bad medical outcome, the doctor must be to blame. But contrary to what we see on TV, where patients are regularly brought back from the brink, doctors aren't miracle workers. CPR has a success rate of less than 30 percent. Patients die in ambulances and on operating tables all the time, and it's no one's fault.

That means a doctor can only be liable for malpractice if the actions he took were negligent, or below the reasonable standard of care. In other words, a lawyer must prove that the patient's suffering resulted from an unforgivable error, not just from the imperfect nature of medicine. Unfortunately, this minor detail has been lost on many an eager plaintiff. To these vexatious victims, reality is a kaleidoscope; with one good twist, mere happenstance becomes medical negligence. Consider the woman who turned an unlucky trip to the dentist into a laundry list of trials and tribulations.

Open Wide and Say *Uggh!*

A Los Angeles school administrator visited her dentist three times in 1992 for emergency crown repair. On the third visit, the dentist injected her with a local anesthetic, the same type and dosage he had used without a problem on her two prior visits. On this occasion, however, the woman began to have a hard time breathing. The dentist called an ambulance, and the woman was taken to UCLA Medical Center, where she was diagnosed with an "idiosyncratic" reaction to the injection and released in apparent good health.

That didn't stop the patient from suing her dentist for $5 million in damages. Among her many grievances, she claimed the incident caused her to suffer from depression and a syndrome that affected the tendons in her hands. But that's just the beginning. The forty-four-year-old woman also claimed she was pregnant at the time and that the injection had caused her to miscarry. All this despite her inability to prove she was ever pregnant. Not only had the woman failed to see an obstetrician before or after the dental visit, but a doctor's exam found she had entered menopause.

Nevertheless, the plaintiff put on a bravura performance. Apparently worried about not getting enough stage time, she decided to represent herself. Within the first minutes of her opening statement, she was sobbing and warning the jury that she suffered "traumatic dementia" and could black out at any moment. Then things really got out of hand. The pitiful plaintiff put herself on the stand and testified for a full day about her "irreversible loss." She called her friends to the stand to sing her praises. During one break, she collapsed into the arms of a pal in the hallway and wailed within earshot of the jurors, "[The judge] won't let me tell my story!" A strange complaint, given that the case dragged on for two full weeks.

Outcome In the end, it took the jury less than three hours to find in favor of the dentist. The fact is, for all her Oscar-caliber melodrama, the woman had failed to prove one essential thing: that her myriad injuries (if they even existed) were the result of some failing on the dentist's part, not just a bizarre event that occurred beyond the reach of reason or skill. Her difficulty in breathing was an iatrogenic injury—one caused by the medicine the dentist administered. But it doesn't necessarily follow that the practice was unreasonable or that the dentist should pay for what turned out to be an inexplicable mishap. Maybe he should have used laughing gas.

Short-Circuited

A self-proclaimed psychic in New Castle, Delaware, said she used to be able to read client's auras, conduct séances, and help police find missing people. But after undergoing a CAT scan at Philadelphia's Temple University Hospital in 1976, she claimed she got headaches whenever she tried to look into either the past or the future. So the thirty-two-year-old woman sued the hospital and a neuroradiologist for malpractice, alleging that the brain X ray had ruined her psychic business.

The plaintiff convinced police officers to testify on her behalf, supporting her claim that she had used her clairvoyance to help them solve cases. (Strangely, while her powers of perception were strong enough to collar criminals, they didn't warn her away from the hospital.)

Outcome In March 1986, a jury granted the plaintiff $1 billion after less than an hour of deliberation. Five months later, however, an appellate court judge threw out the award, ruling that it was so "grossly excessive as to shock the court's sense of justice."

INSULT OR INJURY?

Along with proving negligence on the doctor's part, a "good" malpractice case also requires the finding of serious, permanent injury to the patient. But in our let's-sue-them society, bruised egos and hurt feelings too often suffice for physical suffering. So do injuries that could have happened, but didn't. Where does it stop? Will doctors face suits from patients who could have died but didn't? Or from patients who shouldn't have recovered but did?

Believe it or not, they already have.

Unthankful to Be Alive

In a bizarre case of "wrongful life," a brain-damaged woman and her suspiciously supportive husband sued two doctors and a hospital in March 1997—for keeping her alive. The forty-nine-year-old woman was admitted to John Muir Medical Center in Walnut Creek, California, in September 1994. She was suffering from seizures and pneumonia due to a then-undiagnosed disease. Knowing the woman was not beyond hope, doctors treated her pneumonia with antibiotics and inserted feeding tubes that eventually saved her life. She recovered—and sued.

Now the strange part. The woman's husband testified during their seven-week trial in Contra Costa County Superior Court that doctors had disregarded his repeated requests to stop medical treatment. He also admitted that he no longer loved his wife because she was not the same person he had married. In other words, he thought he deserved compensation because doctors hadn't allowed his old ball-and-chain to kick the proverbial bucket.

Now for the even stranger part. His wife then told the court that she was glad to be alive. She was diagnosed in February 1995 with a degenerative neurological disease. Doctors gave her up to fifteen years to live. In essence, the woman wanted to continue living but demanded compensation for not being dead. (Boy, these two make a great couple, don't they?)

Outcome After five hours of deliberation, the jury unanimously sided with the physicians and the hospital. They concluded that the husband had agreed to treatment when he signed a hospital admission form authorizing the use of such things as antibiotics and intravenous tubes. The couple's lawyer, though, planned to appeal. According to the *San Francisco Chronicle,* he said the doctors had failed to acknowledge and document the husband's wishes to let his wife die. "It's a disappointment," he said.

Better Off Dead?

In another bizarre case of wrongful life, a seven-year-old girl with spina bifida, a debilitating spinal defect, sued her parents' doctors in 1990 because she believed she never should have been born. She claimed that, because the doctors knew she would likely be born with birth defects, they were negligent by not having aborted her.

Outcome The Ohio Supreme Court dismissed the lawsuit in a 4–3 vote, ruling that the doctors had not caused the girl's birth defects and couldn't have prevented them.

Surprised Parent

A woman in Revere, Massachusetts, sued her doctor in 1996 for a "wrongful birth." The thirty-three-year-old plaintiff claimed that the doctor had botched a sterilization operation, leaving her with a healthy but "unplanned" daughter, who was already three by the time the suit was filed. She demanded that the obstetrician cover the lifetime costs of raising her child—including tuition at a private college. In court testimony, the plaintiff called her daughter "angelic" and denied that she was unwanted. "This is really to make sure she gets soccer and Girl Scouts and college, all the things that I didn't have," she said.

Outcome A Middlesex County jury dismissed the case in June 2000, deciding that if the woman truly wanted her daughter, as she had claimed, than she couldn't cash in on the fact that the child was unplanned.

Very Unplanned

In another case of "wrongful birth," an Akron, Ohio, couple sued their doctor for a faulty tubal ligation he had performed on the woman in 1993. A year after the sterilization procedure, the woman gave birth to a son, who had a heart defect. The child died fifteen months later after several open-heart surgeries. The couple demanded that the doctor pay their medical bills and reimburse them for the emotional distress of losing their son.

Outcome The Ohio supreme court dismissed the case. The justices ruled that, while the doctor had botched the tubal ligation, he had not caused the child's heart defect. "Although a negligently performed sterilization is a proximate cause of a subsequent birth, it is not a proximate cause of the birth defect, and, therefore, the negligent doctor cannot be held liable for the costs associated with that defect," one justice wrote in his majority opinion.

Aborted Abortion

It was December 30, 1994. A woman in Boston had gone to the Preterm Health Services Clinic to have an abortion. But before the procedure could be performed, an antiabortion zealot named John Salvi III burst in, wielding a semiautomatic rifle. The madman pumped bullets into three employees, killing one of them, then chased the horror-stricken woman outside. With bullets whizzing by her head, she narrowly managed to escape.

Months later, the thirty-one-year-old woman gave birth to a developmentally disabled daughter, the child whom she had planned to terminate on the day Salvi went on his murderous rampage. The horrible experience, she said, left her so traumatized that she had been unable to go through with the abortion. And for that, she sued Preterm Health Services to recoup the cost of having to raise an unwanted child.

The plaintiff sought between $100,000 and $500,000, claiming that the clinic had failed to protect its clients from madmen like Salvi and had foreclosed on her option to have an abortion. The clinic's lawyer called the allegation patent nonsense. The fact is, he said, "[the plaintiff] chose not to have an abortion after December 30, 1994. She was free to go to any clinic of her choice and have an abortion. She chose not to do so and is, therefore, responsible for her decision."

Outcome In September 1998, a Massachusetts judge rejected a request by the clinic to dismiss the suit, allowing the case to go forward even while pronouncing himself "very, very, very, very skeptical" of the arguments. No news on the final verdict.

ONE THING LEADS TO ANOTHER— SOMETIMES

The final reason many malpractice suits don't hold together is that they lack causation, the glue between what the doctor did and what the patient suffered in consequence. Take the woman who sued her psychiatrist after injuring her arm during a tennis match, thus crippling her career as a musician.

The Spurned Patient

A psychiatrist was sued for malpractice by a patient who claimed he was the reason for the demise of her successful career, which in turn caused her to become even more depressed than when she initially consulted him.

The patient happened to be one of the world's preeminent violists, having held a long and distinguished career with the Los Angeles Philharmonic and as a studio musician. Sadly, she fell into a deep depression after her mother's death and went to the psychiatrist for treatment. She ended up in intensive psychoanalysis with him for the next six years.

During this period, the musician, who was in her fifties, saw the doctor two to five times a week. Somewhere in the course of these frequent visits, she started to develop "profound feelings of erotic transference" toward him. She believed she was in love with the doctor and that he felt likewise. After all, according to her lawsuit, he called her at home on fifteen hundred occasions. He said she was exaggerating, that it was a mere five hundred times, and that they were return calls made mainly to keep her from becoming suicidal.

The musician testified that the therapy sessions continued to focus on her eroticized transference, which seemed like a further indication of his feelings for her. Soon her life began to revolve around him. He allegedly suggested that she should give up her career as a musician because it caused her to become "narcissistic" and furthered her "borderline personality disorder." The advice-spewing doctor also supposedly encouraged her to take up tennis instead, which she quickly did. But this only caused her to suffer a torn rotator cuff in her arm, which effectively ended her ability to play the viola.

Then came the straw that broke the camel's back. The heartless doctor denied any love for her. This crushing revelation sent the patient fleeing to another psychiatrist for consolation. After several sessions with this new professional, she regained the fighting spirit to file a lawsuit in 1998 against the impertinent doctor who had spurned her feelings. And she wasn't about to let him off easy. She demanded $230,000 in medical costs and $1.75 million for loss of earnings. But in an effort to compromise, the plaintiff offered to settle for $1.5 million prior to trial. A fair sum, she thought, for the careless treatment and bad advice she received from the intrusive yet somehow lovable psychiatrist. The doctor declined to settle, and the case ultimately went to trial.

Outcome Ten experts, including psychiatrists, psychologists, economists, music contractors, and orthopedic surgeons, all testified over twenty-one days. After deliberating for forty minutes, the jury dismissed the case, ruling that neither the woman's tennis injury nor her broken heart could be blamed on her psychiatrist.

Prodigal Son

Three days after walking out of the psychiatric unit at Inova Fairfax Hospital in July 1998, a Virginia man drove his car through the front wall of his family's Reston home, then beat his mother to death with a baseball bat. The man pleaded not guilty to the murder by reason of insanity and was committed to a state mental hospital.

A year later, however, the man's father sued the doctors and nurses at Inova Fairfax for wrongful death. He claimed that they were responsible for his wife's murder because they had allowed his mentally ill son to leave the hospital. The hospital pointed out that the twenty-one-year-old man had voluntarily checked himself into the hospital after threatening his mother and attempting suicide. On the morning after his admission, he told nurses, "I feel better now. I need to deal better with my mother." Then he signed a form indicating that he was leaving "against medical advice" and left. "He was an adult who refused medical treatment and got up and walked out the door. And legally, there is nothing anyone can do to stop him," the hospital's lawyer said.

Outcome A Fairfax County jury rejected the widowed plaintiff's claims in May 2001. The jurors ruled that, although the hospital was indeed negligent, it had in no way caused the brutal murder.

A Flush with Death

A California woman was rushed to an emergency room in 1996 after overdosing on medication in a suicide attempt. Doctors treated her, and hours later the woman was allowed to go to the bathroom. There, dizzy from the drugs, she slipped off the toilet and cut her forehead.

Days later, the woman sued the hospital, claiming negligence and infliction of emotional distress. Okay, the nurses may have been remiss in allowing the patient to venture into a bathroom stall by herself; we'll give the prosecution that. But isn't it safe to assume that the plaintiff—given that she had just tried to kill herself—was already more than a little emotionally distressed before her toilet-seat mishap?

Outcome Fortunately, a jury decided there was no correlation between the "wrongdoer" and the woman's emotional "injuries," other than the fact that she had bumped her noggin while under the hospital's care. Even so, the three-day trial cost taxpayers about $18,500 in court costs. So who really took a fall?

LEGAL MALPRACTICE

Medical professionals aren't the only ones running for cover from malpractice lawsuits. Lawyers, too, are seeing their fair share of litigious clients.

No Such Thing as an Honest Mistake

Lawyers, stay on your toes; the slightest slipup these days can leave you buried beneath a landslide of litigation. Take the Atlanta attorney who, in 1997, was sued for more than a quarter million dollars—for failing to check his phone messages.

The unlucky lawyer was hired by National American Insurance Company to represent a trucking firm and driver sued for running over a pedestrian. The case was "on call" on a Fulton state court judge's two-week calendar. On October 5, 1993, a member of the judge's staff left a message on the lawyer's office answering machine after 5:00 P.M., instructing him to report for trial at 9:00 the next morning. National American's claims supervisor, informed of the trial schedule by the company's separate counsel, also left messages for the lawyer after business hours.

Unfortunately, the attorney didn't learn of the messages until 10:00 A.M. on October 6, when his secretary phoned him at a deposition he was attending. By then, however, the presiding judge had already entered a $400,000 default judgment against the lawyer's clients.

Needless to say, National American was spitting mad. Not only did the insurance company appeal the settlement on the grounds that it lacked proper legal representation, it also filed a $275,000 malpractice suit against their absentee attorney.

Outcome In an 8–1 decision, a Georgia appeals court ruled in favor of National American. We suspect the attorney has since taken to wearing a pager.

Death Becomes Them

A Florida man died in the 1991 derailment of an Amtrak train in Lugoff, South Carolina. Three of the victim's adult children sued the railroad for wrongful death and, after a 1994 trial, won $2.8 million in compensatory damages. When the award was upheld on appeal, the court said it had set a state record for wrongful-death cases with adult survivors. Needless to say, the siblings were elated with the outcome—that is, until they read about another case stemming from the same train wreck in which the victim's survivors had received several times more.

In that other case, a jury awarded $50 million in punitive damages to the widow and seven small children of a deceased Miami policeman. Learning of this handsome award, the plaintiffs in the original case soon decided the cash was greener on the other side. They sued their former attorney in 1997 for "a couple million dollars," claiming he had committed malpractice by not getting them enough money. Their new attorney told the *Fort Lauderdale Sun-Sentinel*, "I don't see

why [their] lawyer did any less than what the [other plaintiffs']
lawyers did."

Outcome A three-judge federal appeals court dismissed the
case in May 2001. The judges ruled that the siblings, in fighting for the cash they should have won, forgot what they had
really lost—a father.

Getting Down to Business

Unquestionably, a good many malpractice lawsuits are completely valid. Then there are those that are legitimate yet entail
such strange circumstances that they still qualify as outrageous. Take the South Carolina man who sued his lawyer for
what some might call mixing business with pleasure. According to the malpractice suit, the cocky lawyer failed to inform
the plaintiff that he was having an affair with the plaintiff's
wife while under retainer. The lawyer, who also persuaded his
cuckolded client to buy his wife expensive gifts, had been
hired to provide the two with marital advice.

Outcome The plaintiff was awarded $7.3 million in October
1995.

Preemptive Strike

A group of lawyers in Edinburg, Texas, beat their ex-clients to
the punch by filing a lawsuit against them before the ex-clients
filed suit against the lawyers.

As it happened, a group of a hundred homeowners sued
their lawyers in April 1998, accusing them of committing malpractice, negligence, and fraud while representing them in
1996 in a lawsuit against Fina Oil and Chemical Company. In
that 1996 case, the homeowners sued the Austin-based petro-
chemical company for $255 million over structural damage to

their houses caused by Fina's seismic testing for natural gas. The case was ultimately settled for $25.5 million, of which the lawyers kept almost 50 percent. Outraged by their paltry takings, the homeowners sued their lawyers in 1998 for broad wrongdoing.

Imagine the homeowners' surprise, however, when they learned that their ex-lawyers had filed a lawsuit against them just two weeks earlier. The lawyers' suit asked a federal district court to declare that nothing improper had happened during the original lawsuit against Fina!

Outcome No news on the result on this lawsuit-upon-a-lawsuit-upon-a-lawsuit. But it sure sounds like someone's got a guilty conscience, doesn't it?

14

DON'T BLAME ME: INMATE LAWSUITS VII

The man who can smile when things go wrong has thought of someone he can blame it on.

—Jones's Law

Crazy lawsuits have become an effective way for inmates to strike back at prison officials and perhaps win a few personal privileges. But above all, they're a means for antisocial convicts to shirk responsibility for their own acts—and earn a pretty penny in the process. Here's some proof positive.

Poor Aim

A New York inmate sued for $8.5 million in damages because he smuggled a gun into prison and then accidentally shot himself. He claimed the city was "negligent" to "allow" firearms in prison cells.

But All I Did Was Shoot

A prisoner sued the city of Albuquerque, New Mexico, and its police department after receiving a life sentence for the murder of a police officer. He claimed that he wouldn't have been guilty of murder if the officer hadn't allowed him to surreptitiously "gain access to his handgun" or if the officer had been wearing a bulletproof vest. An appeals court dismissed the case in March 1993.

Taking the Fall

An inmate at the Pima County Jail in Arizona filed a lawsuit against prison officials, seeking damages for a botched suicide attempt. He claimed the guards were negligent by furnishing his cell with bedsheets, which he used to tie around his neck and jump out a jail window. He obviously didn't know the difference between a square knot and a slip knot, though, because the sheet gave way and he plummeted to the concrete below, injuring himself.

Before the case could appear before a judge, however, the inmate saved the court some time by attempting suicide a second time—and succeeding.

Taking the Plunge

A New Jersey inmate died while awaiting trial on a murder charge. Apparently, he decided not to let the jury decide his fate: he slipped and fell on his head while trying to escape out a third-story prison window. His family sued jailers for not maintaining a "reasonably safe facility."

Ouch!

A Connecticut inmate sued the state for $20,000 for the pain and suffering he experienced after he cut his hand on barbed wire while trying to escape from jail.

Double Ouch!!

A New Mexico inmate, who claimed that the prison failed to treat his persistent groin pain, sued the state after taking the matter into his own hands—by cutting off his own testicles!

It Has a Mind of Its Own

A Pennsylvania prisoner claimed that he was deprived of due process when he was disciplined for having oral sex with a visitor. He alleged that his penis had "accidentally fallen out of his pants."

Break a Leg

A lawsuit was filed against Buchanan County, Missouri, alleging that the county should award damages to an inmate who broke his leg while trying to bust out of prison.

Break Another Leg

Then there's the drug offender in Colorado who sued after he broke his leg during a prison-yard softball game. He said no one "warned" him that he could be hurt playing softball. It seems no one warned him he could be arrested for selling drugs, either.

But He Was Only Borrowing It

Another Colorado prisoner sued after he was docked some of his "time off for good behavior" hours. He apparently thought stealing computer equipment from a prison classroom was still within the realm of good behavior.

Can We Reschedule?

A Mississippi inmate sued the state because he didn't receive his scheduled parole hearing. Never mind the fact that he had escaped and was hiding from authorities at the time the hearing was held!

Driven to the Edge

In New York, a prisoner sued for $15 million, claiming that the Department of Motor Vehicles had forced him into a life of crime by denying him a driver's license.

The Perfect Crime

An inmate in Indiana sued to collect the life-insurance settlement of the woman he was convicted of murdering.

All Fired Up

Two Michigan men, who were convicted of setting an arson fire in their store in order to collect on their insurance policy, sued the insurer for not covering the damage caused by the blaze. The duo admitted that they had intended to simply create a small, smoky fire that would damage their inventory, which wasn't selling very well, but that the flames had gotten out of control and spread into the adjoining building. The inexperienced arsonists argued that, because the blaze next door had been accidental, their insurance company should be required to pay for the damage done to the neighboring property.

Amazingly, a court of appeals reversed the trial court's decision to dismiss the case. But in a unanimous ruling, the Michigan Supreme Court eventually upheld the original decision, stating that the conflaguration "cannot be characterized as an accident."

Circular Reasoning

A Texas inmate, who had pulled more than twenty armed robberies at restaurants across the state, sued when he was re-arrested after being mistakenly released on bond due to a clerical error. When the authorities caught up with him a few weeks later, he was charged with more stickups, which he had committed during the time he was running free. His grievance? If the jail staff hadn't released him, he wouldn't have been facing more robbery charges.

Lack of Reasoning

A Colorado prisoner sued for early release because, according to his lawsuit, "Everyone knows a con only serves about three years of a 10-year sentence."

CREATIVE CONVICTS

Vexatious prisoners are pretty good at leveling blame at others. But what do they do when they can't find a legitimate entity to sue? Simple. They make their assailants up.

The Devil Made Him Do It

An inmate at a Pennsylvania state correctional facility filed a lawsuit against "Satan and his staff" for violating his civil rights. He claimed the devil and his demonic helpers had, on several occasions, "caused him misery, made unwarranted threats against him, placed deliberate obstacles in his path, and caused his downfall" and subsequent arrest and incarceration. After thoughtful deliberation, a district judge dismissed the God-awful suit for two very practical reasons: first, the defendant (that is, Beelzebub) was not a resident of Pennsylvania; and second, the plaintiff failed to include directions as to where Satan lived so that the U.S. marshal could serve him/her with papers.

To Thine Own Self Be True

A California inmate filed a $5-million lawsuit against himself, claiming that he had violated his own civil rights. The prisoner, who was serving twenty-three years for breaking and entering and grand larceny, claimed, "I partook of alcoholic beverages in 1993, July 1, [and] as a result I caused myself to violate my religious beliefs. This was done by my going out and getting arrested." To top it off, the smart-alecky convict then asked the state to cover the damages for him because he had no income in jail. His filing read, "I want to pay myself $5 million, but ask the state to pay it on my behalf since I can't work and am a ward of the state."

The case was dismissed almost two years later.

15

DOG EAT DOG: LAWYERS SUING LAWYERS AND OTHERS

I do not care to speak ill of any man behind his back,
but I believe the gentleman is an attorney.
—Samuel Johnson

If we improvised on the Chinese calendar, we could create our own attorney calendar and have, say, the year of the weasel, the leech, the ass, the hog, the vulture, the rat fink . . . the possibilities are endless. Okay, so maybe we're being a little hard on lawyers as a group, but then again, who can resist taking a poke at them, especially since they often deserve it and have been good-naturedly thick skinned about the ribbing? That is, until the California Bar Association objected to the far-too-frequent barbs, claiming that they were blemishing the profession's reputation.

Either way, whether deservedly or not, attorneys are not enjoying the deference they would like. We certainly have no intention of adding to the problem by making them out to be a pack of shifty-eyed carpetbaggers—not as a group, at least—so we'll offer this disclaimer: There's a thriving population of attorneys in this country because there's an abundance of legal problems that require their skills. The truth is, despite Shakespeare's tongue-in-cheek suggestion to kill all the lawyers, society would have a tough time getting by without them. Many lawyers are actually doing some demanding and valuable work, but this isn't what's perceived by Joe Public. And it's easy to see why. When the good, the bad, and the ethically ugly are all dumped into the same cauldron, it's the shrewd defense demagogues and slick TV attorneys who inevitably float to the top. So even though there are various breeds within the barrister species, most doing some arduous albeit humdrum work, it's usually the infamously brash and shamelessly brazen who catch our interest.

A prime example of lawyering gone haywire is the southern California ex-attorney disbarred for conspiring to commit grand theft auto.

Going for the Gold

The vanity plate on his car reads DISBARD, and with his track record of legal antics, it's no surprise. Since being ejected from the California Bar Association in 1974, this ex-attorney has filed more than one hundred lawsuits.

Among his claims to fame: He sued Slim-Fast for putting diet bars in packages he thought were deceptively big, United Parcel Service for ruining his Star Trek posters, a California hardware store for allegedly saying it had a certain tile in stock when it didn't, and a dog-training service that he said failed to train his German shepherd to obey. He sued his ex-wife. He convinced his current wife to sue her hairdresser for cutting her tresses too short before their wedding. He sued the wedding photographer—four times.

Ironically, our compulsive litigant claimed he sued out of a passion for justice rather than money and, according to the *Los Angeles Times,* wanted to be viewed as a "cross between Don Quixote, Ralph Nader, and Charles Keating." Funny, he seems to come across more like a parts bin of Walter Mitty, Torquemada, and Dennis the Menace.

Many of the serial suer's claims began in incidents much like the one that set off his suit against the Mintz Concrete Company. Mintz was hired to dig footings for cement work at his home in Woodland Hills, California, but when he complained that the job wasn't done correctly, the company owner allegedly retorted, "Pay me or sue me"—words the defendant denied ever saying. No matter, the concrete company was slapped with a $3,500 breach-of-contract suit and later settled for $500 after their insurer told owners the case was too costly to fight.

There are others, such as Mastercraft Door & Window Center, that swapped lawsuits with this infamous lord of lawsuits. The ex-attorney alleged that much of the $10,000 worth of equipment he bought from Mastercraft was defective; conversely, Mastercraft claimed he owed the company money. In fact, at least six California businesses filed their own lawsuits against the former attorney for taking their merchandise or services and refusing to pay.

Yet, as he did in other cases, this Walter Mitty of the tort system picketed Mastercraft offices and its booths at trade shows, handing out leaflets accusing the company of fraud. He also sent a friend—whom he once sued in small-claims court—to solicit Mastercraft employees' comments about him. The alleged replies, captured on tape, were later cited in a $25,000 defamation suit against the owner's son.

So what's our compulsive litigator up to these days? Well, he's laughing it up with his own book, *Sue and Grow Rich: How to Handle Your Own Personal Injury Claim Without an Attorney.*

Beer-Bladdered Barrister

Another California lawyer attended a Rolling Stones concert in 1994 at Murphy Stadium in San Diego, California. During the concert he had a few beers and eventually ambled into the men's room to relieve himself. But to his horror, he found several women also using the men's room. Apparently, the lines at the women's rest room were long so, rather than relieving themselves in some public area, they chose to invade the men's room. This intrusiveness irked the lawyer and part-time political consultant, but he toughed it out and managed to endure the indignity.

The following year, the music lover attended another concert at Murphy Stadium, this time featuring Elton John and Billy Joel. And once again, a couple of beers later, he found himself in the men's room. Suddenly, a group of women barged in. To make matters worse, the intruders also "giggled." This made it impossible for the beer-laden lawyer to perform the desperately needed function that had led him to the men's room in the first place. Instead, he returned to his seat and had to "hold it in" for the remaining four hours of the concert.

Afterward, he did what any self-respecting attorney would do in his place. He filed a federal lawsuit over the uncomfortable experience he was forced to endure—an ordeal suffered not once, but twice. His lawsuit named the city of San Diego and the beer vendor. Yes, he sued the beer vendor, Service America, because according to his convoluted logic, if the company had not sold him the beer, he wouldn't have had to go to the rest room in the first place. He demanded $5.4 million in compensation.

Outcome Needless to say, neither defendant chose to settle, and wisely so. In March 1996, the court dismissed the case and ordered the attorney to pay the city and the beer vendor $2,000 apiece for the costs they incurred defending themselves against the ridiculous lawsuit.

This legal professional, however, chose to appeal the decision to the U.S. Supreme Court. Fortunately, the judges had better things to consider and declined to hear the case.

Big Lawsuits Come in Small Packages

A San Francisco attorney blasted Silicon Valley with $9 million worth of lawsuits after learning that there's often less than meets the eye. He sued several software makers, including Xerox, Symantec, and Verisoft/Quarterdeck, in 1997 claiming that the companies packaged their software in boxes that were deceptively "too big."

The plaintiff based his multimillion-dollar claims on two California laws, the Fair Packaging and Labeling Law and the Unfair Competition Law, which were originally enacted to protect consumers from companies that packed small amounts of food in oversized boxes. The lawyer alleged the software makers were being equally dishonest by packing their products, which take up little space, in big, colorful boxes.

Now, most consumers know that software packages virtually always consist of a couple floppy discs or a CD-ROM, and maybe an owner's manual thrown in for good measure. So did this guy really assume he was getting something more just because the box was a bit on the large side?

Outcome No news on the outcome of this lawsuit, but we'd wager that it went nowhere, because not even the most active consumer groups were willing to sign on to this cause.

Poodle Bouncing

Apparently, every dog will have his day—in court. In May 1996, a Los Angeles lawyer filed a discrimination lawsuit on behalf of his three-year-old black miniature poodle. Poor Fifi, it seems, was ejected from a café's outdoor patio. This didn't set well with the poodle's owner, who was dining there at the time. Especially since there were pigeons and other wild birds on the patio that weren't as readily escorted off the premises.

The indignant attorney argued that if the "dirty birds" were allowed to roam freely on the restaurant's property, why couldn't his little pooch? Per the lawsuit, the restaurant's blatant poodle prejudice was a violation of the U.S. Constitution's equal protection clause.

Outcome A judge dismissed the case, ruling that the Constitution didn't cover man's furry and/or feathered friends.

LAWYERS VERSUS LAWYERS

Animal Crackers

Unhappy claimants have often likened lawyers to animals. But a couple of Tennessee attorneys must have really taken these aspersions to heart. One of them sued his partner for damages in 1995, claiming the latter "oinked like a pig, brayed like a mule and howled like a hyena" in the office suite they shared in Memphis. The lawsuit also alleged that the attorney displayed a "rotten, molded, stuffed head of a huge boar" where clients could see it. The defendant bit back, denying that the boar's head, which he took home for Halloween, was moldy or rotten. He also argued that his behavior was neither strange nor improper.

Outcome No news on the outcome. We suggest, though, that the plaintiff call animal control.

Dueling Deadhead

Another office tiff (and subsequent lawsuit) involved a "humiliated" Los Angeles attorney and self-proclaimed "Deadhead" who, in 1995, was in the throes of grieving the death of bandleader Jerry Garcia.

Deadhead, for those unfamiliar with the term, is the name for a faithful fan of the rock-and-roll band the Grateful Dead. Garcia, who headed up the band for some thirty years, had a reputation for overindulging in certain deleterious habits such as alcohol, tobacco, and a variety of drugs. His death by heart attack in a rehabilitation clinic stirred a public reaction similar to "the deaths of presidents, John Lennon, and Elvis Presley," the grieving attorney said. And Garcia, according to the Deadhead lawyer, was "a folk hero and musical genius" whose death was deeply mourned by his fans.

So when a colleague jokingly displayed a cardboard tombstone inscribed with the words R.I.P. JERRY GARCIA (A FEW TOO MANY PARTIES, PERHAPS?) in the high-rise office suite the two lawyers shared, a grievous blow was struck. The Deadhead attorney suffered nothing less than "humiliation, mental anguish, and emotional and physical distress" due to the thoughtless gag. Naturally, his only recourse was a lawsuit.

Outcome The case was ultimately dismissed by the court because the plaintiff failed to pursue it in a timely manner. Despite suspicions that the brooding barrister had actually lost interest in his suit due to the negative publicity he was receiving, he insisted that his case was legitimate but promised to be lengthy and would have interfered with his regular caseload.

Sue Thy Neighbor

One afternoon in March 1989, a lawyer was playing hoops with his son on a basketball court he had built in the backyard of his Encino, California, home. His next-door neighbor, who also happened to be a lawyer, leaned out of his bedroom window and asked them to stop playing. The dribbling of the ball, he said, produced a "percussion noise that was highly annoying." But the ball-bouncing attorney, knowing that he had a legal right to make a "reasonable" amount of noise between 8:00 A.M. and 10:00 P.M., refused to quit his shooting match. So the irritated neighbor, knowing that his rights allowed him to take action to stop a nuisance, sprayed water from his garden hose over the fence and onto the basketball court.

Suit and countersuit. The first lawyer sued because his neighbor had allegedly threatened to come over and personally put a stop to the basketball game. The suit was filed to protect his children's right to play safely in their own backyard, he claimed. He also alleged that he, his wife, and their two children subsequently suffered from mental stress. And to drive the point home, he filed a restraining order prohibiting the water-squirting attorney from coming into contact with them.

The second attorney then filed his own lawsuit seeking more than $2 million. He named not only the ball-playing attorney, his wife, their thirteen-year-old son and eleven-year-old daughter, but also their psychologists and attorneys! He claimed that his property had been devalued and that he "was haunted by the fear of being suddenly awakened by the obnoxious sounds" emanating from his neighbors' basketball court—all of which caused injury "in his health, strength, and activity." If that weren't enough, he then went on to file a product-liability suit against the manufacturer of the backyard basketball hoop and conducted sound tests to determine the noise level of bouncing basketballs. And, not to be outdone, he filed his own restraining order limiting the hours of the day during which his neighbor could play. The court records showed that the water-spraying attorney also had videotapes of his neighbor playing basketball—and that the ball-playing lawyer had videotapes of being taped by his neighbor!

Outcome The cases were ultimately dismissed by a superior court judge. "I guess if nothing else, it's a great opportunity for newspapers to make lawyers look silly," concluded the noise-sensitive attorney. You betcha.

Another Dousing

An attorney—who was suing the Tampa Bay Buccaneers on behalf of season-ticket holders, believing that they were short-changed by the football team in 1999—apparently took the case a little too personally while in a mediation session the following year.

According to a lawsuit filed by the Buccaneers' defense attorney, the aggressive plaintiffs' counsel threw a cup of luke-warm coffee at him. So the drenched attorney had to sue the coffee-flinging attorney. All the while the two remained locked in combat over the gypped season-ticket holders.

Outcome No news on the outcome of this case, but if history is any indication, the two attorneys have probably joined forces to sue the coffee company.

OFFENDED LAWYERS

Sensitive Shyster

It's amazing how many attorneys—who make their livings in an adversarial environment—are prone to being hypersensitive. A Philadelphia attorney, for instance, filed a libel suit against a city magazine because it had referred to him as a "slip-and-fall lawyer" in one of its articles. The lawyer felt this unflattering epithet for a personal-injury attorney was equivalent to being called a "shyster" or "ambulance chaser." So, darn it, he was defamed, he claimed.

Outcome Not so, according to the judge, who dismissed the case in May 1998.

Gracious Winner

In January 1999, a plaintiff's attorney won a $120.5-million wrongful-death verdict against health-insurance giant Aetna. But rather than sit back and relish his victory, the lawyer had more important things to do. He sued Aetna chairman Richard Huber for griping about the verdict by saying, "You had a skillful ambulance-chasing lawyer, a politically motivated judge, and a weeping widow. That's no way to get justice and certainly no way to manage a trillion-dollar industry." The attorney didn't take kindly to being called an "ambulance-chasing lawyer." (Maybe he figured it was the equivalent of being referred to as a slip-and-fall lawyer.)

In his lawsuit filed in Los Angeles Superior Court, the victorious but insulted attorney "claims to fear that he will be shunned by the legal community and haunted throughout his career," stated an Aetna spokeswoman. She went on to say, "This reaction seems excessive in light of the fact that he was nominated for the 1999 Trial Lawyer of the Year and was honored on July 20 in San Francisco" at a meeting of the Association of Trial Lawyers of America.

Outcome Does anybody really believe that an attorney who won a $120.5-million verdict is going to be shunned by the legal community? In the meantime, Aetna has appealed the wrongful-death judgment, the now-former chairman has apologized to the widow—but not to her attorney—and the insurer has vowed to fight the lawsuit.

Big Ones, Too

It seems attorneys of every caliber are sensitive about their reputations. Even big guns like Johnnie Cochran (Mr. If-It-Doesn't-Fit-You-Must-Acquit) don't take kindly to having their reputations tarnished.

In 1997, Cochran filed a $10-million libel lawsuit against a *New York Post* columnist who wrote that the world-famous defense attorney "will say or do just about anything to win, typically at the expense of the truth." Cochran claimed that the column was defamatory because it wrongly implied that he had a record of unethical conduct.

Outcome A judge threw out the case, ruling that the columnist's opinions were "absolutely protected by the First Amendment." In other words, if it's only a dis, you must dismiss. (Maybe Aetna's bitter former chairman has a chance after all.)

Hissing Mad

A Fullerton, California, attorney filed a $100,000 lawsuit against GTE phone company because she was incorrectly listed in its yellow pages under the heading of REPTILES. Her lawsuit, filed in Orange County Superior Court in April 2000, claimed that the mix-up had subjected her "to a great many jokes and hostile phone calls, hissing sounds as she walks by, and other forms of ridicule." Even comedians Jay Leno and Paul Harvey made cracks about her on their shows.

Representatives from GTE said they had inadvertently listed her in the December 1999 yellow pages under REPTILES—above Prehistoric Pets and Radical Reptiles—because she had the same phone number as that used by a now-defunct Fullerton company called Reptile Show. Other yellow pages editions have her correctly listed.

Outcome No news is good news. Hissss.

REJECTED LAWYERS

Discriminated Attorney

Another California attorney and his wife tried to buy a site for a new home but were rejected because the developer allegedly didn't trust lawyers and had "a rigid policy of not selling to them," the *CalLaw* legal journal reported in an April 1999 article. "Too litigious," continued the article, so the couple, "at the risk of proving [the builder's] point, promptly sued the developer in Kern County Superior Court."

The rejected couple's lawsuit accused the developer of discriminating against them in violation of the state's Unruh Civil Rights Act, a law named after the late California House speaker Jesse Unruh and designed to protect Californians from discrimination based on sex, color, religion, ancestry, national origin, and disability. The developer's lawyer argued that his client's policy wasn't arbitrary but was a legitimate business interest, because experience had shown that lawyers in fact were more likely to threaten litigation.

Outcome If the developer has any money left after the lawsuit, he should build a moat.

Marry This, Buddy!

Many a jilted bride or groom has undoubtedly sworn vengeance upon the heartless fiend who dared dump them after a promising engagement of marriage. Most eventually manage to get over the trying, not to mention ego-shattering, episode. Yet there are always the diehards who manage to turn a bust-up into a victory.

Witness the three-time-divorced Chicago attorney who

sued her former fiancé, a wealthy Oregon rancher, in 1992—for breaking off their seven-week engagement. She must have been mighty persuasive in her role as the castoff bride-to-be, given that the jury found the fiancé in violation of the Illinois Breach of Promise Act and awarded her $60,000 for loss of income, $25,000 for psychiatric counseling expenses, and $93,000 for "pain and suffering."

Outcome All totaled, she won $178,000. And yes, she also kept the $19,000 engagement ring, which was subsequently put up for sale at a Loop jewelry store.

No Need for Attorneys Here

Another castoff attorney, this one ejected from an island by her fellow *Survivor* contestants, sued the makers of the hit TV reality show for $5 million. In February 2001, the disgruntled twenty-eight-year-old barrister claimed that she was voted off the premier season of *Survivor* by her co-contestants because they were coerced into doing so by the show's producer, Mark Burnett. According to her lawsuit, "the Survivor contest was unfairly and fraudulently pre-arranged."

Apparently, Burnett had suggested to another contestant that he vote the plaintiff off because it would be better to keep a different contestant, an ex–Navy Seal, around for the future. Another contestant on the *Survivor* program, filmed in the South Pacific in 2000, claimed that Burnett just told them to "vote your conscience."

Outcome None yet, but Burnett said, "If she's trying to say this thing was rigged, she's crazy." He may have a point, too. Is it really that hard to believe that an attorney would be voted off an island by fellow survivors?

INJURED ATTORNEYS

Amazingly, lawyers can be injured while on the job and end up collecting workers' compensation benefits, too.

Quite a Stretch

A lawyer won $35,000 in workers' compensation after he hurt his shoulder reaching into the backseat of his car for his brief-case.

Do Not Operate Heavy Equipment

Another lawyer was awarded nearly $108,000 in workers' compensation after he hurt his back lifting and inspecting the underside of his leather office chair.

Tricks of the Trade

A third lawyer was working for New York's Workers' Compensation Division when he sprained his back reaching for a statute book on the top shelf of the state's supreme court law library. He sued under the workers' compensation law and won $30,000. Can you smell the irony?

Pretrial Jitters

Yet another lawyer won an $85,000 disability payment from an insurance company because he allegedly became "allergic to courthouses" and could no longer practice his profession. He claimed that after being arrested for insurance fraud two years earlier, exposure to the criminal justice system made him physically sick.

LAWYER MOTHERS

Wouldn't it be fun to have a mother for an attorney, er, an attorney for a mother? Well . . .

Curveball

The mother of a sixteen-year-old boy sued a youth baseball league for $600,000 when she discovered her son was not allowed to play on a team designed for older boys.

The boy's mother, a New York attorney, sued the North Colonie Baseball League in Albany, its president, and its commissioner in June 1997, claiming that her son would be "irreparably deprived of the opportunity to enjoy baseball as a sport" if he couldn't play that summer on the Connie Mack team, generally reserved for seventeen- and eighteen-year-olds. North Colonie officials had initially ruled that the kid should remain in Mickey Mantle, a team for teenagers sixteen and younger. But she insisted her son, a junior in high school who would be turning seventeen that August, was talented enough to play on the varsity squad. "The college scouts are going to be looking at the Connie Mack players. They're not going to be looking at the Mickey Mantle players," the mom told the *Albany Times Union.*

Even after North Colonie eventually invited the boy to join its Connie Mack team, his mother wasn't satisfied. She argued that being limited to just one team—even if it was one for older boys—would crimp her son's plans of rising to baseball stardom. She demanded that he be given permission to "shop around" for a Connie Mack team in another town—where she believed he had a better chance of being put in a starting lineup. "Why should he not be able to play at the most competitive level to improve his skills?" she complained to the media. "Connie Mack [initially] declined to invite him. So at that point he should be eligible to become a free agent."

Given the mother's scenario, imagine if the amateur club adopted a rule that let everyone go wherever they wanted, whenever they wanted. "It would create absolute chaos," said the league's lawyer. "If they let him do it, they're going to have to let every single kid who asks go," he said. "They want special treatment for this kid." What's more, letting younger boys play out of their age brackets could bump eligible older kids from the roster or spark recruiting wars, in which teams scout around for the best players. Hardly the intramural experience such leagues are designed for.

And what of the hundreds of thousands of dollars in damages our lawyer mom demanded? The high figure, she claimed, was intended for "shock value." True to her profession, however, she quickly added that she would not automatically drop the claim if North Colonie came up with a fair solution. "Everything is subject to negotiation."

Outcome The case was settled out of court in February 1998. The teen athlete was allowed to play on the team of his choice, but won none of $600,000 his mother had sought.

All in the Family

In 1997, a Los Angeles attorney (and mother) was at a family gathering at her daughter's house, sitting on the couch playing with her daughter's dog. The dog, which was later described as a "mutt" only slightly larger than a lapdog, became excited and bit the mother on the nose. Blood was drawn, photos were duly taken of the shaken and grief-stricken barrister still clutching her nose, and the mutt was promptly put outside.

Given the old adage of never representing yourself lest you end up with a fool for a client, the injured attorney then retained what she described as "one of the best trial attorneys in the Los Angeles area." She needed somebody good, after all, to represent her in a lawsuit against her daughter. Apparently, she found a good attorney, too, because he managed to wrest $25,000 out of the daughter's homeowner's insurance company.

There's more. Since the incident occurred at a family get-together, the lawyer's son also happened to be present at the "mauling." And despite the fact that he was in his thirties, he sued his sister, claiming to have suffered severe emotional distress at the sight of his mother being nipped on the honker by Fido.

Outcome The distressed plaintiff received $2,000 from his sister's insurance carrier for his grief. The bottom line: some people just don't know when to stop mothering, while others simply don't know when to stop lawyering.

VACATIONING LAWYERS

After all that suing, attorneys need a few days of rest and relaxation . . .

Hey, Was That a Lobster or a Lawyer?

A Milwaukee attorney filed a lawsuit in October 1997 claiming that his sun protection factor 2 sunscreen "provided no prevention of sun burning." The roasted plaintiff demanded that the manufacturer of Nivea Sun lotion pay him $5,000 as reimbursement for his red-hot vacation.

Maybe our fair-skinned filer should have read the label on the lotion before stepping out of the shade. It states that factor 2 is suitable only for people who rarely burn or already have deep base tans.

Outcome The plaintiff found no relief in court. The judge dismissed the case with prejudice.

Going Overboard

A southern California attorney went for a morning sail on his friend's boat in 1999. The weather was fair, the sea breeze gentle. Yet it wasn't long before the pair hit some stormy legal seas. As they approached the boat slip, the attorney decided he would help out by tying the craft to the dock. But as he leaped ashore, he slipped and injured himself.

Now, it doesn't take the keen eye of a sailor to see what lay over the horizon. The friend claimed the attorney had jumped on his own free will. The lawyer, however, contended that he was "ordered by the skipper" to jump, thus constituting negligence on his friend's part.

Outcome The trial took five days and cost $30,500 in court fees. And in the end, the lawyer had to walk the proverbial plank: it took the jury just forty-five minutes to decide in the friend's favor.

Messy Briefs

Another leisurely lawyer resorted to suing her travel agency for $100,000 after her 1993 vacation left her with an uncomfortable malady. According to her lawsuit, the fifty-year-old attorney had bought an "all meal included [sic]" tour package to Jamaica from FDR Holidays. Unfortunately, while in Jamaica the island's electricity went out overnight. The next day, the vacationing barrister sat down to one of her prepaid tropical meals and ordered a local fish dish. She was prescient enough to ask the waiter whether the fish was still fresh, given that the island had been without refrigeration for much of the previous night. The waiter assured her that the fish was "okay," so she ate it.

Back on the mainland, the lawyer claimed she subsequently developed "permanent diarrhea." She claimed she was unable to digest foods and could no longer enjoy the meals she used to relish. So, in other words, she sued the travel agency because a restaurant in another country allegedly served her bad fish.

The defendants, on the other hand, called the plaintiff's allegations fishy. During the three-day trial, FDR Holidays pointed out that none of the runny attorney's medical results had revealed any microbes that could have caused a permanent digestive disorder. (Besides, how could the company foresee the plaintiff would eat fish she thought had spoiled?) Therefore, the defense argued, she was just in midlife and, according to their independent medical examiner, had become lactose intolerant.

Outcome In May 1998, after a three-day trial, the court failed to buy the woman's fishy tale and dismissed the case.

> *Why does a hearse horse snicker,*
> *Hauling a lawyer away?*
>
> —Carl Sandburg

TRIALS AND TRIBULATIONS: A POTPOURRI OF OUTRAGEOUS LAWSUITS

The ultimate result of shielding men from the effects of folly is to fill the world with fools.

—Herbert Spencer

Mr. Spencer may have a point, since by now it should be apparent to the reader that the idea of zero accountability is becoming an increasingly popular notion. If nothing else, the preceding few hundred lawsuits have shown not only how wacky some people's thinking can be, but also how personal responsibility is a concept that's too burdensome for far too many. The sad part is that the lawsuits we have listed aren't even the tip of the proverbial iceberg; they're more like the frosty mists wafting about the tip. After all, for every lawsuit in this book, there are thousands of others, on the surface perhaps not quite as inane, but in essence favoring the same nonaccountability idea as the others. All this, unfortunately, seems to be filling our world with the fools Mr. Spencer foretold.

Yet it appears we are all fools, in a way, because everybody is now paying higher prices for products and services that are passed along to us via an unseen lawsuit tax. Unseen perhaps, but certainly felt. It's estimated that the additional costs of this lawsuit charge in California alone come to $10 billion per year. The levy, for example, comes out to about 20 percent of the cost of a stepladder, half the cost of a football helmet, and 40 percent of the cost of a dose of DPT vaccine.

Additionally, aside from compensating millions of plaintiffs each year, these unseen costs also manage to support an entire community of professions. Aside from the attorneys, with their entourage of paralegals and legal secretaries, there are the process servers, insurance adjusters, appraisers, negotiators, investigators, accident reconstructionists, biomechanical engineers, doctors, chiropractors, court clerks, court reporters, and even the bailiffs and the judges—all living off the lawsuit industry. Add to this the peripheral support services these positions require, and we have a continent-sized iceberg hidden beneath those frosty mists.

And all the while, we continue to propagate more fools by rewarding half-witted conduct, by condoning finger pointing, and by eliminating all individual responsibility. Essentially, we're breeding ninnies by shielding people from the effects of their own follies with our benevolent notions of helpful intervention. Not surprisingly, with the myriad lawsuits being bandied about for every conceivable reason, there are now many that have gone beyond simple foolishness and are treading the bounds of absurdity.

SUPERNATURAL SUITS

Serving God

A Pennsylvania man sued God in 1996 for failing to take "corrective action" against his former employer, USX Corporation, which had fired him thirty years earlier. His lawsuit also asked the Lord to return the plaintiff's youth, resurrect his dead mother, and give him guitar-playing skills. Named as codefendants were former presidents Ronald Reagan and George Bush, Congress, all fifty states, and every single American.

Outcome A federal judge left the man's prayers unanswered yet again when he dismissed the case in March 1999.

Beware of Ghosts

A resident of Wilder, Kentucky, was drinking, line-dancing, and having a good old time at a local country music bar. Little did he know that his high spirits would soon be dashed by a . . . well, spirit.

The man sued the bar in 1993, claiming that he was beaten up by a ghost in the little boy's room. According to his account of the fateful night, the poltergeist "punched and kicked him" while he was trying to relieve himself. The plaintiff demanded $1,000 in damages and insisted that a sign be prominently displayed in the rest room to warn innocent patrons of the abusive apparition.

Outcome The lawyer for the bar managed to get the case exorcised from court. He cited the great difficulty of serving the specter with a subpoena to testify at the trial.

House of Horrors

Another man bought a large Victorian house in suburban Nyack, New York, then later claimed it was haunted by ghosts that rattled chains in the attic. He sued the former owner in 1989 seeking to undo the $650,000 sale and to collect damages for not being forewarned of his unwelcome house guests.

Outcome In 1991, the state supreme court ruled for the buyer, saying his contract was violated because the house was "possessed by poltergeists" and, therefore, was not vacant at the time the sale closed. He got his $32,000 down payment back and quickly fled his haunted house.

Aborted Flight

A twenty-five-year-old man with high hopes joined the Maharishi International University of Fairfield, Iowa, which promised to teach him several valuable skills, including how to fly via self-levitation and to reverse the aging process. But after spending the next eleven years at the school, it finally dawned on him that his guru's promises had not materialized. He sued the school in 1987, arguing that he had only learned "to hop with his legs folded in the lotus position." He claimed to have suffered psychological and emotional damage upon realizing that his twice-daily routine of chanting a single note had neither taught him to levitate nor made him any younger.

Outcome After meditating on the case for a while, the jury decided that the university had, indeed, misled the plaintiff. They awarded him $137,890, but denied the $9 million in punitive damages that he had sought.

Dead Woman Walking

A woman in Manchester, England, sued a stage hypnotist in 1996 for allegedly turning her into a zombie. The forty-year-old mother of seven attended an hour-long hypnotism show at Wyresdale Amateur Soccer and Social Club in February 1994 and volunteered to participate in the performer's skit. The hypnotist put her in a trance and asked her to act like a child. That age-regression suggestion, however, apparently reawakened the woman's memories of sexual abuse by an uncle when she was eight. Consequently, when she went home, she suffered from panic attacks and depression and twice attempted suicide. The plaintiff, who later fully recovered, blamed the hypnotist for negligence, saying, "I went to that stage show as a normal, happy, healthy, energetic woman and came out a zombie."

Outcome A high court in London sided with the plaintiff in May 2001 and ordered the hypnotist to pay her $9,000 in damages.

SCHOOL DAZE

Top of the Class

The mother of a gifted high school student sued a Pennsylvania school district in June 1999 when her son wasn't named valedictorian. According to her lawsuit, the family had agreed to forfeit the seventeen-year-old's chance of being valedictorian at William Tennent High School if he were allowed to skip his senior year to take some college courses instead. (The school's policy dictates that the valedictorian must complete his or her junior and senior years at the high school.) At the end of the year, however, the mother had second thoughts. She filed a lawsuit to force the school to recalculate her son's grade-point average, counting his A's at Pennsylvania State University as comparable to A-pluses in high school, and to name him valedictorian if he came out as the highest-ranking member of the graduating class. (He got one B in physics.)

Outcome A Bucks County Court judge refused to order a hearing on the case but gave the mom an A for effort.

Dummkopf

A student at the University of Michigan apparently thought it was easier to sue than to study. He filed a lawsuit against the school in 1990, demanding $853,000 for being given an F in German.

Outcome The plaintiff flunked out of court, too. His case was dismissed in less than an hour.

Making the Grade

Believe it or not, there's another student who took to the courts over an unacceptable grade. This time, a woman sued her professor and the University of San Jose, California, in July 1993 to gain a grade change from a B-plus to an A-minus.

Outcome The judge dismissed the lawsuit, remarking that he was responsible for upholding the law, not grade-point averages.

Add It Up

When a sixteen-year-old high school student brought home a report card with a disappointing C in math, his parents didn't ground him or send him to a tutor. They sued his teacher and San Ramon Valley High School.

The Danville, California, couple took issue with the math teacher's grading policy. Under it, no student in his precalculus class could get a higher grade than his or her homework assignments. But when the student scored an A on his final exam, he expected to receive the same grade on his report card. His homework, though, was worth only a C, and that's the grade he ended up with.

The school district's attorney argued that it wouldn't make

sense for any teacher to give students the option of taking their final exam grade as the grade for the class; that would leave students with no incentive to do their homework. But the parents held firm. "We went in and tried to make a deal. We wanted an A, they wanted a C, so why not compromise on a B," the student's father said. "But they dug in their heels and here we are." *Here* being court, of course.

Outcome In December 1993, after a year and six different appeals with the school district, another year of court proceedings, $4,000 in legal fees paid by the couple and another $8,000 by the district, the plaintiffs finally got their own report card from a Contra Costa County Superior Court judge. They flunked their lawsuit. The C stood.

Ironically, the grade had ceased to be of any importance to the plaintiffs' son long ago. By the time the verdict was in, he was already halfway through his freshman year at the University of San Diego. Yet his father vowed to fight on with an appeal.

Nothing to Cheer About

A student in Wellington, Ohio, sued her high school for a mind-boggling $1.5 million because she was cut from the cheerleading squad. The suit, filed in 1999, alleged that the teen was kicked from the team not because of poor pom-pom skills, but because of arbitrary evaluations by her teachers.

In October 1999, a Lorain County common pleas judge ruled that the plaintiff had no guarantee of a spot on the squad and that she had mistaken privileges for rights. But the undaunted cheerleader pressed on, demanding to be both reinstated to the team and granted a jury trial.

Outcome The plaintiff ultimately dropped her claim in January 2000 at the request of her lawyer. "We're going to take a break," the cheerleader's mother said at the time. "Most likely we'll go back [to filing suit] again, but we want to see what happens in court and at school."

Tha Man Kan't Spel

A Michigan man who used guesswork instead of a dictionary sued a Detroit tattoo parlor in February 1999 over a misspelled tattoo. The plaintiff, a former marine and student at Wayne State University, went to Eternal Tattoos in 1996 to get the word *villain* emblazoned on his right forearm. Before the procedure, workers at the tattoo parlor debated how to spell the word; the plaintiff wasn't sure either, so they finally settled on *villian*. The guy didn't notice the misspelling until three years later, when friends made fun of him. At that point, he had the tattoo surgically removed. Claiming that the plastic surgery had cost him $1,900 and left a scar on his arm, the man sued the tattoo parlor for $25,000.

Outcome No news on this case. Maybe he should try a simpler tattoo, like MOM.

Cut to the Chase

When a sixteen-year-old student was caught carrying three knives at her Escondido, California, high school, she did what any red-blooded gal would do. She sued the vice principal.

The litigious teen was one of several students searched after being caught smoking on campus in April 1994. She never argued whether or not she was entitled to bring knives to school, but rather claimed the vice principal had acted unreasonably in searching her—and thus discovering the knives.

Outcome Her complaint made it all the way to the Ninth Circuit Court of Appeals before being struck down once and for all. In his cutting decision, the judge called the delinquent's lawsuit "vexatious" and "a triumph of petulance over common sense." He faulted the plaintiff's parents for misleading her into feeling wronged when she was caught carrying a small arsenal of weapons. Rather than filing suit, the judge lectured, her parents "might profitably have pondered their own culpability and considered what they might have done to prevent their child's misconduct."

What a Gas!

A former student at California Polytechnic University at San Luis Obispo filed a lawsuit in September 1993, claiming the school unfairly dismissed him from its teaching certification program. The school maintained that it had dismissed the student because he had failed most of his classes. But the plaintiff alleged that the real reason for his ouster was "unsubstantiated rumors" that he ate cookies in a sloppy manner and suffered a rather irksome flatulence problem. According to his lawsuit, "There is no physical evidence that any gas was passed, nor . . . any authentication as to [its] point of origin."

Outcome The judge thought the plaintiff's lawsuit was full of hot air. Dismissed!

Blew It

A West Virginia high school marching band was practicing its moves on a muddy field during a weeklong band camp in August 1995. The instrument-laden students trudged in time to the band leader's commands: *Right-two-three-four! Left-two-three-four! Now backward!* Just then, the trombonist's feet slipped out from under him and . . . splat! He fell on his buttocks and back.

The sixteen-year-old brass-wind blower claimed he suffered spinal injuries that resulted in $20,000 in medical bills. So he sued the Kanawha County school board and county commissioners for compensation—to the tune of $250,000, or more than twelve times the cost of his treatment.

Outcome No news on this lawsuit. Good thing, though, that he wasn't playing a tuba.

Pristine Versus Sistine

A Northwestern University art student filed a lawsuit in 1998 after school officials threatened to turn his ornate fresco into another bland, off-white dormitory ceiling.

The collegiate dustup began when the sophomore painted his own version of Michelangelo's Sistine Chapel, complete with cherubs aplenty, on the ceiling of his campus dorm room. The university, however, said that marking school property— artistically or otherwise—was prohibited and that the mural had to be covered over. So rather than seeing his masterpiece obliterated, the aspiring artist hired a lawyer. This master of the legal arts, in turn, argued that the mural was protected by a little-known 1990 amendment to the Visual Artist's Rights Act, which allows for the preservation of unique works of art. Besides, the lawyer added, the university's regulations banned students from decorating the walls, woodwork, doors, and furnishings—but didn't explicitly mention anything about ceilings. (Talk about drawing fine lines.)

Outcome Northwestern University settled the lawsuit out of court by agreeing to let the painting remain on the dorm room ceiling until the end of the school year. Ironically, the much-publicized controversy caught the eye of a wealthy art lover, who offered to pay the cost of having the ceiling taken down and preserved for posterity.

COPS AND ROBBERS

A Blue Sues

An off-duty Los Angeles police officer was riding his bicycle down an eight-foot-wide bike path in sunny southern California when he came upon a pair of cyclists riding side by side in the opposite direction. In order to avoid a potential smashup, the pedaling patrolman swerved into a driveway and fell.

Apparently he was a lawman who didn't limit his lawsuits to on-duty incidents, because he immediately sued the city, which built the bike path. His lawsuit claimed the bike path was too narrow for two-way traffic. The city, on the other hand, felt the path was just fine and that the hasty cop had simply picked the wrong place for his hard-core workout. After all, the defense argued, his tumble took place on a ten-mile-per-hour bike path, on a crowded Saturday afternoon in the middle of June. Further, Mr. Tour de France was wearing toe clips, which locked his tootsies into the pedals. In short, he was being a danger to everybody on the bike path, and it's a good thing he didn't cause a pileup.

Outcome After an eleven-day trial, the officer took another fall in 1997 when the jury found in favor of the city. The case, though, cost taxpayers $66,500.

To Protect and to Serve . . . Drinks?

In 1995, four masked robbers entered a Hayward, California, bar brandishing weapons. Two of the gunmen forced the patrons to lie on the floor and relinquish their wallets, while the other two emptied the cash register and rifled through the storage room. But before they could make a clean getaway, the police arrived. After an officer shot and wounded one of the gunmen, two others ran back into the bar to take hostages. One courageous patron whipped out a pocketknife and stabbed one of the gunmen, who later died from the injury.

You'd think this would be the end of the story, but no. An attorney sued the bar on behalf of the dead robber's family, alleging that it had failed to provide a "safe environment" for the gunman. He also sued the city, claiming the police were rough in their handling of the situation.

Outcome The lawyer eventually dropped the suit against the bar when he realized it was a patron, not an employee, who had stabbed the robber. The bar's insurance company, however, still had to pay $2,500 to cover its legal fees. The suit against the city was also dropped when the lawyer saw a surveillance tape proving the robbers had acted far more roughly than the police.

Give Me the Money or I'll Sue

A man who robbed an Atlantic City bank twice over three days in June 1997 filed a $1.5-million defamation lawsuit against the teller he held up. The twenty-two-year-old robber, who listed his occupation as a professional gambler, claimed the bank clerk had falsely told police officers that he had threatened to shoot her, an allegation that resulted in more serious charges against him. His lawsuit urged the court to hold the teller "accountable for her crimes."

Outcome In June 1999, the plaintiff was sentenced to twenty-four years in prison on two counts of robbery. His defamation suit against the bank teller has yet to go to trial.

Villain Come Victim

A cab driver was parked on a side street in San Francisco in May 1989 when he spotted a tourist being robbed. He threw his taxi into gear, sped after the fleeing mugger, and managed to pin him against a building with the cab's bumper until the police arrived four minutes later.

Although the community applauded his valiant efforts, it wasn't long before the courageous cab driver regretted his good deed. The purse snatcher, whose leg was broken in the incident, sued the cabby for what he alleged was "excessive force and negligence in effecting the citizen's arrest."

Outcome In February 1992, a California jury took the cab driver for a ride by assessing him $24,595 for the mugger's injuries. The award was later overturned, but by then the taxi company had spent $68,000 defending its driver.

You Get What You Don't Pay For

In 1994, Toronto-Dominion Bank in Ontario, Canada, filed a lawsuit against a client who had borrowed $3.5 million for his business and then defaulted on his repayments. The cash-strapped client promptly filed a countersuit for $30 million. His reasoning? The bank had loaned him too much money. If the loan officers had been more prudent, he claimed, he wouldn't have been able to borrow so much.

Outcome In July 1995, a judge found in favor of the bank and ordered the debtor to pay his due.

PENNY PINCHERS

Wisdom Comes with Age

A Los Angeles man sued Sizzler restaurant in 1990 after the cashier refused to give him the $1.25 senior-citizen discount advertised on its menu. The plaintiff—who was thirty-one years old at the time—claimed that he was a victim of age discrimination.

Outcome The judge ruled in favor of the restaurant and ordered the plaintiff to pay $8,601 for "making a mockery of the system."

Video Game

In 1987, a man in Oakland, California, sued a video-rental club that issued him "one free video per month" coupons. He claimed the club defrauded him when it refused to give him two free videos in one month after he pointed out that he had not used his coupon the prior month.

Outcome A frustrated judge threw out the case, scolding the plaintiff for trying to nickel-and-dime the courts.

A Penny Saved Is a Penny Lost

The same Oakland, California, man sued a local grocery store in 1989 for swindling him out of two whole cents. The frugal plaintiff argued that the store committed fraud when it accepted his coupon for thirty cents off a six-pack of Mug root beer, but charged sales tax on the posted price, thereby cutting his savings to twenty-eight cents.

Outcome The judge threw in his own two cents when he not only dismissed the case but also prohibited the plaintiff from filing any more suits without paying a filing fee, despite his claim of being a pauper.

The Grand Poobah

There's a seventy-three-year-old New Yorker who seems to make a hobby of being a nuisance. Or, as a Queens Supreme Court justice said, "Apparently, he uses the courts to amuse himself and as part of his modus vivendi [way of life]."

The man has filed at least sixteen lawsuits in the Queens Supreme Court over the past eight years. In one, he claimed to have lost several teeth on a bad batch of tuna. In another, he sued a card store for selling him allegedly defective film. In a third, he sued a deli for not buying back his used cans and bottles. Then there was the lawsuit that claimed he suffered severe burning in his throat and chest after gulping bottled water. He even sued a cemetery for $999 billion, alleging that gardeners had interfered with his mother's burial. The guy has never won a single case.

Outcome It seems this grand poobah of the litigation world finally went a bit too far. In January 1999, a supreme court judge barred him from filing any more lawsuits until he went to a psychiatrist and proved he wasn't crazy.

PLANES, TRAINS, AND AUTOMOBILES

Objects May Shift

A Texas woman was on a Delta Air Lines flight from the Caribbean to Miami in 1990 when another passenger opened an overhead storage compartment and a case of rum fell on her head. She sued the airline for negligence.

Outcome No news on the outcome—though it's not the first time alcohol has given somebody a headache.

Bridge Over Troubled Lawsuits

The families of two aviators who died while trying to fly a small single-engine plane under a low-lying bridge filed a lawsuit in 1999, claiming the city should have prevented the accident. The pilot and his passenger had made one successful pass under the South Padre Causeway, but crashed on their second attempt. It's surprising they even made it the first time, given that autopsies revealed illegal substances in the bloodstreams of both men. That, and the fact that neither was legally certified to fly, although the plane was owned by one of the decedents. Regardless, the plaintiffs charged the city and its airport with failing to "verify" that the men were up to flying at the time they took off for their half-hour flight.

Outcome A judge threw out the case in September 1999.

Sign of the Times

Two Texas men were driving through Dallas–Fort Worth International Airport in 1993 when they crashed into the back of another motorist who had stopped outside the American Airlines terminal to read flight information posted on a large electronic board. The two men sued American Airlines, blaming their injuries on the distraction created by the company's fourteen-hundred-square-foot sign. The airline argued that the sign offered a valuable service and blamed the accident on driver inattention.

Outcome In 1996, a jury agreed with the plaintiffs and forced American Airlines to pay $20 million in damages. Strangely, the jurors also made the rear-ended motorist pay $5 million to the men who hit him.

A Bad Sign

Another misplaced sign caused a car to barrel into a freight train—if you believe the plaintiff, that is. According to the motorist's 1988 lawsuit, a bus-stop sign—which was ten inches by ten inches large—obstructed his view of the approaching train as he drove over the tracks. (Apparently, the huge railroad markings and the flashing red warning lights were only there for ambience.) The motorist, who survived the crash, sued the local bus company for placing the sign in a dangerous place.

Outcome A judge dismissed the case when he discovered that the plaintiff had also been watching a portable television perched on his passenger seat at the time of the accident!

Pole Position

A Los Angeles motorcyclist lost control of his bike and hit a curb. Thrown from his bike, he was airborne until touching down against a bus-stop sign. He sued the bus company in 1994 for bad placement of the pole.

Outcome Yeah, we know, if the pole hadn't been there it would have been a perfect three-point landing, and everything would have been just fine. The case was dismissed.

Space Case

A schoolteacher sued her condominium association in 1993 for swindling her out of eighteen inches of prime Chicago real estate. Without seeking her permission, the association had narrowed the woman's parking space from 111 inches to 93 inches in order to accommodate a new space for the board president's car. The woman complained about the unilateral decision but was ignored. So rather than ding a few car doors, she filed a lawsuit against the housing association, the board president, and three board members.

Outcome In August 1996, a Cook County Circuit Court judge put the squeeze on the defendants. The condo association was ordered to add nine inches to both sides of the woman's parking space, pay her $51,006 in punitive damages, and pick up her legal fees of $166,171! The board president now parks around the block.

Enter at Your Own Risk

The family of a slain Dutch tourist sued Alamo Rent-A-Car in Florida for failing to warn the victim about the dangers of Liberty City, a low-income, high-crime area near Miami. The forty-one-year-old victim was shot by robbers in 1996 when her husband stopped their rental car at a Liberty City gas station to ask for directions. The death was a tragedy, but the tourists had rented the car across the state in Tampa!

Outcome Regardless, a jury ordered Alamo to pay the plaintiffs $5.2 million in May 2000. (We wonder what kind of legal trouble Alamo would have gotten into if it had warned customers to stay out of certain neighborhoods?)

Sailor Suit

In February 2001, the family of a deceased boater filed a wrongful-death lawsuit against the city of East Providence, Rhode Island, arguing that the sailor's fatal 1998 heart attack was caused by the city's assistant harbor master. According to police reports, however, all the harbor master did was yell at the sailor, who was maneuvering his boat without using the required navigational lights. Among the sailor's last words was this comment to the harbor master: "Mind your own [expletive deleted] business."

Outcome Ahoy there. No news on this case yet.

THE FAMOUS AND THE INFAMOUS

Long Live the King

A retired air force major in Fort Worth, Texas, sued the estate of Elvis Presley in July 1993 for cutting into his business. He alleged the estate's "claim" that Elvis died in 1977 was false and interfered with his attempts to sell books on the famous rock-and-roller's current whereabouts. "That company has made hundreds of millions of dollars perpetrating fraud," said the plaintiff, who produced some of Presley's early records in the mid-1950s. "There is no bit of proof that Elvis is dead. I have to do what I can to get the truth out."

Outcome No news on the outcome of this lawsuit, but we figure it's as dead as Elvis.

Picking on the Pope

It was a case that rocked Texas. A Catholic priest from San Antonio was accused of child abuse. The attorney for the child argued that not only was the priest liable, but so was his employer—Pope John Paul II. She pointed to a 1976 Supreme Court ruling that allowed for employers to be held responsible for the actions of their employees. According to that ruling, the lawyer argued, she should be able to name the pontiff as a defendant.

Outcome In March 1994, a Texas judge dismissed the case, ruling that the pope was not only the head of the Catholic Church but also a head of state, the Vatican. Therefore, he said, it wouldn't be appropriate to subpoena His Excellency to testify in a lawsuit in Texas.

This Bomb's for You

Isn't there something odd about self-avowed enemies of the state insisting on exercising their once disdained constitutional rights by filing lawsuits? Well, that's precisely what Ramzi Yousef, who committed one of the worst terrorist attacks on American soil, proceeded to do in January 1999.

The mastermind behind the 1993 bombing of New York's World Trade Center, Yousef sued the federal government from his cell in a Florence, Colorado, superpenitentiary. According to his sour-grapes lawsuit, the prison's rules "vexed, harassed, annoyed, intimidated, and infringed upon" his rights. It seems his fellow inmates—who included the likes of Timothy Mc-Veigh (the Oklahoma City bomber) and Ted Kaczynski (the Unabomber)—were enjoying more privileges than he was. So the disgruntled terrorist, believed to be an Iraqi native, demanded $1.1 million on the grounds that he had more rules to live by—namely, speaking only in English with immediate family members and being barred from communicating by mail with anybody outside the prison.

Outcome No news on the outcome of this lawsuit yet. We think he should be grateful that he hasn't been given the same treatment that Timothy McVeigh was ultimately afforded.

Funny Bunny

A former *Playboy* cover model and ex-girlfriend of Hugh Hefner sued the author and publisher of *Inside the Playboy Mansion* in March 1999, claiming the book offended her new-found piety. The book featured several photos of the ex-bunny au naturel, though that in itself was not the cause of her consternation. Rather, she objected to a photo taken of her in the bedroom she once shared with Hefner during the mid-1980s. "I have a seven-year-old daughter, a nine-year-old stepdaughter, and a thirteen-year-old stepson, and that son is at a very vulnerable age," lamented the uncovered cover girl.

Of course, the mortified bunny's morality had its limits. It turns out that the protective mother had a business on the side: she ran a Web site that featured X-rated pictures. So sometimes she's shy, sometimes she's not. Apparently, it depends on if there's somebody to sue.

Outcome None at this time. We don't suspect, though, that this lawsuit will spare the plaintiff's kids from the gory details of her past escapades.

Nothing to Hide

It's amazing how previously cherished nudie shots tend to haunt those in the limelight. Just ask Marsha Clark, Laura Schlessinger, or the lead singer of the rock band Aerosmith. The latter, much like the ex-bunny, was also in the throes of a lawsuit—except he was considerably more concerned about his exposed privates. His ex-wife wanted to publish a tell-all book called *Dream On,* in which she planned to include a nude photo of the long-famous singer.

He filed a lawsuit in August 1998, claiming that his ex-wife had promised to return the photo as part of their divorce settlement in 1987. His objection to the snapshot, he said, was a moral concern that his children would feel "severe embarrassment" if they saw it. The ex-wife, however, had a different theory. She claimed it wasn't the kids who would be mortified, but rather ex-hubby himself. "He's embarrassed because he's no Tommy Lee, you know what I'm saying?" she said, referring to Pamela Anderson's rocker ex-husband. "The only big thing he has in the world is his career."

Outcome The judge, however, must have felt that the belittled rock star had *something* worth hiding. In March 1999, he enjoined the defendant from using the controversial photo in her memoir.

Aerosmith Live

In October 1998, a man from Walnut Creek, California, sued Aerosmith and the Concord Pavilion, the open-air amphitheater that hosted the rock band's concert, claiming that the show had caused him permanent hearing loss. The loud amplifiers, coupled with He's-No-Tommy-Lee's crooning, supposedly left the man with a constant ringing in his ears. Amazingly, none of the other thousands of fans suffered similar problems. Yet the tender-eared fan sought an unspecified amount for medical costs and loss of wages. Maybe he was one of those dedicated fans who like to sit inside the speakers.

Outcome The case is probably headed for court, lining up behind all the other Aerosmith lawsuits.

Public Beeper Number One

There's a roadside attraction in Los Angeles who calls himself the King of Beepers. His sunny face grins down from billboards, usually with a bikini-clad woman straddling a giant pager, enticing passersby to try his wares.

This "king" definitely enjoys his fame and isn't shy about having his mug displayed in larger-than-life likenesses around the city. So why did a guy like this sue for libel and invasion of privacy? Apparently, he didn't like how an HBO documentary about Heidi Fleiss had insinuated that he was "Cookie," the famed Hollywood madam's former bodyguard. The movie had shown a close-up of the King's face on one of his billboards as the narrator said, "With Cookie on my mind, I imagined I saw him everywhere." The King said he didn't even know Fleiss, but yes, he did know Cookie. Either way, he claimed the documentary had represented him in a light inconsistent with his true character. So he sued the filmmaker.

Outcome A superior court judge tossed out the lawsuit in July 1997, ruling that the self-proclaimed King of Beepers was a public figure who evidently took great pleasure in his celebrity. As such, he should expect some rumors about his background.

Can't Stand the Commotion

The wealthy neighbors of Martin Frankel, the famed financier who fled to Germany in May 1999 with hundreds of millions of dollars in other people's money, sued the former fugitive for lowering their property values. In a lawsuit filed in July 1999, three homeowners claimed Frankel's illegal dealings and subsequent disappearance attracted hordes of law enforcement officials and journalists to their stony cul-de-sac in suburban New York. They sought millions of dollars in damages from the now-imprisoned Frankel, alleging that the international manhunt he had caused ruined the tranquillity of their upscale neighborhood and depreciated the value of their multimillion-dollar homes by 20 percent. "These people have paid a premium to enjoy the privacy and seclusion that Frankel took from them," said the plaintiffs' lawyer.

Outcome The angry homeowners are still waiting to have their day in court. It seems their disrupted neighborhood failed to take precedence over the federal charges of racketeering, securities fraud, and money laundering that are pending against Frankel.

WHOOPEE WOES

Maybe She Was Only Borrowing It

A man in Albuquerque, New Mexico, filed a lawsuit accusing his ex-girlfriend of stealing his sperm—and not from a vial at a donor clinic either.

The thirty-six-year-old plaintiff tried to dodge a paternity suit by claiming his live-in lover committed breach of contract, fraud, and conversion of property (his semen) by getting pregnant against his will. According to his lawsuit, filed in September 1998, the man agreed to have sex with his thirty-seven-year-old girlfriend only if she took birth-control pills—but she abused his princely offer by "intentionally acquiring and misusing his semen" when she secretly discontinued her contraceptive medication.

The woman, however, said taking the pill was her idea and that the pregnancy was an accident. Her lawyers had a slightly more elaborate take; they argued that the man had, in essence, given his sperm to the defendant as a "gift" and had "surrendered any right of possession . . . when he transferred it . . . during voluntary sexual intercourse." (Maybe his girlfriend should have gotten a receipt.)

And as if this theft-of-bodily-fluids charge wasn't enough to make a judge's head spin, there was the plaintiff's mercurial behavior: He urged his girlfriend to abort after learning of the pregnancy, then offered to marry her. When she refused, he threw her out. Then, despite having filed a lawsuit against being named the father, he demanded visitation rights. And that's not all. The plaintiff went on to seek monetary compensation. He claimed that his ex-girlfriend—who by then had given birth to a girl—should reimburse him for the "economic injury" he would sustain by having to pay child support. In other words, he wanted her to pay him the money that he paid her to take care of his daughter.

Outcome The judge didn't go for it. "I think the argument is clever," he admitted, "but it has been the experience of this court that cleverness has its limitations." The judge dismissed the case in order to prevent "misappropriation of sperm" from becoming the latest tort du jour: "The issue of use of birth control is better left to consenting adults."

Headboard-Banging Fun

One more whoopee tribulation. A thirty-six-year-old man sued the Red Roof Inn in Hartford, Connecticut, claiming that a flimsy headboard had caused the loss of a small portion of his index finger. According to his 1998 lawsuit, the man was making gentle and passionate love to his girlfriend when the wooden headboard came crashing down on them and fractured his digit. The injury ultimately led to the removal of his fingertip.

The plaintiff offered to settle the suit for $50,000, but the Ohio-based hotel chain refused, arguing that it was the man's questionable behavior that had caused the 1996 accident. According to the hotel's attorney, "In order for [the headboard] to fall, there had to be some serious acrobatics taking place."

Outcome No news on the outcome of this case, but as far as we know, the girlfriend survived in one piece.

TRESPASSERS BEWARE

Quite a Shocker

In 1996, a Florida man was shocked by thirteen thousand volts of electricity after breaking into a utility substation and climbing up a power transformer in a drunken stupor. Even more shocking, however, was the lawsuit he filed four years later against the Tampa Electric Company and six local bars that had allegedly sold him alcoholic beverages on that fateful night. The suit charged the utility company with failing to prevent the man from slipping into the fenced and locked substation. The liquor vendors were accused of negligently selling him booze even though he was "unable to control his urge to drink alcoholic beverages."

Outcome We're anxious to hear the outcome, if any. But in the meantime we'll be pondering what, if anything, the plaintiff figures he is responsible for.

A Midsummer Night's Suit

On a warm July night in 1985, seven friends squeezed through a hole in a fence to take an illegal dip in the Bronx municipal pool. Given that it was one o'clock in the morning, the lights were off and no lifeguards were on duty. One of the trespassers, a thirty-two-year-old woman, stepped into the shallow end, slipped under the surface, and drowned.

The deceased woman was later determined to have had a blood-alcohol level of 0.23, twice the legal limit for driving. Regardless of that—and the fact that she had broken onto private property—the departed's survivors sued the city of New York. They claimed the city was negligent for failing to keep trespassers out of the pool area or to have a lifeguard on duty after the park was officially closed!

Outcome The jurors must have been a little tipsy themselves, because they awarded the family $2 million. In October 1994, however, an appellate court threw out the award, determining that the woman had assumed the risk of her actions and was thereby solely responsible for her own death. The five-judge panel ruled that her "reckless and culpable" behavior was an unforeseeable event that absolved the city of any blame.

Running Wild

After mistakenly letting his two dogs slip from the house, a Michigan man chased his furry friends across a neighbor's property. While in hot pursuit, the frenzied dog owner stepped into a snow-covered hole, tripped, and fell. He filed a negligence lawsuit against his neighbor in 1998 for failing to maintain a hazard-free yard.

Outcome An appeals court agreed with the lower court's decision to dismiss the case, ruling that the property owner wasn't to blame for mishaps that befell trespassers on his yard.

BAD SPORTS

Second-String Suit

While some parents have long been notorious sideline coaches at their kids' sporting events, there may be a new game in town—lawsuits. An outraged couple in Gibsonberg, Ohio, sued the coaches of their son's high school baseball team because the boy allegedly spent too much time "warming the bench." The parents, who claimed they were "humiliated" by their son's lack of playing time, filed suit in 1998 on the grounds that the coaches' decision to designate some kids as substitute players violated the U.S. Constitution.

Outcome Although there's no news yet, we figure the case is going to make some groundbreaking precedent. Now, let's see, was it the First or Fourth Amendment that guaranteed kids equal time on the playing field?

You're Outta There!

A Texas high school baseball player filed a federal lawsuit in August 1997, claiming his constitutional rights were violated when he was benched before a key playoff game for making disparaging remarks about his coach. The plaintiff, a starting pitcher for the Cypress Falls High School baseball team, said he was kept out of the game after blaming the coach for a losing season that he claimed cost him his scholarship. "To Coach [name omitted], I leave a $40,000 debt. I figure you cost me that much with your 3–7 season," the athlete wrote in his 1996 senior prom "Memory Book." The plaintiff and his parents also sought compensation for the "humiliation" of having to explain why he was benched during the big game.

Outcome A U.S. district court judge ruled that the punished pitcher didn't have the constitutional right to take the mound. In his decision, the judge wrote, "Federal judges issue opinions and orders, not starting lineups."

Take a Bow

A mother and stepfather in Bellevue, Washington, sat in the bleachers watching their nine-year-old daughter's judo competition in sheer horror. They braced one another, barely able to contain themselves. No, it wasn't because the young girl had been pinned to the floor and punched silly. It was far worse: the fourth-grader had been forced to bow before approaching the mat.

That sportman's gesture, the peeved parents complained, was a violation of their child's religious freedom. And though others in judo insist that bowing is no more religious than shaking your competitor's hand after a tennis match, the parents sued the U.S. Judo Federation in 1997. Apparently, they believed a kid ought to be able to get on the mat and try to kick his opponent's teeth out without the tremendous personal affront of having to bow.

Outcome In the end, a federal judge had to play referee. He dismissed the case, ruling that the plaintiffs and the judo federation should wrestle over the issue outside of court.

The Windup

A teenager in Levittown, Pennsylvania, who said bad coaching cost her a college scholarship sued her former softball coach in May 2001, seeking $700,000 in damages. The nineteen-year-old athlete claimed that her pitching coach taught her an incorrect technique that meant she couldn't pitch in college. She also said the coach used favorite players, causing her emotional distress. "This is ridiculous," said the school board's president. The lawsuit "will do nothing but hurt a lot of innocent people who volunteer their time to try and help kids."

Outcome It's too soon to know the outcome of this case. Let's face it, kid, you either have it or you don't.

Lather, Rinse, Litigate

Don't expect to leave smelling good after a workout at the Town Center Club of Bonaventure and Century Village in

Pembroke Pines, Florida. Citing liability concerns, the club-house has banned the use of soap in its gym showers. "We do not provide soap in the shower because, God forbid, someone might slip," said the club's vice president.

These precautions aren't as extreme as they may seem. The Town Center Club paid out $50,000 to settle just such a claim after a resident who slipped in the shower filed suit in 1998. The clubhouse has removed all soap from its shower stalls and has posted signs warning bathers not to dare smuggle in their own. "We'll document the people using soap," said the club's executive director, "so if they slip they'll know the warnings won't look good in a jury's eye."

THE OUTRAGEOUSLY OUTRAGED

Playground Battleground

A three-year-old girl was playing in the sandbox at Charles River Park in Boston when a three-year-old boy kicked sand at her. The mother of the young girl scolded the naughty as-sailant. But the boy's mother, not one to allow her son to be taken to task by another parent, yelled back. The war of words culminated in a lawsuit. In 1996, the girl's mother sought a "citywide" restraining order against the other mother and her troublesome tyke—one that would cover "all times and places."

Outcome As petty as the argument sounded, a Suffolk Superior Court judge actually granted the restraining order over the sandbox skirmish. The media accused both the judge and the plaintiff of small-mindedness and expressed hope that, for the child's sake, "a lack of common sense is not hereditary."

A Rare Beef

A Chicago insurance agent decided he needed to get away for a while and relax due to his high blood pressure. So in 1995 he took a vacation with a couple of friends to Lake Geneva, Wisconsin, where the group went to a steakhouse for dinner.

Here, the high-strung plaintiff ordered a steak medium-well done, but was allegedly served meat that was well done. Obviously accustomed to having his way, he launched into a full-scale tirade. According to the restaurant's owner, the ranting patron began "running up and down the main dining room with his cellular phone and complaining to the waitress about the table, the salads, the meal, everything. . . ." He even smarted off to the customers and "went up to a local business owner and told him he probably didn't know what a cellular phone was." Then the troublemaker dialed 911 and summoned the local police. This strategy proved equally fruitless when the responding officers told him to eat his food, pay the bill, shut up, and leave.

Not having achieved the results he had hoped for, the man resorted to seeking vindication in the hallowed halls of the federal courts. Claiming the incident caused, among other things, his blood pressure to rise, he sued the restaurant owner, the police officers, the chief of police, the police department, the town of Lake Geneva, and the town's board.

Outcome When a district court judge dismissed his case, the relentless plaintiff turned to a federal appellate court. Here, the judge had some choice words for the discriminating steak connoisseur. He called the appellant a "wise guy," and opined that his "goofy" lawsuit "trivializes the constitutional rights he asks us to vindicate. If your meal is not tasty, you do not throw a tantrum, upset the other diners, and then sue the mayor of the town." The court ordered the plaintiff and his attorney to pay $16,082.74 to cover some of the legal costs of the people they had sued.

For Your Amusement

One thousand tickets at the Boomer's Family Recreation Center in Florida could buy handfuls of candy, yo-yos, plastic men with parachutes attached to their backs, and a slew of other trinkets. No wonder, then, why one Boca Raton parent filed a lawsuit when his now "emotionally traumatized" six-year-old son was cheated out of 850 redeemable tickets.

The saga began in March 2000, when the father and son spent a rainy day at Boomer's, a recreation center and game arcade. While playing one game, the boy won 1,000 tickets; the machine, however, apparently spit out only a voucher worth 150 tickets. The father asked Boomer's employees to give him another voucher for the 850 tickets that weren't counted. When he was turned down, he got belligerent and began shouting profanities. The mad dad and his son were asked to leave the arcade and never return.

In December 2000, the man sued Boomer's for one thousand tickets and to have the company pay for his legal fees. He claimed that his six-year-old "was traumatized, began crying uncontrollably, felt ashamed and was embarrassed" when the pair was escorted out by Boomer's employees. (The fact that he was shouting obscenities apparently had nothing to do with the boy's upset.) As the fuming father so aptly put it: "It does seem ridiculous that a parent would spend a couple thousand dollars to see his son get a $10 prize back, but what would I be teaching him if I just let it go?" Self-restraint, perhaps?

Outcome The case is still winding its way to court. In the meantime, we hope junior is learning a valuable lesson.

Bottom's Up

A Georgia auto mechanic sued his seventy-eight-year-old mother, seeking $2,613 as payment due for repairing her truck. The miffed matron agreed that her son should indeed get what he deserved: She filed a countersuit in 1991 stating, "The plaintiff is indebted to the defendant for 40 years of services rendered as a mother, guidance counselor, cook, maid, banker, nurse, bail bonds-woman, baby-sitter, laundry worker, and psychologist, all of which the plaintiff has not paid for." It went on to read, "As a mother, and provided the law will allow me, I would publicly [like to] give my son the whipping that he so rightly needs and which I failed to give him as a child."

In case the judge wouldn't allow her to take the spanking into her own hands, she provided an alternative. The spitting-mad mother suggested the court "appoint a bailiff or other official to apply to my son the hickory whipping."

Outcome She ultimately won the lawsuit, but the judge suspended the spanking, sparing the wayward son one heck of a sore bottom.

THAT NASTY HABIT

Second-Paw Smoke

Flight attendants and waitresses apparently aren't the only victims of secondhand smoke. A woman in Pasadena, California, has added a new "breed" to the rash of tobacco-related lawsuits flooding the courts. She sued her condominium association in 1998, claiming her neighbor's taste for cigarettes not only bothered her but killed her dog. She alleged that the poisoned pooch died of bronchitis, although no veterinarian would confirm her grim diagnosis.

Outcome No conclusion to this lawsuit yet. What was the dog doing? Hanging out at the neighbor's place?

Waiting to Inhale

For more than twenty years, a retired army colonel in Chicago had begged his wife to quit smoking. Nothing worked. So he sued her. The sixty-nine-year-old man claimed that smoke from his wife's cigarettes violated the Clean Air Act and requested that the court force her to kick the habit. Although tobacco smoke is not regulated under the Clean Air Act, the man was undeterred. He claimed he filed the suit because he loved his wife of forty-three years and didn't want to see her die from cancer.

The man's lawyer, however, had other things in mind besides the defendant's health. He said he hoped the wife didn't quit, so that federal courts could begin to regulate cigarette smoking by individuals: "I'd like to see this issue resolved by the courts."

Outcome Much to the chagrin of his lawyer, the worried husband dropped his lawsuit in October 1997 when his wife finally agreed to curb her nicotine habit.

To Love, Honor, and Light Up

A Medina, Ohio, couple claimed that their daughter's wedding day was ruined by smoking restrictions at the reception. Apparently, the banquet hall had banned smoking a week before their daughter's August 1999 nuptials. That meant some of the guests missed the newlyweds' cake cutting and the traditional flinging of the garter because they were puffing outside. It also caused the bridal dance to be held up while the bride's own father was brought in from the parking lot, where he too, was smoking. "We basically had two parties," the father lamented.

The couple were so upset, in fact, that they sued Vell's Party Center for breaching its contract when it put a stop to indoor smoking. Vell's owner, however, argued that the local fire marshal had ordered him to restrict smoking to the entrance of the building because of a prior reception at which a guest had become ill from cigarette smoke.

Outcome A Medina Municipal Court magistrate stubbed out the case in January 2000, saying he couldn't put a monetary value on smoking. "As for the guests who were smokers and missed important events that occurred at the wedding reception," he added, "perhaps they should have remembered why they were there or have been paying attention."

INTERNATIONAL INCIDENTS

Hug a Goose, File a Suit

Whether it's storming whaling vessels or chaining themselves to trees, conservationists have been known to take some pretty desperate measures when it comes to saving wildlife. But in 1995, an environmentalist group in Mito, Japan, turned "desperate" into downright dumb when they attempted to secure government funding for wetlands preservation.

Believing that the best advocates for the cause were those who actually inhabited the wetlands, the group filed a $214,290 lawsuit on behalf of a flock of geese. The group argued that since the migratory birds were recognized under wildlife protection laws, they should be accepted as a party to the lawsuit.

Outcome The judge dismissed the case, citing that the geese had not hired anyone to represent them and would mostly likely fail to appear at trial.

Divorce Canadian Style

A Canadian woman convicted of shooting her estranged husband in the face filed suit in January 2001 to receive spousal support from the man she nearly killed. The fifty-one-year-old woman used a .22-caliber hunting rifle to shoot her spouse at close range as she moved her belongings out of their Ontario home in November 1995, shortly after they separated. The victim was left with severe facial disfigurement and a bullet lodged in his spine. The woman was paroled in April 1999. But rather than continue to live off the monthly $535 welfare checks she was receiving, she sued her ex-husband, who was earning $40,000 a year as a security guard, for financial assistance.

Outcome The case has yet to go to trial. But as bizarre it seems, the plaintiff may actually win. The fact that she tried to murder her husband may be a moot point, because Canada's divorce law is "no fault" and does not take prior behavior into account. Nor is there any statute of limitations for filing a claim. "Her conduct isn't admissible under the Divorce Act," said a Toronto family lawyer. "Technically speaking, the fact that she shot him in the face doesn't bar her from a support case."

Holy War

Three theologians in Germany filed a defamation lawsuit against the Protestant and Catholic Churches for allegedly bringing the name of Jesus into disrepute. The plaintiffs, who called themselves Christ's "brothers in spirit," sued under a vague law that permits people to defend their dead relatives' reputations. They argued that the churches' role in wars had disqualified them from calling themselves Christian. "In view of their bloody history, it's a fraud," one of the men told a court in Munich.

Outcome The judge threw out the case in May 2000, citing the German constitution's guarantee of religious freedom. Showing himself to be a better theologian than the three wise men, the judge also noted that since Christians believe Jesus rose from the dead, his "brothers" had no grounds to bring a suit on His behalf.

Try to Relax

A spa masseuse in Australia filed a workers' compensation lawsuit against her boss in 2000, claiming that she suffered stress and depression from having to hear clients gripe about their personal problems.

Outcome It's probably the plaintiff's boss whose griping now. A jury awarded the tense masseuse the equivalent of $15,600 in compensation for her work-related "injuries."

Taste Test

A man who worked for a beer company in Brazil sued his former employer in 1999, claiming that years of "tasting" up to 3.2 gallons of beer a day turned him into an alcoholic. The plaintiff knew what the job would entail when he accepted the position of senior brewer for Brahma twenty years before. In his suit, he said he had to conduct quality tests on the company's products by sipping from the beer vats each day. All that imbibing finally got to the guy, and the company forced him to retire at age forty.

Outcome A court in Brasilia ruled that Brahma should have warned its taste-tester of the risks associated with his job. The plaintiff was awarded $30,000 in damages and a monthly pension for life equal to his old salary of $2,600.

Tissue Trauma

A Hong Kong man was eating hash browns at a McDonald's restaurant in 2000 when he felt something odd in his mouth. He spit out his food and found a tiny piece of tissue paper mixed with it. The man quickly called state authorities to complain, asked that the paper be tested for germs, and checked himself into a hospital complaining of a sore throat and, in the words of the *South China Morning Post,* "an urge to be sick." Discharged from the hospital the same day, he sued McDonald's.

Outcome A magistrate threw out the case in January 2001, ruling that it was a "trivial matter" and that the plaintiff had been "overanxious." The judge also ordered a state bureaucracy, which had brought the case on his behalf, to reimburse the restaurant for $30,000 in legal costs.

ANIMAL CRACKERS

But Is He House-Trained?

In 1992, an Israeli man took his wife of twelve years to divorce court because she had named her fluffy white poodle after him. For the husband, it was the final insult in a troubled marriage. Howling mad, he demanded the court to order her to stop calling the dog by his name.

Outcome No news on this case. How do you suppose the dog felt being called by the husband's name?

Catfight

A California man sued the Escondido Public Library for $1.5 million after his dog was clobbered by the library's feline mascot L. C. (short for Library Cat). The dustup occurred in November 2000, when the handicapped man entered the library with his assistance dog, Kimba, a fifty-pound Labrador mix. Seconds later, L. C. pounced from his perch atop some books and launched a full frontal attack on Kimba. The dog was later treated for scratches to his face, amounting to a $38 veterinarian bill.

Kimba's owner, however, wasn't so easily pacified. He claimed that he was emotionally traumatized by the cat attack and suffered from "flashbacks, terror, nightmares, and other problems" as a result. Besides the $1.5 million in damages, he demanded that L. C. be declawed and that signs be posted in the library warning patrons of potential danger.

Outcome No news on the outcome of this case, but we suspect that Kimba's owner is barking up the wrong tree.

Pet Peeved

Rocky was a miniature Chihuahua with machismo. The moment he laid eyes on Canella, a fine female rottweiler tied to the deck of her owner's home across the way, he knew he had to have her. So as soon as Canella's owner stepped inside, tiny Rocky made his move. He sidled up to the object of his desire, mounted her, and, well, you can guess the rest. At that very moment, a passing animal-control agent noticed the consummating canines and stopped to watch, fascinated by the disproportionate pair. Once he had gotten an eyeful, he alerted Canella's owner, who ran outside with a camera to take photos. The animal-control officer turned a garden hose on the passionate pair, ultimately separating them.

A month later, Canella's owner was shocked to learn that his ravaged rottweiler was pregnant. He sued Rocky's owner, claiming that the feisty Chihuahua had stolen Canella's virtue, thereby limiting her chances of being bred to "an acceptable male so that a litter might be sold." But Rocky's owner fought back at the 1994 trial, presenting character witnesses who shed a dark light on Canella's alleged chastity. Several witnesses testified that other dogs in the neighborhood had also "known" Canella, including a small shih tzu with a bad hip.

Outcome Even so, Rocky's owner was ordered to pay $2,600 for the loss of Canella's future "acceptable" breeding possibilities. As for Rocky, he's got reason to brag: he's living proof that size doesn't matter.

Black Magic

A man in Hatfield, Massachusetts, sued the state electric company in May 2001 over the death of his "lucky" pet cat. Apparently, the man's wife had taken the year-old black cat, named Venus Viola, to work, where the animal was accidentally electrocuted by an uninsulated wire. The plaintiff claimed that Venus Viola was "a good luck charm" and said "she would have gained me $250,000 if she had lived." He sought reimbursement for that lost $250,000.

Outcome Failing to believe that the cat's unfortunate demise warranted a quarter-million-dollar award, a superior court judge sent the case to district court, which handles small claims and cases involving less than $25,000 in damages. No news on the final outcome of the catty claim.

A Whale of a Suit

The parents of a drifter who was found dead in the killer whale tank at SeaWorld sued the Florida marine park in September 1999 for having portrayed the orca as "lovable." The deceased man, whose last known address was a Hare Krishna temple in Miami, had apparently hid out overnight at SeaWorld to take a late-night skinny-dip with the whale, named Tillicum. The next morning, his lifeless body was found draped naked over the back of the enormous mammal. Authorities concluded that he had suffered from hypothermia and drowned. The grieving parents sued SeaWorld in Orange County Circuit Court, seeking $60 million for their pain and suffering. Their lawyer claimed the marine park was responsible for the accident because it portrayed Tillicum "as being a huggable, kissable, human-loving, friendly, I'll-let-you-ride-on-my-back whale."

SeaWorld, however, thought the facts spoke for themselves. "A fellow trespasses on our property, scales two very clear barriers, takes off his clothes, and jumps into 50-degree water with an 11,000-pound killer whale," the park's general manager said. "This is an incredibly unwise thing to do."

Outcome The plaintiffs dropped their lawsuit one month later, apparently realizing that orcas are called *killer* whales for a reason.

Catfight Redux

A man in Vancouver, British Columbia, sued his own mother for closing a car door on the paw of his cat, Daisy.

Outcome In November 1993, the court awarded the son $632 in medical costs and other expenses. His mother, in turn, lost her 40 percent "good driver" insurance discount due to the auto-related mishap. Ironically, Daisy didn't benefit much from the award; she was subsequently run over by a car.

BARFLIES

Limit Schmimit

A tavern owner sued the state of Arkansas in 1992, claiming that its sobriety checkpoints caused people to drink less and thus cut into his business. (We bet he ends up walking the line every time he steps into his car.)

Outcome A judge tossed the case out.

Undesignated Driver

In June 1995, the family of a deceased radio station executive sued a Bridgeport, Connecticut, pub and one of its waiters for causing the man's death. According to the suit, a waiter at Cobb's Mill Inn committed negligence when he decided to drive the blitzed businessman home as a favor. Apparently, when the Good Samaritan dropped off the man, he merely let him out of the car and failed to accompany him into the house. The drunken man tripped on the front steps of his home, hit his head, and died.

Outcome Nothing on the results of this one.

Money Tree

A California teenager was sitting in the backseat of his friend's car after a heavy night of drinking in 1996. On the drive home, the eighteen-year-old stuck his head out the window to vomit. Just then, the driver veered off the road, ramming his passenger's head into a pine tree. Severely injured, the teen and his parents sued Shasta County for $700,000, claiming it was the county's fault that the tree was so close to the road.

Outcome No news on the outcome, but the driver must be thanking his lucky stars that no one noticed *his* role in the accident.

Drunk of the Irish?

A "stereotypical" lawyer in Orlando, Florida, sued the Dollar Rent-A-Car company in March 1999 on behalf of the family of a woman who was killed when her boyfriend, an Irish tourist, crashed their rental car. The thirty-three-year-old Irishman, who was drunk at the time of the accident, was eventually charged with manslaughter and driving under the influence. As such, the attorney alleged that Dollar Rent-A-Car should be liable for the woman's death because the company "either knew or should have known about the unique cultural and ethical customs in Ireland which involve the regular consumption of alcohol at pubs as a major component to Irish social life." The lawyer went on to charge that the company "knew or should have known [the Irish driver] would have a high propensity to drink alcohol."

The attorney was immediately greeted with a barrage of incensed phone calls from Irish Americans who didn't appreciate someone turning a crude cultural stereotype into a barometer for individual behavior. So in May 1999, he amended his lawsuit to focus on Ireland's different driving conditions and the duty that should be imposed on rental-car companies to make sure Irish drivers can handle American roads.

Outcome No news on the outcome. Can you say *faux pas*?

Blame My Boss

In 1994, a receptionist in Ontario, Canada, drank at an afternoon office party, drank more at a bar afterward, and then tried to drive home in a snowstorm, refusing offers of a ride. Shortly into her drive, she lost control of her car and crashed into a truck, seriously injuring herself. So what did she do next? She sued her boss, the owner of a local realty company, for failing in his duty to protect her from harm.

For his part, the boss argued that he had not only offered the woman a cab ride home but had also asked whether he could call her husband to pick her up. In addition, a coworker had offered the plaintiff a lift, which she had promptly refused.

Outcome In February 2001, a judge assessed the plaintiff's injuries at $1.2 million, but graciously cut that figure by 75 percent to reflect her own fault in the accident. Still, $300,000 is a steep fine for an employer who did just about everything except wrestle his tipsy receptionist to the ground.

FAIR-WEATHER LITIGANTS

Struck by an Idea

A man in Arlington, Virginia, was sitting on the roof of his apartment building during an electrical storm in 1991, his feet dangling precariously in a puddle of water. The next instant—wham! A bolt of lightning knocked his socks off.

No sooner did his hair stop smoking than the twenty-seven-year-old filed a $2-million lawsuit against the building's manager and owner. He claimed the management was negligent in maintaining the rooftop and should have hung brighter signs warning him of the possible dangers of his actions.

Outcome Nothing on the result of this one. But we think the plaintiff has a better chance of getting hit by lightning than winning a favorable verdict.

Singing in the Rain

In 1996, a disgruntled woman in Israel sued a Tel Aviv television station and its weatherman for forecasting a sunny day when instead it rained. Because of the inaccurate prediction, the plaintiff left her home lightly dressed, caught a cold, missed four days of work, and suffered "severe anguish and stress." She demanded $1,000 and an on-air apology.

Outcome Though the results aren't in yet, we trust the jury will award her just compensation—namely a pair of galoshes and a hot toddy for her troubles.

An Uncommon Cold

A Michigan man sued the state for $1 million, claiming he caught a cold in the drafty rotunda of the state's capitol while viewing an art exhibit there in 1997.

Outcome No verdict yet, but a spokesman for the governor said, "The irony is we've heard for years that the capitol is full of hot air. I don't know where the cold air is coming from."

Rough Seas

A Florida man set off on a fishing trip on what appeared to be a perfect spring day. The sun was shining and the water looked as placid as a wading pool. But before the first fish could bite, the weather took an abrupt turn for the worse. The winds picked up and a heavy rain began to pelt the water. The tiny boat rocked precariously on the choppy seas as the fisherman tried to maneuver back to port. Suddenly a huge wave struck. The panicked man was thrown overboard and, tragically, drowned.

So what did the victim's survivors do? The grieving family sued the Weather Channel for $10 million, claiming the deceased man had relied on a storm-free forecast early June 1, 1997, when he left his Big Pine Key home on the fateful outing. Filed in June 1998, the lawsuit alleged that the Atlanta-based TV station had a "contractual obligation" to provide "correct weather information in a timely manner" and was negligent in not doing so. Apparently, the Weather Channel had broadcast news about inclement weather conditions approaching the Florida Keys, but not in time for the drowning victim to take heed.

Outcome A federal judge, however, said that broadcasters could not be held responsible for the fate of people who make plans based on their weather predictions. If that were allowed, just imagine the flood of suits that would ensue—from farmers whose crops dried out, beachgoers who met with fog instead of sunny skies, tourists who were rained on during their trip to Disneyland. . . . The judge ruled that the drowned man was merely a viewer and had no enforceable contract with the Weather Channel. "It is well established that mass media broadcasters and publishers owe no duty to their general public who may view their broadcasts or read their publications," he wrote in a nine-page decision dismissing the family's lawsuit.

SICK AND TWISTED

Morbidly Ironic

A California man sued the operator of Bear Mountain ski slope for failing to maintain a safe environment. The skier was injured in 1994 after crashing into a steel pole holding up a sign that read, BE AWARE—SKI WITH CARE.

Outcome In November 1998, a district court of appeals allowed the plaintiff to proceed with the case despite a state law barring most skier lawsuits. No news on the final verdict.

Morbid Motorist

In February 1996, a woman was driving down a country road in Jacksonville, Wyoming, when a snowmobile suddenly cut out of the fields directly into the path of her car. The two vehicles collided and, tragically, the snowmobile rider was killed. A police investigation determined the deceased man was at fault since he had cut out onto the roadway.

Tragic, no matter how you look at it, but raised to the level of macabre by the lawsuit that followed—one filed by the driver of the car against the *widow* of the snowmobile rider! According to her lawsuit, the thirty-six-year-old plaintiff suffered "grave psychological injuries" due to witnessing the death of the defendant's husband. Therefore, the driver claimed, she should be compensated by the grieving widow for the mental anguish she suffered as a result of the accident.

Outcome No news yet, but we know there aren't going to be any winners in this case.

How Low Can You Go?

The city of San Carlos, California, filed a lawsuit against a seven-year-old boy who was hit by a municipal truck while riding his bicycle. City officials claimed the boy caused the 1987 accident by darting out in front of the truck near his family's home. The boy suffered some bruises and a bump on the head. City officials, however, said the truck driver strained his back when he jammed on the brakes to try to avoid hitting the youngster. He missed seventy-one workdays recuperating. The city's lawsuit demanded $13,000 for the driver's medical bills, workers' compensation, and repairs to the truck.

Outcome Outraged, the boy's parents filed a $100,000 countersuit against the city two weeks later. They claimed the boy was forced to ride his bicycle in the street because of poorly maintained sidewalks in the neighborhood. For all we know, they're all still duking it out.

Parental Guidance Suggested

A woman lost her two little girls in October 1997 after they wandered out of their Upland, California, apartment onto nearby railroad tracks. The three-year-old and twenty-two-month-old were killed by a passing commuter train. No sooner were her daughters laid to rest, however, than the grieving mother filed a $30-million lawsuit against the local transportation authority. She claimed the agency was to blame for the deaths of her children because it had neglected to fence off the track to prevent such a tragedy. Never mind that investigators proved she had been high on methamphetamines and had fallen asleep with the apartment door wide open, allowing her children to wander the neighborhood alone for more than an hour.

Outcome Six months after the tragic accident, the plaintiff was caught drinking and using methamphetamines in a motel room with two juveniles. She was sentenced to 150 days in jail for drug use and contributing to the delinquency of minors. Her lawsuit against the transportation authority has yet to go to court.

Family Affair

Here's a family you don't want to know. In the summer of 1992, a northern California man murdered his wife with a shotgun, then called his son to announce, "I just blew your mother's head off, and I am going to blow my head off." The son and his wife immediately drove the short distance to the father's home. They found the desperate dad in the driveway "with a shotgun pointed at his chin, and the butt on the ground with a stick in the trigger mechanism area."

The son pleaded with his father not to kill himself and eventually edged close enough to lunge for the gun. The two wrestled over the weapon and it discharged, grazing the son's wife. The homicidal dad was taken into custody, convicted of killing his wife, and sent to prison. The son and his siblings then sued their incarcerated father for the wrongful death of their mother. The case was settled by stripping the father of all his assets and dividing the entirety of his property among his children.

Yet, apparently dissatisfied with the outcome of the legal melee, the son went on to sue his captive father for negligent infliction of emotional distress. After all, the lawsuit said, his father had intentionally subjected him to emotional distress by inviting him to the scene of the shooting. In so doing, the father had breached a parental duty not to inflict emotional distress on his son, a duty that arises out of a typical family relationship.

The court conducted a bench trial and entered a defense judgment for the incarcerated father. The verdict was immediately challenged by the son's attorneys, and the case was eventually heard in an appeals court. Clearly concerned about opening a Pandora's box of claims over family disputes, the court first pointed out, "Where only emotional distress is claimed, the degree of certainty that the plaintiff suffered injury is diminished." The court then went on to say: "Heartache and emotional pain are an inherent staple of the parent-child relationship. . . . Only in families that are not close are the members sufficiently indifferent to one another's personal failings not to feel emotional distress. To inject the cold, impersonal logic of the law into such an arena could lead to the destruction of close family relationships."

With that, the appellate court upheld the trial court's judgment and effectively blocked a new avenue for pursuing compensation. In so ruling, the court mandated that emotional distress caused between family members, be it major or minor, should remain in the home and outside the domain of the courts.

It should be noted that the appellate court's decision was not unanimous, merely a majority of two to one. Therefore, future forays into this area can undoubtedly be expected, despite the exasperated tone of the ruling, which quoted former U.S. Supreme Court Justice Oliver Wendell Holmes Jr. in stating: "There are occasions in the course of judicial decision making when it becomes necessary to stand athwart the relentless march of logic and shout, 'Enough already!!' "

SOURCES

NEWSPAPERS, MAGAZINES, AND OTHER PERIODICALS

AAP Newsfeed
Albuquerque Tribune
Arizona Republic
Asheville (N.C.) Citizen-Times
Associated Press
Atlanta Journal & Constitution
Austin American-Statesman
Boston Globe
Business Journal (Charlotte, N.C.)
Business Wire
California Lawyer
Chicago Sun-Times
Chicago Tribune
Commercial Appeal (Memphis, Tenn.)
Corporate Detroit
Daily Appellate Report
Daily News (N.Y.)
Dallas Morning News
Denver Post
Denver Westword
Des Moines (Iowa) Register
Evening Standard (London)
Forbes

Fresno (Calif.) Bee
Herald (Rock Hills, S.C.)
Houston Chronicle
Independent (London)
Indianapolis Star
Iowa State Daily
Kansas City Star
Ledger-Star (Norfolk, Va.)
Legal Intelligencer
Liability Week
Los Angeles Daily News
Los Angeles Times
Media Daily
Medical Economics
Milwaukee Journal Sentinel
Nation
New York Post
New York Times
News & Observer (Raleigh, N.C.)
News Tribune (Tacoma, Wash.)
Newsday
Newsweek
Orange County (Calif.) Register
Orlando Sentinel
Ottawa Citizen
PC/Computing
Pittsburgh Post-Gazette
Cleveland Plain Dealer
Portland Oregonian
Professional Liability Litigation Reporter
Reader's Digest
Record (N.J.)
Reuters

Rocky Mountain News
Sacramento Bee
San Antonio Express-News
San Diego Union-Tribune
San Francisco Chronicle
Seattle Post-Intelligencer
Seattle Times
South China Morning Post
St. Louis Post-Dispatch
St. Paul Pioneer Press
St. Petersburg Times
Star-Tribune (Minneapolis/St. Paul, Minn.)
Stuart (Fla.) News
Sun-Sentinel (Ft. Lauderdale, Fla.)
Supermarket News
Syracuse (N.Y.) Herald-Journal
Telegram & Gazette (Worcester, Mass.)
Time
Times Union (Albany, N.Y.)
Tri-Service
Tucson (Ariz.) Citizen
U.S. News & World Report
USA Today
Verdicts & Settlements
Virginian-Pilot
Washington Post
Washington Times
Weekly Standard
Wisconsin State Journal
Workforce

BOOKS

Frank, Leonard R. *Webster's Quotationary*. New York: Random House, 1999.

Gregory, Leland H., III. *Presumed Ignorant: An Uncensored Guide to Disorder in the Courts*. New York: Dell Publishing, 1998.

Lieberman, Jethro K. *The Litigious Society*. New York: Basic Books, 1981.

O'Connell, Jeffrey, and C. Brian Kelly. *The Blame Game*. New York: Lexington Books, 1987.

Howard, Phillip K. *The Death of Common Sense*. New York: Random House, 1995.

ORGANIZATIONS AND WEB SITES

American Tort Reform Association
American Consulting Engineers Council
The Association of California Tort Reform
The Association of Trial Lawyers of America
California Citizens Against Lawsuit Abuse
Chuck Shepherd's News of the Weird
The National Center for Public Policy Research
Product Liability Coordination Committee
Texans Against Lawsuit Abuse

ABOUT THE AUTHORS

Attila Benko is currently a fraud investigator for a national insurance company. He has also worked as an insurance claims administrator in both Annapolis, Maryland, and Los Angeles, where he handled countless claims and gained vast experience investigating, negotiating and directing litigation through defense counsel. Attila has a bachelor's degree in criminal justice. He lives in Sierra Madre, California.

Laura B. Benko is presently a reporter for *Modern Healthcare* magazine. She has also served as an editor at *Investor's Business Daily* and as a reporter for the *Los Angeles Times* and the *Seattle Times*. Laura has a bachelor's degree in English from the University of California, Los Angeles; a master's degree in print journalism from the University of Southern California; and a master's degree in clinical psychology from Antioch University, Los Angeles. She lives in Santa Monica, California.